Palgrave Studies in Music and Literature

Series Editors
Paul Lumsden
City Centre Campus
MacEwan University
Edmonton, AB, Canada

Marco Katz Montiel
Edmonton, AB, Canada

This leading-edge series joins two disciplines in an exploration of how music and literature confront each other as dissonant antagonists while also functioning as consonant companions. By establishing a critical connection between literature and music, this series highlights the interaction between what we read and hear. Investigating the influence music has on narrative through history, theory, culture, or global perspectives provides a concrete framework for a seemingly abstract arena. Titles in the series, both monographs and edited volumes, explore musical encounters in novels and poetry, considerations of the ways in which narratives appropriate musical structures, examinations of musical form and function, and studies of interactions with sound.

More information about this series at
http://www.palgrave.com/gp/series/15596

Nduka Otiono • Josh Toth
Editors

Polyvocal Bob Dylan

Music, Performance, Literature

palgrave
macmillan

Editors
Nduka Otiono
Institute of African Studies
Carleton University
Ottawa, ON, Canada

Josh Toth
MacEwan University
Edmonton, AB, Canada

Palgrave Studies in Music and Literature
ISBN 978-3-030-17041-7   ISBN 978-3-030-17042-4   (eBook)
https://doi.org/10.1007/978-3-030-17042-4

Cover illustration: Todd Strand / Alamy Stock Photo

This Palgrave Macmillan imprint is published by the registered company Springer Nature Switzerland AG
The registered company address is: Gewerbestrasse 11, 6330 Cham, Switzerland

To Idzia Ahmad: Friend, tortured soul poet, and Dylan devotee who followed his line and succumbed to "the inclement teeth of the weather..."
and
To Jeff Toth: A Dylan fan, a brother,
"a strong foundation / When the winds of changes shift"

ACKNOWLEDGMENTS

These edited collections are always more difficult than, perhaps, they should be. On some level, to get to the finish line, you need to "pay in blood"—although, if you're lucky (or if you play your cards just right), you "pay in blood, / but not [your] own." We've had some luck in this regard. So we have some reparations to make. To begin, we'd like to thank the series editors of Palgrave Studies in Literature and Music (Paul Lumsden and Marco Katz). They had the vision to get this project off the ground, and the forbearance to let the two of us manage it. We'd like to thank, also, the helpful editors at Palgrave (Allie Troyanos and Rachel Jacobe); the hawkeyed research assistants at MacEwan University (Cassie Digout) and Carleton University (Bissy Waariyo); and a table-of-contents-worth of great contributors. At a more personal level, our gratitude goes also to our families for their support and patience... "If not for you."

And finally, the debt we all—as editors and contributors—owe to the enigmatic and polyvocal Bob Dylan, the subject of this book, is immeasurable.

All Dylan lyrics referenced in this collection, unless otherwise noted, come from BobDylan.com.

CONTENTS

CHAPTER 1

Introduction: The Foreign Sounds of Dylan's Literary Art

Josh Toth and Nduka Otiono

On 13 October 2016, Professor Sara Danius, Permanent Secretary of the Swedish Academy, announced that the Nobel Prize in Literature had been awarded to Bob Dylan. Asked (in the wake of the announcement) if, in choosing Dylan, the "Swedish Academy [had] widened the horizon of the Nobel Prize in Literature," Danius quickly and cleverly compared Dylan to Sappho and Homer. Both, she notes, wrote poetry *so as* to perform it; Dylan's role as musician is, therefore, in no way inimical to his role as poet. And yet she goes on to insist that "he can be *read* and should be *read*, [for he] is a great poet of the English tradition" (our emphasis). Let's not overlook Danius' subtle shift in focus here—from celebrating Dylan's work as a form of ongoing performance to justifying it as readable text. Danius (and, by extension, the Swedish Academy *en masse*) clearly realizes and accepts that Dylan's identity as musician, as performer, needs to be defended. Awarding Dylan the Nobel *in literature* is not the same as awarding it to Yeats or Eliot. Dylan isn't *really* a poet because he's *really* a

J. Toth (✉)
MacEwan University, Edmonton, AB, Canada

N. Otiono
Institute of African Studies, Carleton University, Ottawa, ON, Canada

© The Author(s) 2019
N. Otiono, J. Toth (eds.), *Polyvocal Bob Dylan,*
Palgrave Studies in Music and Literature,
https://doi.org/10.1007/978-3-030-17042-4_1

1

musician. And while it is true, as Danius notes, that some of the most famous poets have been performers (and that some of the most famous poems are remnants of an oral tradition), the litmus test (today) for "literary" greatness is efficacy in print: Dylan (like Homer, like Sappho) "can and *should* be *read*." The fact that he (like Homer, like Sappho) writes *so as to* perform is therefore mentioned only to be muted, or subsumed by the fact that what Dylan *writes* can also be *read*.

In large part, the purpose of this collection is to interrogate the ways in which Dylan's work engages or provokes this odd anxiety about the nature, or finite boundaries, of the literary—an anxiety that became ever more apparent in the hours and days and weeks that followed Danius' announcement. While various journalists and bloggers and fellow musicians and writers published or posted or tweeted congratulatory "defenses" of Dylan, just as many (if not more) lamented or mocked the Swedish Academy's "surprising" decision. Either way, Dylan's status as Nobel laureate was approached as a notable exception—something that challenged (for good or ill) the very definition of "literature." It's hard not to hear in these various defenses and condemnations an echo of the anxiety surrounding the novel's growing popularity in the late eighteenth century. A new form was suddenly challenging the static parameters of the literary—one, moreover, that could not be taken as a serious or valuable artistic endeavor. Consider, for instance, Rev. William Jones' ([1780] 1810) assertion that novels "vitiate the taste, while they corrupt the manners." This is because, as Jones goes on to assert,

> many of them are but the waking dreams of those, who know neither the world nor themselves. Many of them also are mean imitations, which affect the style and manner of more successful compositions. Some of them are void of all regular design, and made up of heterogeneous parts, which have no dependence upon one another.
> —*late qui splendeat, tinus et alter*
> *Assuitur pannus*—
> And thus they become like the party-coloured jacket of a little disordered fool upon the stage of a mountebank, who sets the rabble a-gape with the low and insipid wonders he has collected, to detain them in his company, and draw the money out of their pockets. (307–8)

Such commentary—focused, as it is, on the way in which certain popular literary forms draw our attention away from, and then corrupt, that which is better, more rigorous, and more authentically homogeneous—is surprisingly, if ironically, apropos in *this* contemporary context. Recall Gary Shteyngart's (2016) scathing "response" on Twitter to Dylan's Nobel win: "I totally get the Nobel committee. Reading books is hard." While the irony of such an indictment may or may not be lost on Shteyngart (and the vast majority of his Twitter "followers"), it's worth perseverating somewhat on just how neatly an eighteenth-century condemnation of the novel (as a mutation of *proper* literary forms) anticipates the current unease about Dylan's status as a literary "master." For good or ill, Dylan often seems to present himself as a "fool upon the stage," one who refuses (or repeatedly exposes us to his inability) to express or "know himself" *in full* and who offers up compositions largely "void of regular design, and made up of heterogenous parts."[1] And most certainly a vast majority of his works can be called "mean imitations," pastiche-like arrangements that play with and "affect the style and manner of [what many might call] more successful compositions." It is hardly surprising, then, that, in a manner that is all too familiar, Dylan's retractors have felt the need to imply—or to state outright—that Dylan should have been ineligible for the award. He is not a writer, and certainly not (ironically) a novelist. He is a musician—and not even a *great* musician. His win thus speaks to a certain diminishment of what is truly literary and (therefore) of society. And surely, on this point, Rev. William Jones would agree.

These strange appeals to a certain absolutism, or a sense of literary "purity," are best represented by a now infamous tweet from the popular American novelist, Jodi Picoult: "I'm Happy for Bob Dylan. / #ButDoesThisMeanICanWinAGrammy?" (2016a). While Picoult quickly went on to clarify that this initial response was "just a gentle joke" (2016b), her question remains a likely symptom of the "unease" Dylan's win effected within the literary and academic community. Picoult, who has (as far as we are aware) zero presence in the world of musical performance, feels warranted to suggest that Dylan has as much "right" to the Nobel Prize in Literature as she does to a Grammy. On the one hand, this is simply a ridiculous suggestion (joke or not). Besides the fact that Dylan has written books and screenplays, he is not merely or only a "composer" of

---

[1] These aspects of Dylan's artistic identity are touched upon in the following chapters—but they are, for the most part, largely assumed (at this point) in most discussions of Dylan's work. Take, as just a few representative instances, approaches to Dylan such as Aidan Day's *Jokerman* (1988), Stephan Scobie's *Alias Bob Dylan* (2003), or (more recently) Louis Renza's *Dylan's Autobiography of a Vocation* (2017). See also the final chapter of Josh Toth's *Stranger America: A Narrative Ethics of Exclusion* (2018)—that is, "Bob Dylan's Autoplasticity."

music. He is a lyricist. Picoult, however, deals *only* in printed words—although, notably, she started her career writing issues of *Wonder Woman*. But surely suggesting that, because she is an author of books, Picoult is more "worthy" of the Nobel than Dylan is just as absurd as insisting that what Dylan does is (simply or only) a form of "literature."

On the other hand, however, Picoult's suggestion is utterly compelling—insofar as it implies an understanding of literature that Dylan's body of work (when taken as whole) *compels* us to accept. Is not Picoult, also, like every other writer, a type of composer? Is not her work, in some sense, caught up in a type of performance—or, at the very least, susceptible *to* performance? Is it not necessarily imbued, or haunted, by the affective senselessness of musical polyphony? Such questions are, of course, justified most obviously by Mikhail Bakhtin's famous effort to privilege novelistic discourse over poetic hegemony, an effort which implies (also and again) that Dylan has always been more of a novelist than a poet anyway. (We'll return to this idea in a moment.) And while we are quite certain Picoult wasn't thinking of Bakhtin when she posted her Tweet, the question she asks clearly belies her anxiety (even as it opens up the possibility) that the line between a mercurial performance and the fixity of print (as literature proper) is only ever a type of hysterical fantasy. For this very reason such a line needs to be policed. This is precisely the reason, as we already noted, why Dylan's Nobel win provokes a sense of unease that is readily comparable to the unease sparked by the rise of the novel at the close of the eighteenth century. Not surprising, either, then, is the Swedish Academy's attempt to forestall this anxiety by stressing the *readability* of Dylan's work—the fact that it "can be and *should* be read."

What we are suggesting, however—and what we hope the following chapters work to demonstrate in their respective ways (and especially when read together)—is that there is something absurd about such a move, that it (ultimately) does more to undermine Dylan's win than it does to justify it. Most obviously, we cannot simply "read" the vast bulk of Dylan's work. Reading the lyrics to one of his songs (silently and on a page) is akin to reading only every second line, or only every second page, of a novel. Or better, it is akin to reading a comic after removing the art. As a number of our contributors suggest (explicitly or implicitly), Dylan constantly stresses the manner in which lyrical meaning (or affect) occurs in the moment of a given performance—which is to say that Dylan's "poetry" cannot be disentangled from issues of musicality and vocal expression. This is not to suggest that it is never useful to consider Dylan's lyrics in silence and on the page. But it does mean that Dylan's literary importance is in no way tied, merely, to his ostensible "readability." We are always in danger of missing the point, or the value, of Dylan's work if we view him, simply, as another "great poet of the English tradition"—a fact Dylan frequently intimates in interviews.[2] Dylan is not a "poet"—not, anyway, in any traditional sense; nor is his writing (in isolation) comparable to the work of "great poets" like Yeats or Eliot. It's simply not the same thing—even if, at the same time (and however paradoxically), it works to confuse the very possibility of making such a distinction. We are not, in other words, interested in suggesting that Dylan's work simply marks a unique space for itself anterior to a clearly delimited field of "literature." Nor are we interested in "recovering" Dylan's work as traditionally literary and, for that reason, of value. Our position is that it is unique insofar as it functions, rather (or finally), to straddle and confuse any number of modalities, any number of genres, any number of forms: it is literary only insofar as it is also musical; readable only insofar as it must also be heard; new only insofar as it is haunted by tradition. It is, we are saying, polyvocal.

Indeed: Dylan's oeuvre seems, always, to be confronting the exhaustion (or false restrictiveness) of literary forms as such. By singing, by performing (his songs as well as himself), he constantly evokes the inherently dialogic and polyphonic nature of the literary. As Picoult's tweet accidently suggests, a work of literature is always a kind of disharmonious singing—a performance tied to its moment of utterance, possessed by (in Roland Barthes' terms) "the thousand sources of culture" ([1967] 1977, 146), and perpetually susceptible to future recontextualization, to new dialogic encounters, new translations between addresser and addressee. Dylan thus imbues—by implication (if nothing else)—even his books and screenplays (and maybe even his sculptures and his paintings) with a spirit of musicality, of polyphony. For confirmation we need only recall that when he finally submitted to giving the lecture mandated by the Swedish Academy,[3] Dylan decided to focus on the ostensibly tenuous relationship

---

[2] Again, a number of our contributors (like various critics before them) address these interviews—which are almost always defined by Dylan's various frustrating and humorous evasions. For, though, a succinct summary of Dylan's refusal to be defined by terms like "poet" or "songwriter"—or, rather, to refuse any specific definition of those terms—see the second section of Chap. 2 (i.e., Damian A. Carpenter's "Restless Epitaphs").

[3] For a slightly more robust discussion about Dylan's "delayed" response (and the frustration it provoked) see Emily O. Wittman and Paul R. Wright's discussion of Dylan's autobiographical tendencies—in, that is, Chap. 8.

between literature and song. Accompanied by a jazzily haunting piano composition,[4] Dylan reads potentially plagiarized[5] (yet poetically reassembled) summaries of three canonical texts: *Moby-Dick*, *All Quiet on the Western Front*, and *The Odyssey*. All the while, he shifts between first, second, and third person—placing (and confusing) himself and his listener in the heart of the action, demonstrating how what is past is always still affective in the present. As he asserts, while discussing the trials of Odysseus, "some of these same things have happened to you.... You too have shared a bed with the wrong woman. You too have been spellbound by magical voices, sweet voices with strange melodies.... And you've had close calls as well. You have angered people you should not have. And you too have rambled this country all around." But who is "you" in this instance? Is it some *other* Odysseus? Is it Dylan? Is it the listener (who might also be a reader)? And who is speaking? Homer or Dylan? Or even Homer as distilled over thousands of years and (now, today) on innumerable internet summaries? Regardless, the larger implication here (as in any number of other Dylan works) is that these other voices are always also his voice, or *our* voice—as he, she, I, or you, *we* are always "tangled up in blue." Of course, in the final moment of his lecture (or is it a song?), he again frustrates any easy conflation of song and literature—and we'll need to come back to this peculiar moment. For now, though, we'd like to draw out the broader implications of Dylan's career-spanning effort to embrace and endorse a certain type of polyvocality.

To a degree, Dylan's career is wholly tangled up in a mid-century repudiation of aesthetic and cultural modernism—the utopian desire of the isolated genius to "make it new." As Brian McHale (2008) notes, while

---

[4] The music playing in the background was composed and performed by Alan Pasqua—who was, unexpectedly, and at the 11th hour, contacted by Dylan's manager. According to Pasqua, Dylan requested something that was "not really melodic, not cocktail, not super jazzy, but sort of background-y piano music" (Pasqua as qtd. in Sisario 2017). Dylan did not offer Pasqua any other information. Pasqua thus composed the music having never read Dylan's lecture. He was not even told that the requested music was *for* the lecture. Given that Dylan is a proficient pianist himself, it is unclear why he gave this particular task to Pasqua. However, the odd and ambiguous nature of the request seems to betray a desire on Dylan's part to imbue the lecture with a certain musicality *and* a certain dissonance, to stress a certain discordant yet ineffaceable relationship between words and music.

[5] On the possibility that Dylan "plagiarized" parts of his lecture—from, of all places, *SparkNotes*, see Andrea Pitzer's 2017 article, "The Freewheelin' Bob Dylan," in *Slate.com*. Of course, Dylan's tendency to borrow—or to "lift" wholesale—parts (or aspects) of other works is relatively well documented at this point.

trying to pinpoint the moment postmodernism began, Dylan's release of *Blonde on Blonde* in 1966 (i.e., the first double rock album) articulates and participates in a larger cultural "breakdown." This is a distinctly postmodern breakdown of identities and aesthetic forms. Such a breakdown is first and most clearly identified and then embraced by the preeminently postmodern writer, John Barth ([1967] 1984)—who, in his most famous essay, "The Literature of Exhaustion," repudiates the modernist refusal to overcome its own perceived dead ends and (in turn) celebrates the fact that "an artist may paradoxically turn the felt ultimacies of our time into material means for his work—*paradoxically*, because by doing so he transcends what had appeared to be his refutation" (71). For Barth, this paradoxical act (exemplified most overtly in the works of Borges) entails a willingness to skillfully engage (as Menelaus desperately wrestles Proteus in *The Odyssey*) the infinite library, or labyrinth of discourses and/or aesthetic forms, that constitutes reality. What, for Barth, makes Borges' "stance" so "interesting" is that, for Borges, as one of his editors once noted, "'no one has claim to originality in literature; all writers are more or less faithful amanuenses of the spirit, translators and annotators of pre-existing types.' Thus his inclination to write brief comments or imaginary books: for one to attempt to add overtly to the sum of 'original' literature by even so much as a conventional short story, not to mention a novel, would be too presumptuous, too naïve; literature has been done long since" (73). But Barth does not see this, simply, as some perverse game. Borges, like Menelaus, isn't in it "for kicks." Rather, he "illustrates a positive artistic morality." He represents "the chosen remnant, the virtuoso, the Thesean *hero*, who, confronted with Baroque reality, Baroque history, the Baroque state of his art, need *not* rehearse its possibilities to exhaustion… He need only be aware of their existence or possibility, acknowledge them, and with the aid of very special gifts—as extraordinary as saint- or herohood and likely not found in The New York Correspondence School of Literature—go straight through the maze to the accomplishment of his work" (75–6).

It's certainly not difficult to argue that Dylan engages in such Borgesian heroism from the start. Even his early "folk" albums are subtly self-aware of their redeployment of past literary and musical influences and forms—a self-awareness that certainly begins to peak in the various comical songs that make up *Another Side of Bob Dylan* (1964). This is the album in which, also, Dylan begins to turn increasingly inward (and away from overt political engagement); it is the first time he overtly suggests that he can *only* articulate himself—*even if* the "inner 'thing' he thinks to 'translate' is itself only a ready-formed dictionary" (Barthes [1967] 1977, 146). Dylan's very identity as a musical/literary artist becomes inextricably linked to the performance of his work. In constantly composing, he is constantly tracing and exposing an infinite and labyrinthine network of connections between himself, the traditions that *affect* him (as an artistic subject), and his equally complex and unknowable listener. For instance, as the singer of "I Shall Be Free No. 10," Dylan is "just average, common too / I'm just like him, the same as you." For this reason, "It ain't no use a-talking to me / It's just the same as talking to you." And, of course—and, one is certainly inclined to think, *because* of this articulated lack of individualistic privilege (which we can easily associate with modernist elitism)—the singer mocks his role as "poet": "Yippee! I'm a poet, and I know it / Hope I don't blow it."[6] But, and even if we accept McHale's decision to privilege *Blonde on Blonde* as the apotheosis of Dylan's "break" with specific and delimiting traditions (musical or literary), it is the albums between *Another Side* and *Blonde on Blonde* that most clearly articulate and perform Dylan's desire to confront the "Baroque state of his art" and "go straight through the maze to the accomplishment of his work." After all, *Blonde on Blonde* can be viewed as the final entry in a thematically and stylistically linked set of albums (including *Bringing It All Back Home* [1965] and *Highway 61 Revisited* [1965]). The major ruptures or breakdowns McHale identifies are therefore anticipated by Dylan in 1965, when he released his first "electric" album and then alienated his fan base at the Newport Folk Festival.

In the liner notes for *Bringing It All Back Home*, Dylan clearly addresses a crisis in American cultural production, one that necessitates an effort to overcome the declining efficacy of *both* musical and literary forms. He asserts that he does "not want t' be bach. mozart. tolstoy. joe hill. Gertrude stein or james dean / they are all dead. The Great books've been written. the Great sayings have all been said" (1965). Neither music nor literature nor popular culture can address the crisis he perceives. The implied alternative is to transgress, or simply abandon, the current boundaries of aesthetic delimitation. For this reason, it would seem, Dylan embraces while distancing himself from specific categories of artistic production: "a song is anything that can walk by itself / i am called a songwriter. a poem is a

---

[6] Keith Nainby discusses this moment of self-mockery in Chap. 4. And, in Chap. 3, Charles O. Hartman offers a close reading of the song's opening verse.

naked person … some people say that i am a poet" (1965). Instead of suggesting a type of hierarchy (with songs reigning over poems or vice versa), Dylan expresses a desire to work as *both* poet *and* songwriter (and therefore as neither). His songs need to "walk all by themselves" while remaining, also, *intentionally* pure (or "naked"), governed solely by a singular "poet" who can articulate nothing but himself. In this sense, Dylan's effort to identify and then refuse the restrictions of (folk) music and (traditional) literature echoes and then calls into question, as we suggested above, Bakhtin's efforts to maintain a distinction between novelistic and poetic discourse—the former being polyvocal; the latter, hegemonic and authorial. As Bakhtin states, "the possibility of another vocabulary, another semantics, other syntactic forms and so forth, to the possibility of other linguistic points of view, is… foreign to poetic style" (285). The *prose* writer, however, according to Bakhtin, is not interested in apprehending and articulating (an illusion of) "the virginal fullness and inexhaustibility of the object itself." Instead, such a writer

> confronts a multitude of routes, roads and paths that have been laid down in [their] object by social consciousness. Along with the internal contradictions inside the object itself, the prose writer witnesses as well the unfolding of social heteroglossia *surrounding* the object, the Tower-of-Babel mixing of languages that goes on around any object… [T]he object is a focal point for heteroglot voices among which his own voice must also sound; these voices create the background necessary for his own voice, outside of which his artistic prose nuances cannot be perceived, and without which they "do not sound." (278)

It is, in other words, precisely because (and not in spite) of a polyphonic disharmony of voices that the literary artist's voice "sounds." But, of course, then, also, this sounding is simultaneously corrupted or effaced by the very thing that makes it possible. It is never pure. It can only be heard *in concert.*

What this means for Bakhtin—and, we are suggesting, Dylan—is that only a certain type of artistic discourse (what Bakhtin calls "novelistic discourse") can expose and embrace "a critical qualified relationship to one's own language (as merely one of many languages in a heteroglot world)" and, by extension, "the incomplete commitment of oneself, of one's full meaning, to a given language" (1981, 285). We might in fact say that Dylan's work functions, primarily, as a frustration of those various "forces that struggle to overcome the heteroglossia of language, forces that unite and centralize verbal-ideological thought, creating within a heteroglot national language the firm, stable linguistic nucleus of an officially recognized *literary language*, or else defending an already formed language from the pressure of growing heteroglossia" (Bakhtin 1981, 270–1, our emphasis). But Dylan goes, it often seems, even further than Bakhtin—for in Dylan even the poetic (when conceived and performed *as song*) is inherently novelistic, capable of giving the artistic self by announcing its perpetual incompletion, its perpetual loss to the vocabularies (or sounds) of otherness. Dylan, we might say, positions his particular forms of *"literary music"* as a *novelistic* (because *polyphonic*) balance of song and poetry, forms that do not simply abandon the author to the vagaries of cacophonous potential *or* insist upon a finite or hegemonic (i.e., authorial) perception of a socio-political reality, or "object." In other words, the liner notes that preface the radical sounds of *Bringing It All Back Home* outline, or stage, an artistic project that goes beyond a postmodern sense of "exhaustion" by insisting upon a fluid and unpredictable blend of musical *and* literary styles. Dylan's vast knowledge of such styles—and his willingness to mimic and manipulate them—is, as several of our contributors note, carefully and playfully implied throughout his much later and distinctly *novelistic* memoir, *Chronicles* (2004).

But let's go back, instead, to the Nobel lecture. At the end of the lecture, and after trying to articulate what is "literary" about his work, Dylan (while still accompanied by the sounds of a piano) recalls Odysseus' conversation with Achilles in the underworld. Achilles, Dylan notes, is filled with regret. He now recognizes the pointlessness of dying young—even if he died as a great hero. He realizes, now, Dylan states, "that whatever his struggles of life were, they were preferable to being here in this dead place." This brings Dylan to his penultimate point: "That's what songs are too. Our songs are alive in the land of the living. But songs are unlike literature. They're meant to be sung, not read. The words in Shakespeare's plays were meant to be acted on the stage. Just as lyrics in songs are meant to be sung, not read on a page." On some level, this assertion seems to contradict our argument; and it most certainly undermines Danius' effort to validate Dylan's win by stressing his readability. Dylan, after all, suggests here that songs—*"unlike* literature"—are "alive in the land of the living." There is, in this sense, nothing literary about them. And there is, in turn, nothing musical, nothing alive, about literature—that which "can and should be read." It's simply a mistake, then, to call Dylan a poet. But

Dylan goes on to say that he "hope[s] some of you get the chance to listen to *these* lyrics the way they were intended to be heard: in concert or on record or *however people are listening to songs these days*. I return once again to Homer, who says, 'Sing in me, oh Muse, and through me tell the story'" (our emphasis). The ambiguity in these lines is striking—especially insofar as they function to disrupt the meaning of Dylan's earlier phrasing (i.e., "unlike literature"). Suddenly the "un" takes on the same dual function it takes on in words like "unconscious," uncanny," or "undead." Rather than simply negating, it *sublates*. The sublative function of the "un" is implied the moment Dylan forces us to wonder which lyrics he means. He has, after all, just discussed an epic poem and two novels. He has also quoted some particularly obscure lines from Donne—so as to show how words can affect us even when we are uncertain of their meaning. On some level, though, we can assume that, in saying "*these* lyrics," he means the lecture itself—*even if* he means also *The Odyssey, All Quiet on the Western Front, Moby-Dick*, all his own works, and (by extension) all that might be called "literary." And therefore, in linking "however people are listening to songs these days" to *how* such lyrics "were intended to be heard," he opens up the possibility that even reading can be (or always has been) a form of listening. It's just a matter of what we are given (and, in turn, *willing*) to hear.

CHAPTER DESCRIPTIONS

Therefore, and although (or, better, *because*) each is distinct in style, length, and approach, the chapters in this volume come together to comment upon the cultural and aesthetic effects of Dylan's "songs"—his musical *yet literary* forms—while further defining the specific nature of Dylan's transgressive artistic ingenuity. Each chapter focuses on the function and implications of a certain polyvocal confusion in Dylan's work—a confusion, subversion, and overcoming of various aesthetic traditions. Combined, they explore (as fully as possible) the multigeneric nature of Dylan's oeuvre—his tendency to employ, mix, and question musical and literary traditions—and thus interrogate the subversive and perpetually unpredictable nature of his extensive catalog. Or, more simply, the various chapters that constitute *Polyvocal Bob Dylan* develop our understanding of Dylan and place his textual and performative art within a larger context of cultural and literary studies.

The book is divided into two sections: *Literature and Music* and *Performance and Literature*. The first section opens with Damian A. Carpenter's "Restless Epitaphs: Revenance and Dramatic Tension in Bob Dylan's Early Narratives." This chapter explores, in the author's words, "two ways in which Dylan makes use of epitaph in his work and what this use symbolizes in regard to his identity as an artist: (1) as a performative, dramatic rhetorical space and (2) as an existential threat." The author engages Dylan's debts to traditional poetics while also insisting upon (and stressing the importance of) his unique role as a writer of songs/music. Carpenter deploys an intriguing idea of "revenance," defined in this context as "a portmanteau term that encompasses notions of the revenant (in terms of both a ghostly presence and simply meaning one who returns to a place), resonance and presence." Central to his analysis is Dylan's tendency to embrace a social/aesthetic past he simultaneously seeks to overcome. The cumulative effect of these qualities, writes Carpenter, "generate[s] a narrative space/performance in which the past (which we should also consider in terms of 'tradition' [...]) resonates in a present moment and can draw the present audience into the past moment as if it were present and thereby effect a present response."

To fully unravel the thematic and dramatic tension in Dylan's early work, Carpenter draws from T.S. Eliot's essay, "Tradition and the Individual Talent," as well as from Robert Frost and Dylan's own autobiography, *Chronicles* (2004). Significant in his theorizing is the relationship between "historical sense" and "mechanical craft"—and, as Carpenter argues, "the way in which Dylan views history and folk tradition can be viewed in terms similar to Eliot's 'historical sense.'" This chapter demonstrates how Dylan carves out his own space as a poetic songwriter by reordering tradition to speak to his present. Beyond Carpenter's rigorous engagement with Dylan's folkloric and performative poetics, the technical nature of this chapter is remarkable. This chapter is enriched by Carpenter's in-depth knowledge of musical theory which he deploys in his readings (especially) of "Ballad of Hollis Brown" (1964) and "North Country Blues" (1964). As Carpenter declares, "what makes Dylan's restless epitaphs so effective and felt, what makes them matter, is precisely the dramatic bond and shared burden they expose, the listener's active role in the drama of the narrative."

Dylan's various debts to (and frustrations of) poetic tradition—along with his tendency to place a significant burden of responsibility on listeners—is largely the focus, also, of Charles O. Hartman's chapter. Hartman, however, is primarily concerned with "Dylan's Deixis." By offering a careful analysis of deixis in Dylan's song-writing, Hartman ties that songwriting to a poetic tradition that Dylan both embraces and disregards. This chapter, to appropriate the author's felicitous expression, sorts through the sometimes-fugitive operations of deixis in Dylan's songs. Hartman carefully establishes "the core but easily overlooked operation of language called *deixis*" which "Dylan's song lyrics have in common with the traditions and concerns of poetry in the usual, narrow sense." Throughout the chapter, Hartman offers remarkable examples of "how Dylan uses deixis to create character and setting, draws parallels with how poets use it, and points out the ethical work that these manipulations enable." As Hartman argues, "Although the most basic vehicles of deixis are pronouns ('I,' 'you'), demonstratives ('this house'), and adverbs ('here,' 'now'), in storytelling deixis can permeate the language less obviously." He compares Dylan's deictic manipulations with the use of deixis by literary "greats" such as Robert Browning, Gwendolyn Brooks, and Philip Levine. Recognizing the primacy of live performance, Hartman emphasizes Dylan's reliance on deixis to captivate his audience as he keeps "performing, around the world, dozens or hundreds of times every year." Hartman argues that "live performance entails and generates its own deixis, distinct from any deixis contained within the fiction of the song itself." He illustrates these unique engagements with commanding examples from Dylan's work—focusing specifically on the "unstable" nature of Dylan's "deictic choice[s]," as well as his frequent "refusal to acknowledge the claims of deixis."

Dylan's tendency to compel exegesis via striking deictic manipulations connects his work to a larger tradition of poetic expression *even as* it results in songs that are far more novelistic than poetic, more polyphonic than hegemonic. But it also connects his *writing* to the peculiarities of his various vocal performances. This latter connection is the focus of the following two chapters. Both Keith Nainby and Astrid Franke help us to see that Dylan has always striven to be, in the most literal sense, polyphonic—employing, throughout his career, strikingly different voices, accents, and singing styles. Nainby's chapter—"Not Just Literature: Exploring the Performative Dimensions of Bob Dylan's Work"—explores "the connection between Dylan's vocal performance and his texts, focusing on how this connection generates meanings for the listener." As do the contributors already discussed, Nainby foregrounds Dylan's provocation of complex aesthetic responses in his listeners. He combines concrete examples and rigorous textual analysis of Dylan's vocal performances to highlight the manner in which language communicates experience by necessarily obfuscating it. What emerges from this painstaking unpacking of some representative Dylan songs and compelling performative strategies is what Nainby identifies as "Dylan's use of vocal attack." Defined as "the rate at which he breathes sound into the microphone and the rate at which he allows that sound to decay," Dylan's vocal attacks extend his work beyond the literary into intricate performative dimensions. Nainby's emphasis on Dylan's artistic manipulation of words and polyvocality reminds one of Dell Hymes' (1974) theory of the "ethnography of speaking." But beyond drawing attention to Dylan's ingenious stretching of the situational context of language usage, Nainby's essay concludes that Dylan's "vocal performance choices are an integral element of his poetic treatment of human relationships, relationships he frames as troublesome and beautiful because they are fraught with the paradox at the heart of communication."

Dylan's interest in, and negotiation of, this specific paradox is considered, also, by Franke, who reflects further on Dylan's complex relationship with, and challenge to, the listener. In "The Complexities of Freedom and Dylan's Liberation of the Listener," Franke offers a fascinating analysis of freedom (as it relates to vocal shifts/play) in Dylan's performances—while also aligning Dylan's work with a larger American (and African American) tradition. Focusing on songs from Dylan's gospel phase and his Sinatra phase, Franke argues that the songs "sound different and *are* different in different contexts and thereby acquire cultural significance *in the moment.*" Franke invites us "to think a bit more about the many voices of Dylan, both metaphorically and also literally," and the complexity of his work as he changes his performing self and "continues to present songs he wrote half a century ago in perpetually new ways." Franke draws from Axel Honneth's (2007) theorizing on the paradoxes of individual freedom as well as from Jane Tomkins' (1985) concept of "cultural work" to elucidate how listeners defamiliarize themselves from established aesthetic norms to reengage a work of art anew. She offers an enthralling exploration of Dylan's complicated sense of freedom at the intersection of past, present, and future and compares Dylan's thematic and aesthetic concerns with issues in "immigrant literature and in African American literature, albeit in contrasting ways." Franke concludes that "It is a gift to a culture to have a singer around for so long that he can make us realize the patterns in which we listen to him (and presumably every other song, too)."

The issue of drama and of (therefore) performativity is addressed more overtly in the second section. The chapters in this section tend to focus on the ways in which Dylan's understanding and ongoing exploration of identity (of literature, of music, of America, of "Bob Dylan" as artist) are directly related to the polyvocality that defines his work as both writer and performer. In "'Blowin' in the Wind': Bob Dylan, Sam Shepard, and the Question of American Identity," Katherine Weiss addresses the way both Dylan and Shepard work to destabilize American myths while insisting upon the very necessity of such myths—in the form of masks or always mutating performances. By focusing specifically on Shepard's relation with and effort to understand him, Weiss reveals the significance of Dylan's protean nature (as it relates to America's tendency to get trapped in, or to reify, its necessary myths). At the same time, she shows how Dylan and Shepard collaborated to break down outmoded myths by resurrecting, necessarily, new, albeit more temporary, unstable, performative ones— especially in their interrogation of the concept of American identity. Particularly noteworthy in this chapter is not just how Shepard and Dylan question the validity of a "true West" identity. But how, in Weiss' words, "Along with questioning the historical myths that shape America and its people, Shepard and Dylan tackle the myth we call the American Dream." A major plank upon which this chapter rests is Weiss' analysis of the collaboration of the "two iconic writers"—Shepard and Dylan—in co-writing the song "Brownsville Girl" (1986). As Weiss surmises, "This song explores American identity and myth through American icons torn down by the death of the Wild West—a death brought on by increasing modernization."

John McCombe provides an alternative reading of Bob Dylan's engagement with "westerns" and American "performance" in his contribution: "Bob Dylan's 'Westerns': Border Crossings and the Flight from 'the Domestic.'" This chapter offers a revealing discussion of "western" codes of masculinity in Dylan's work, while further advancing Weiss' reflections on "the heroic cowboys/outlaws that Dylan and Shepard are inspired by and strive to revise." As McCombe declares, his "goal is to demonstrate how Dylan's westerns regularly conform to, yet occasionally subvert, gender-based binaries that distinguish the classical Hollywood western." In so doing, McCombe advances Weiss' identification of both Dylan's and Shepard's "affinity for classic Hollwood westerns" through her analysis of "Brownsville Girl."

McCombe proves how "integral popular music can be to conversations about masculinity, domesticity, and the western genre." At the heart of this chapter's contribution to an understanding of Dylan's transgressive artistic ingenuity is McCombe's key observation that "one of the many tensions in Dylan's art lies in the simultaneous creation of women protagonists who display agency in Dylan's 'song westerns' in conjunction with elements of Dylan's art that reinscribe predominant gender tropes that mobilized second-wave feminists in the period under consideration." For instance, to illustrate his claims, McCombe refers (at one point) to Dylan's "Tom Thumb's Blues" (1965), which "offers a roll call of women." McCombe also explores what he calls "The cinematic turn in Dylan's art," which he sees as being "part and parcel of Dylan's larger efforts in the mid-1970s to inform his songwriting with influences from a range of art forms." This chapter then analyzes a number of Dylan's western-themed songs that are laced at the same time with autobiographical experiences as Dylan struggled to balance career and home life. The association between Dylan's eclectic art, westerns, and domestic life allows McCombe to conclude his discourse by attempting a reconciliation of the gender ideology in Dylan's work with his "occasional misogyny." As McCombe declares, "those increasingly complex song westerns also suggest that a 'Polyvocal Dylan' is a product of the manner in which cinematic discourses collide with gender discourses at a particular moment of ideological crisis for the western and western hero."

Further deepening our understanding of Dylan's ongoing negotiation of an autobiographical impulse and the literary or cinematic tradition we tend to associate with such an impulse, Emily O. Wittman and Paul R. Wright examine, more closely, Dylan's relationship with autobiography in their contribution, "'I Don't Do Sketches from Memory': Bob Dylan and Autobiography." "One thing is clear," writes Wittman and Wright, "when we theorize Dylan's relationship to autobiography—whether in his songs, interviews, or in his ostensibly real memoir, *Chronicles* (2004)—we must turn away from traditional categories." Thus, the appreciation of Dylan's transgressive challenge of orthodox/traditional categories is extended into the autobiographical realm. Whereas the preceding chapters inevitably discuss the affinity between Dylan's life and his art tangentially, it is in this chapter that Dylan's autobiography is writ large. Noting the frustrations in tracking "a linear narrative about Dylan's past and revelations of soul-searching and private moments," Wittman and Wright contend that it is in "alternative forms of life-writing"—such as songs/

lyrics—that pieces of Dylan's life can best be located. Using songs such as "Highlands" (1997), "The Lonesome Death of Hattie Carroll" (1964), "My Back Pages" (1964), and "Idiot Wind" (1975) as case studies, Wittman and Wright demonstrate how Dylan creates "lyrics that could just as easily apply to literary narrative as to songwriting." Throughout this long chapter, Dylan's "strategy of deflection and disruption" provides the lens from which his explicit and implicit autobiography—respectively in *Chronicles* and in his lyrics—is viewed and analyzed. Consistent with this "disruption" of orthodoxy, Wittman and Wright conclude that even while working explicitly with autobiography as a genre (in *Chronicles*), Dylan turns "the logic of the *Bildungsroman* on its head" and establishes "The autobiography as song fragment. The life as lyric."

Very often, and as evident in the foregoing synopsis of the chapters, discourses of Dylan's transgressive art and creative persona understandably focus on his American and European influences. Yet, as Nduka Otiono highlights in "Beyond Genre: Lyrics, Literature, and the Influence of Bob Dylan's Transgressive Creative Imagination," Dylan's life and work have also cast a spell on a generation of African writers from Nigeria. Using a personal essay style, Otiono explores his own encounter with Dylan's work in the context of contemporary writers in the Lagos-Ibadan cultural axis in the late twentieth century, and how this impacted his teaching Dylan at the University of Alberta, Canada. Otiono combines personal reflections by representative Nigerian poets with Khatija BiBi Khan's (2017) unusual theoretical approach called "soetry" to comprehend the influence of Dylan's transgressive creative imagination and multigeneric work. Among others, Otiono highlights Dylan's mid-career album *Oh Mercy* (1989), the release of which was preceded by the landmark publication of six volumes of poetry by the six "Update poets" in Nigeria in 1988. Clearly, Nigeria is one of those "strange countries you have to enter"—to borrow Dylan's (2004, 165) phrasing; and, as it turned out, in "entering" Nigeria Dylan offered a creative spark that ignited the poetry and lifestyle of some of the significant writers born in the roaring 1960s as African countries gained independence from colonial rule. The beautiful words of Uche Nduka, New York-based Nigerian-American author of nearly a dozen books of poetry and one of the Update poets, sums it up thus: "For me and my generation in Nigeria, the music of this inscrutable bard was the soundtrack to our travels throughout the country, our courtships, our flirtations, our political protests. He helped me discover myself as an artistic wayfarer. His example made us refuse to write a poetry of restraint. He is still urging us to zestfully stoke our artistic fires."

An Introductory Conclusion

In all, then, *Polyvocal Bob Dylan* invites us to reassess Dylan's Nobel-winning work as that which is frustratingly "*unlike* literature," as that which is radically polyvocal.

Let's return (one last time) to the Nobel lecture. In the end, and in what might *seem* like an overtly hubristic move, Dylan draws a direct line between his literary art and Shakespeare's. One possible implication is this: expressing an affinity for Dylan's works is little different than expressing an affinity for Shakespeare's. To appreciate either in their intended form (as performance) is to expose ourselves to facile condemnation—that our appreciation is tied to the fact that "reading books is hard." But if Dylan shows us anything it's that the novel, like the political-minded folk singer, is just another exhausted archetype. There is little involved in "reading" a novel *if* we are not encouraged (or willing) to listen as well—that is, to feel, to hear all the residual traces, all the *other* voices that frustrate the possibility of a hegemonic (or easy to "grasp") meaning. Reading in a traditional sense is all about following a straight line of sense. And yet, as Dylan suggests, when we read (or listen to) a writer like Melville, we are not given to know what "it all means": "When Melville put all his old testament, biblical references, scientific theories, Protestant doctrines, and all that knowledge of the sea and sailing ships and whales into one story, I don't think he would have worried about it either—what it all means." What really matters, Dylan asserts, is whether or not "a song moves you"—and, by "song," here, it would seem, Dylan implicitly encompasses *The Odyssey*, *Moby-Dick*, Donne's "Elegy XIX," and every one of Shakespeare's plays. Songs are simply that which incline us toward listening. Or as Dylan declares elsewhere: "A song is like a dream, and you try to make it come true. They're like strange countries you have to enter" (Dylan 2004, 165). And, as the following chapters can help us to confirm, Dylan *writes* songs.

References

Bakhtin, Mikhail. 1981. *The Dialogic Imagination: Four Essays*. Edited by Michael Holquist and translated by Caryl Emerson and Michael Holquist. Austin: University of Texas Press.

Barth, John. 1984 (1967). The Literature of Exhaustion. In *The Friday Book: Essays and Other Nonfiction*, 62–76. New York: Putnam.

Barthes, Roland. 1977 (1967). *Image-Music-Text*. Translated by Stephen Heath. New York: Hill & Wang.

Danius, Sara. 2016. Interview with Sven Hugo Persson. *Nobelprize.org*, October 13, 2016. Accessed May 4, 2018.

Day, Aidan. 1988. *Jokerman: Reading the Lyrics of Bob Dylan*. Oxford: Basil Blackwell.

Dylan, Bob. 1965. Liner Notes. *Bringing It All Back Home*. Columbia.

———. 2004. *Chronicles. Volume One*. New York: Simon & Schuster.

———. 2017. Nobel Lecture. *Nobelprize.org*, June 5, 2017. Accessed May 4, 2018.

Honneth, Axel. 2007. "Verwicklungen von Freiheit: Bob Dylan und seine Zeit." In Bob Dylan. Ein Kongreß. edited by Axel Honneth, Peter Kemper and Richard Klein, 15–28. Frankfurt: Suhrkamp.

Hymes, Dell. 1974. *Foundations of Sociolinguistics: An Ethnographic Approach*. Philadelphia: University of Pennsylvania Press.

Jones, William. 1810 (1790). Letters from a Tutor to His Pupils. In *The Theological and Miscellaneous Works of Rev. William Jones*, ed. William Stevens, 265–280. London: F. C. and J. Rivington.

McHale, Brian. 2008. 1966 Nervous Breakdown; or, When Did Postmodernism Begin? *Modern Language Quarterly* 69 (3): 391–413.

Picoult, Jodi (@jodipicoultPicoult). 2016a. I'm Happy for Bob Dylan. / #ButDoesThisMeanICanWinAGrammy? *Twitter*, October 13, 2016, 5:24 a.m.

——— (@jodipicoultPicoult). 2016b. Actually, as I Said in the NEXT Tweet, I Like Dylan. He Is a Poet. It Was Just a Gentle Joke. #context #relax! *Twitter*, October 13, 2016, 7:06 p.m.

Pitzer, Andrea. 2017. The Freewheelin' Bob Dylan. *Slate.com*, June 13, 2017.

Renza, Louis. 2017. *Dylan's Autobiography of a Vocation: A Reading of the Lyrics 1965–1967*. New York: Bloomsbury.

Scobie, Stephen. 2003. *Alias Bob Dylan: Revisited*. Calgary: Red Deer.

Shteyngart, Gary (@Shteyngart). 2016. I Totally Get the Nobel Committee. Reading Books Is Hard. *Twitter*, October 13, 2016, 6:10 a.m.

Sisario, Ben. 2017. 'A Really Cool Gig': Playing Piano for Bob Dylan's Nobel Lecture. *The New York Times*, June 7, 2017.

Tomkins, Jane. 1985. The Cultural Work of American Fiction 1780–1860. Oxford: Oxford University Press.

Toth, Josh. 2018. *Stranger America: A Narrative Ethics of Exclusion*. Charlottesville: University of Virginia Press.

PART I

Literature and Music

Restless Epitaphs: Revenance and Dramatic Tension in Bob Dylan's Early Narratives

Damian A. Carpenter

> *old north Hibbing …*
> *deserted*
> *already dead*
> *with it's old stone courthouse*
> *decayin in the wind*
> *long abandoned*
> *windows crashed out*
> *the breath of it's broken walls*
> *being smothered in clingin moss*
> *the old school*
> *where my mother went to*
> *rottin shiverin but still livin*
> *standin cold an lonesome*
> *arms cut off*
> *with even the moon bypassin it's jagged body*
> (Bob Dylan, "11 Outlined Epitaphs")

I am quoting this excerpt specifically from the physical album's liner notes because official lyric collections have since edited it.

© The Author(s) 2019
N. Otiono, J. Toth (eds.), *Polyvocal Bob Dylan*,
Palgrave Studies in Music and Literature,
https://doi.org/10.1007/978-3-030-17042-4_2

A typo can speak volumes. Clearly, the above excerpt from the liner notes (more specifically, the second section/epitaph of the eleven) to *The Times They Are a-Changin'* (1964) is purposively full of typos (clearly used to serve as eye dialect), particularly the dropped 'g' in most of the gerunds— as is, of course, the case with the album title.[1] Might we not see these amputated gerunds, like the schoolhouse's "amputated arms," as clipped action, with some outside tension butting up against an ongoing action in which the word's ghost limb we feel—*know* is there—exerts its presence? Time is always chang*ing*, mov*ing* forward, but *the times* certainly do not change without some kind of confrontation between a status quo impediment and a disruptive force for change. Hence the anthemic appeal of the album's title song, a call to seize the day, resonating quite in tune with the temper of the times. And yet many of the "restless epitaphs" on the album present us with narratives in which the times do not change. They are narratives of the "deserted/already dead," yet, like ghost limbs, still exerting their presence, a dramatic restlessness. In this chapter I am considering two ways in which Dylan makes use of epitaph in his work and what this use symbolizes in regard to his identity as an artist: (1) as a performative, dramatic rhetorical space and (2) as an existential threat.

The first notion of epitaph demonstrated in Dylan's work is that it is a present indication of an absence, which essentially makes the absent present. Dylan's epitaphic narratives on *The Times* are imbued with a notion of a present absence, a loss that haunts and affects the present. The narration of this notion effects a quality of revenance, a portmanteau term that encompasses notions of the revenant (in terms of both a ghostly presence and simply meaning one who returns to a place), resonance, and presence. The cumulative effect of these qualities generates a narrative space/performance in which the past (which we should also consider in terms of "tradition," as will be further discussed) resonates in a present moment and can draw the present audience into the past moment as if it were present and thereby effect a present response.

---

[1] This is a characteristic artifice found in the title of his previous album *The Freewheelin' Bob Dylan* and song titles (like "Blowin' in the Wind") on the first three albums. He largely abandons this artifice after *The Times* until the 1990s.

D. A. Carpenter (✉)
East Tennessee State University, Johnson City, TN, USA

There is a typo in the "11 Outlined Epitaphs" excerpt above, which, unlike the amputated gerunds, is obviously a mistake, and it has since been corrected in official lyric collections.[2] The typo in question is the common confusion of "it's" with "its." This mistake points to a quality of revenance in the epitaphic narratives on the album, particularly "North Country Blues" and "Ballad of Hollis Brown." Along with the implication of possession, it also suggests a presence in both present and past (i.e., "it is" and "it has"). It is a ghostly presence that fittingly encapsulates the tone and resonance of the scene in which he describes old north Hibbing: "deserted / already dead." The "dead" town, like a graveyard, possesses the stone court house, which in turn possesses its walls that are covered in moss like an old tombstone; the isolated schoolhouse is dismembered. But because of the typo, the immediacy, the now-ness, of this scene/moment resonates in past and present, and this "already dead" town seems to resonate a presence: the court house *is* decaying; the wall *is* being smothered; and the "jagged body" of the schoolhouse *is* "rottin shiverin but *still livin*" (Dylan 1964, my emphasis).

This consideration makes way for the second consideration of epitaph that is essential to Dylan's work: an epitaph is a threat to the living, a threat of confinement, being buried alive, or drowned (as invoked in the first verse of the album's title track). The physical ruins of old north Hibbing (abandoned in 1919) clearly resonate for Dylan as he returns home in this memory. This resonance is dramatically reified on the album in "North Country Blues." As he comments in "11 Outlined Epitaphs," Dylan could not avoid the felt presence of those ruins growing up in Hibbing, where the town re-established, with a number of buildings moved from the old site to the new: "the winds of the / north came followin an grew fiercer / as the years went by" (1964). The past, the ruins, exert their presence. Their decay threatens to smother and infect the physical and psychological present, an effect we see tragically rendered in "Ballad of Hollis Brown." So, as he further comments in "11 Outlined Epitaphs," Dylan "ran / an kept runnin" all the way to New York City, where he (ironically, perhaps) invested himself in the past, the folk tradition (1964).

---

[2] In addition to correcting "it's," official lyric collections have also added an apostrophe to the amputated gerunds.

Dylan is repelled by the decaying presence of the past, yet drawn to it in another form. Dylan is only, finally, able to achieve a better understanding of this tension by moving forward, the very activity he seems to embrace in the closing of lines of the second epitaph: "running yes ... / but stoppin for a while / embracin what I left / an lovin it—for I learned by now / never t expect / what it can not give me" (1964). Note the full-legged gerund here, "running," the only one not amputated in this particular restless epitaph. It suggests escape. Whereas in the narratives of Hollis Brown and the nameless woman of iron ore country the restless isolation they increasingly and doggedly experience becomes a confinement from which they cannot escape, leading to slow decay and destruction.

This chapter will first visit a key year in Dylan's career, 1965, when his audience sought to define him with the epitaphs of "poet" or "(protest) singer." For Dylan, a label, fixity, is indeed an epitaph, a threat, which he clearly indicates in the ninth section of "11 Outlined Epitaphs" in an exchange with a reporter:

> "come come now Mr Dylan our readers want
> t know the truth"
> "that is the bare hungry sniffin truth"
> "Mr Dylan, you're very funny, but really now"
> "that's all I have to say today"
> "but you'd better answer"
> "that sounds like some kind of threat"
> "it just could be ha ha ha ha" (1964)

Dylan's evasiveness concerning labels (i.e., "the truth") in interviews during this time helps us to better understand how he perceives his unique craft beyond publicly assigned labels. In consideration of his seemingly evasive answers we can then examine the conceptual and mechanical elements of poetry (T. S. Eliot's concept of "historical sense" and Robert Frost's "sound of sense") and songwriting (the folk tradition and the early influence of Hank Williams, Bertolt Brecht, and Robert Johnson on Dylan) that help to conceptualize the quality of revenance and dramatic tension in "Ballad of Hollis Brown" and "North Country Blues."

A POET WHO HAPPENS TO BE A SINGER

In December 1965, little more than two years after he penned his epitaph for Hibbing, and about five years after his "running" led him to New York City, Bob Dylan found himself on the west coast giving a press conference in San Francisco before a string of ten shows in the area to finish out the year. Ralph Gleason, the jazz and popular music critic, begins the conference by introducing Dylan as a "poet who also happens to be a singer," and reiterates (more pointedly) that "Mr. Dylan is a poet" (Route TV 2016). Gleason follows up his introduction by asking Dylan if he thought of himself "primarily as a singer or a poet." Dylan responds that he thinks of himself as more of a "song and dance man," a clear evasion of having to define his work in limited terms. When asked by another reporter what Dylan would call his music, after Dylan contended that he did not play "folk-rock," Dylan responds evasively again: "I like to think of it more in terms of vision music—it's mathematical music" (Dylan 2006, 63).[3] This answer is followed up by a reporter asking him if he saw the words as being more important than the music. Evading again, Dylan responds, "The words are just as important as the music. There would be no music without the words" (63). Near the end of the conference another reporter extends this line of questioning to include the element of content in relation to text and sound: "What's more important to you: The way that your music and words sound, or the content, the message?" The answer? Another evasion: "The whole thing while it's happening. The whole total sound of the words" (74).

Evasiveness has been a distinct trait of Dylan's persona, a trait that speaks to an impulse to avoid being trapped in limited definition, so these answers are not surprising. But Dylan had faced this line of questioning many times over the previous two years, and the evasiveness is probably also a result of weariness. We can even see it on his face, hear it in his voice. For instance, four months earlier interviewers asked Dylan if he was "primarily a poet." His response was an un-evasive "no," but he went on to

---

[3] In a recently discovered recording of an impromptu interview with Dylan and Joan Baez before a concert on March 19, 1965 (conducted by two students of University of North Carolina—Chapel Hill), Dylan also speaks in terms of mathematics when asked how he would classify himself: "I'd say I was a mathematician more than anything else—sort of a socialistic mathematician.... I deal in numbers" (Goldsmith 2018). It is significant that by the end of the year Dylan essentially substitutes the qualifier "socialistic" with "vision," further distancing himself from the "protest" label.

problematize even that answer by calling into question the label of "poet" and calling himself a "trapeze artist" (Dylan 2006, 49). This line of questioning was so pervasive at the time that it was even asked to other folk artists. In a *Broadside Magazine* interview, Phil Ochs (1965), when asked about Dylan's work in terms of poetry or song, comments, "It is a combination of both. I tend to think his music is an integral part—it is poetry in song form. And therefore not really subject to all the disciplines of classic poetry, but subject to the disciplines of the ballad and of music. And he's combined the two" (4). Ochs's response recognizes that placing "primary" importance over any singular element of Dylan's art shifts attention away from the overall effect it achieves. It is the way the text, sound, content, and performance dynamics interact that makes Dylan's work distinctive and effective. The questions that dominate Dylan's interviews during the mid-1960s are thus unsurprising: why is his work so appealing to the public? What is his message? What are his songs about? The interviewers were too focused on singular elements or trying to fit his work into singular categories that ultimately de-emphasize the accumulative effect of its parts. In essence, they were performing amputations on his body of work.

Song and dance man, trapeze artist, mathematical/vision music: these may be playful evasions avoiding labels such as "poet," "protest singer," or "folk-rock," but they also point to better ways to approach the mechanics of Dylan's art. "Song and dance man" explicitly suggests performance as well as the idea of doing two things at once. "Trapeze artist" likewise indicates performance and even more pointedly invokes the concept of performing in a nebulous space between two points, not to mention the amplified dramatic tension in attempting to do so. During the San Francisco press conference, Dylan echoes this vocation again when asked what poets he admired. Listing a variety people, he includes poets (Arthur Rimbaud and Allen Ginsberg), songwriters (Smokey Robinson and Charlie Rich), and *visual* performers (juggler/comedian/actor W. C. Fields and "the trapeze family in the circus") (Dylan 2006, 64). Considering the mention of Ginsberg and a trapeze performer in this response, it is hard not to think of Ginsberg's fellow Beat poet Lawrence Ferlinghetti (who Dylan was photographed with two days later) and his poem "Constantly Risking Absurdity" (1958), which likens the poet to an acrobat and visually represents either the walking of a tightrope with tense, controlled sway of balance or swinging on a trapeze by lines that sway between the margins of the page.

The object of this "super realist" above the heads of the observers is to catch his elusive partner "Beauty" in mid-air:

> And he
>> a little charleychaplin man
>>> who may or may not catch
>> her fair eternal form
>>> spread-eagled in the empty air
> of existence (Ferlinghetti 1958, 30)

And we can easily translate the poem's tension between the dire need for precision of physical mechanics of the poet's craft in order to capture an indefinable abstraction to Dylan's similar notion that his craft is a balance between both the mechanically precise (i.e., mathematical, the craft elements that make up the song) and the abstract (i.e., vision, the physical and felt presence that the song reifies).

Just days before Dylan released *Bringing It All Back Home* (1965), the album which served to spark greater confusion and debate among the public and critics who had been evaluating Dylan strictly in terms of a folk musician/"protest singer" with poetic sensibilities, Paul J. Robbins interviewed Dylan for the *L.A. Free Press*. His first question expresses an awareness of the tension between the mechanics of his songs and their abstract presence as a sum greater than their individual parts: "If you are a poet and write words arranged in some sort of rhythm, why do you switch at some point and write lyrics in a song so that you're singing the words as part of a Gestalt presence?" (Dylan 2006, 37). The basic elements of the question—which highlight the tension between "poet" and "songwriter"—clearly anticipate the line of questioning Dylan would face in the year to come. And Dylan answers in kind: "I can't define that word poetry, I wouldn't even attempt it. At one time I thought that Robert Frost was poetry, other times I thought Allen Ginsberg was poetry, sometimes I thought François Villon was poetry—but poetry isn't really confined to the printed page" (37). He further comments on his songs: "If you take whatever there is to the song away—the beat, the melody—I could still recite it. I see nothing wrong with songs you can't do that with either... Because they're not supposed to do that... Songs are songs" (37–8).

Poems are poems, songs are songs: but of course there's much more that needs to be considered in these simple declarations, which is why people were having such a hard time grasping what Dylan was actually doing in his work. Robbins's mention of "Gestalt presence" speaks to the quality of revenance in Dylan's work, where something happens between text and sound, a dramatic tension, a ghostly restlessness, that creates a quality which seems to be tapping into a character, a world, a time before *and* beyond the actual performance. His songs speak to the present (hence Dylan's early popularity because he spoke to "the times"), but they carry the weight of the past (which is what made his work that people labeled "protest" more effectively felt than the work of his contemporaries)—and the resonant effect, the dramatic restless tension between the past and present, exhibits a quality of human presence.

What is resonance? It is the product of a medium between action/ inflection and reception. You strike a note on the guitar and send forth a vibration that exists independent of the original action as it builds sound within the body of the instrument. The sound has a quality of the string struck and has a quality of the body it inhabits when it leaves, but when it leaves it is altogether something more than the sum of these two points. The physical make-up of the string shades the initial sound, the way it is struck, the "inflection," exerts a certain sound, and the type of wood, its age, and environment exert a certain tonality. In this analogy, in the context of revenance, the initial action/inflection is the present. The product of this as it resonates in the deep recesses of the body and time (present and past) is the revenant, the returning ghost of the original sound that has something to communicate, a "Gestalt presence."

Amid all the questions Dylan faced about his role as either poet and/or songwriter in 1965, a number of poets are referenced. Two who are mentioned a number of times, mostly in a negative light, are T. S. Eliot and Robert Frost. Even Phil Ochs mentions them in the *Broadside* interview. One might hazard to claim that there is a bit of "anxiety of influence" in Dylan's negative comments, particularly in the Robbins's interview, about their work being "bullshit" (Dylan 2006, 39). After all "Desolation Row" (recorded July/August 1965), aside from actually mentioning Eliot (although still clearly in negative terms), demonstrates a quality we see in Eliot's poems like "The Love Song of J. Alfred Prufrock" and *The Waste Land* mixed with elements of a Ginsberg's poem like "Howl." In *Chronicles*, Dylan (2004) claims that Archibald MacLeish, Carl Sandburg, and Robert Frost, "the poet of dark meditations," are "the Yeats, Browning, and Shelley of the New World" (107). But tracking influence is a slippery slope, and as Clinton Heylin (2009) notes, "one must be wary (as others have not been) of reading too much into Dylan's name-dropping of literary sources in midsixties songs" (249). While we may debate about conscious or unconscious influence, the more productive avenue is to take an opportunity to focus on these two poets that Dylan derided early on and consider the resonance of their commentary on poetry mechanics, how they create/participate in a sum other than their parts: specifically, Eliot's concept of "historical sense" and Frost's notion of "sound of sense," which particularly speak to the qualities of revenance and dramatic tension in Dylan's work.

Historical Sense and Folk Sense

T. S. Eliot ([1919]1950) begins his essay "Tradition and the Individual Talent" by noting that in current literary criticism the word "tradition" is rarely used "except in a phrase of censure" (3). When one speaks of a poet as traditional they are indicating that the poet is unoriginal, merely producing "archeological reconstruction" (3). Authenticity and quality, for these critics, stem from individuality born of a poet's novelty, his or her difference from predecessors. And we can liken this perspective to the public attempts to classify Dylan within a category like "protest singer." However, Eliot argues, "if we approach a poet without this prejudice we shall often find that ... the most individual parts of his work may be those in which the dead poets, his ancestors, assert their immortality most vigorously" (4). Eliot's purpose in this essay is to reconceptualize "tradition" in terms of possessing an "historical sense" instead of viewing tradition as a fixed point in the past. Historical sense "compels a man to write not merely with his own generation in his bones, but with a feeling that the whole of the literature from Homer and within it the whole of the literature of his own country has a simultaneous existence and composes a simultaneous order. This historical sense, which is a sense of the timeless as well as the temporal and of the timeless and of the temporal together, is what makes a writer traditional" (4). When an artist produces a work imbued with this historical sense he or she not only carries the weight of the past into the present, but also reorders the nexus of tradition where present speaks to the past and both past and present exist simultaneously in the moment.

It is quite a happy coincidence that Eliot comments that historical sense is "nearly indispensable to any who would continue to be a poet beyond his twenty-fifth year" (4). In 1965, the twenty-four-year-old Dylan was approaching this mark and not only caught up in debates about him being primarily a poet or songwriter but also about whether or not he was abandoning the folk tradition in favor of popular culture. In a larger context, debates about "folk" tradition in America had been ongoing since the nineteenth century: debates that ranged in perspective from viewing folklore as a remnant artifact to viewing it as a living tradition and to concerns with the effects of mass media and popular culture on folklore. More immediately there was a discernible tension in the 1950s/1960s folk revival among strict traditionalists, "protest" singers, and popularizers. Dylan avoided such debates, as he has consistently done over the course of his career. Two decades later, reflecting on the divisions he witnessed during his early apprenticeship in the folk tradition, he comments, "Folk music was a strict and rigid establishment. If you sang Southern Mountain Blues, you didn't sing Southern Mountain Ballads ... It was really pathetic... everybody had their particular thing that they did. I didn't much ever pay attention to that" (1985a, 8). What Dylan did pay attention to when he reached New York City in 1961 was the "historical sense" of folk tradition, and soon "folk songs embedded in [his] mind like religion. Folk songs transcended the immediate culture" (Dylan 2004, 27). The folk tradition he found himself immersed in would provide an archetypal pattern, a timeless "folk sense" to play against and with the simultaneous historical sense of past and present:

> Folk music was a reality of a more brilliant dimension.... I felt right at home in this mythical realm made up not with individuals so much as archetypes, vividly drawn archetypes of humanity... Folk music was all I needed to exist. Trouble was, there wasn't enough of it. It was out of date, had no proper connection to actualities, the trends of time.... Once I'd slipped in beyond the fringes it was like my six-string guitar became a crystal magic wand and I could move things like never before. (236)

Dylan would learn much from fellow performers and acquaintances in those early years, but his reflection on this time in *Chronicles* points to two centers from which he would develop his historical sense: the New York Public Library and Izzy Young's Folklore Center in Greenwich Village.

At the library, he immersed himself in newspapers, zeroing in on the years 1855–1865. Is it a coincidence that the time span he highlights in *Chronicles* implicitly parallels his early years of musical maturation a century later from 1955 when he formed his first full band, the Golden Chords, to 1965 when he would noticeably break from the rigid folk establishment and begin playing with a band again? At the very least,

Dylan saw some kind of parallel between the two historical moments: "The age that I was living in didn't resemble this age, but yet it did in some mysterious and traditional way. Not just a little bit, but a lot. There was a broad spectrum and commonwealth that I was living upon, and the basic psychology of that life was every bit a part of it" (2004, 86). The two key words here, "traditional" and "commonwealth," speak to Eliot's concept of "historical sense," particularly in the way he frames them in terms of a simultaneous presence of past and present. And perhaps he did indeed, forty years later, recognize how the resonance of the past (or certain revenant echoes) would make themselves present in his work: "Back there [1855–65], America was put on the cross, died and was resurrected.... The godawful truth of that would be the all-encompassing template behind everything that I would write" (86). A restless epitaph to be sure and perhaps a parallel to the ghost of old north Hibbing's ruins resurrected further south in the new north Hibbing.

Young's Folklore Center was "a crossroads junction for all the folk activity you could name," and it was only natural that the young magpie Dylan would flock there (Dylan 2004, 19). He immersed himself in Young's eclectic menagerie of printed and recorded folk material inhabiting the past as if it were the present: "The madly complicated modern world was something I took little interest in. It had no relevancy, no weight.... What was swinging, topical and up to date for me was the stuff like the Titanic sinking, The Galveston flood. John Henry driving steel, John Hardy shooting a man on the West Virginia line.... This was the news that I considered, followed" (20). This archetypal "folk sense" is part of the "historical sense" he experienced while reading century-old newspapers at the library. In the context of Eliot's concept, the tradition that forms the medium for Dylan's historical sense is the folk tradition, rather than the poetic tradition. For Dylan, the archetypal, timeless folk narrative was an ur-narrative, the stories subsumed by the larger national narratives, and it provided the key to understanding the past and the present times: "Folk songs were the underground story.... Everything was simple—seemed to make some kind of splendid, formulaic sense" (103).

But all of this talk of historical sense does not speak directly to mechanical craft. One can have all of the historical sense in the world, but that does not make them an artist. As Eliot ([1919]1950) argues, novelty simply for the sake of novelty carries no weight and merely imitating the past is just "archaeological reconstruction" (3). Dylan recognized that harnessing the resonance of the folk and historical senses would require acting as more of a medium, a filter: "I wanted to understand things and then be free of them. I needed to learn how to telescope things, ideas. Things were too big to see all at once, like all the books in the library—everything laying around on all the tables. You might be able to put it all into one paragraph or into one verse if you could get it right" (Dylan 2004, 61). Getting it "right" would require honing his craft.

THE REVENANCE THE SOUND OF SENSE MAKES

In 1959, the year Dylan left Hibbing to "attend" the University of Minnesota, Robert Frost sat down with Robert Penn Warren and Cleanth Brooks to discuss the craft of poetry. The interview was included as a supplement to the third edition of their widely used college textbook *Understanding Poetry*. It is doubtful that Dylan would have been exposed to this in his brief time at the university, or would even care to be. And if we take him at his word in "My Life in a Stolen Moment" (1962), he was apparently "expelled from English class for using four-letter words / in a paper describing the English teacher" (Dylan 1985b, 70). But some of Frost's comments speak directly to the quality of revenance we see in Dylan's work. They can also help us to conceptualize what happens in mid-air as the trapeze artists swing between poetry and song.

Two particular comments are of interest here. The first is prompted by Warren asking Frost about the dramatic quality of the "strain of rhythm against the meter." Frost (1966) responds, "From those two things rises what we call this tune that's different from the tune of the other kind of music. It's music of itself" (200). And later, he somewhat reiterates this comment, adding a simile that compares the effect to playing a stringed instrument: "It's neither the meter nor the rhythm; it's a tune arising from the stress on those—same as your fingers on the strings, you know. The twang!" (203). Thinking back to my guitar analogy, we can translate the elements he highlights in this accumulative process: the meter is the body, the form (of the guitar); the rhythm is the present action/inflection; the tune is the end sound, the result of these elements working with and against each other.

Two decades earlier in the "The Figure a Poem Makes," Frost (1964) makes a similar comment: "The possibilities for tune from the dramatic tones of meaning struck across the rigidity of a limited meter are endless" (v). "Tune," for Frost, is not merely the ability to put a poem to music. In fact, he tells Warren and Brooks, if you can easily do this then it is "bad writing" (1966, 200). For him, tune is tension, dramatic tone, the reso-nance of human emotional presence, a quality that appears to align with what he describes as his ultimate goal in his poetry in a letter to John Bartlett in 1913 (after publishing his first book, *A Boy's Will*): "I... have consciously set myself to make music out of what I may call the sound of sense" (as qtd. in Anderson 1963, 52). In another letter to Bartlett (after the publication of his second book, *North of Boston*, in 1914), Frost further stresses the fact that this sound of sense is an accumulative effect in terms of "sentence sound" that results in a meaning other than the sum of the words: "Remember that the sentence sound often says more than the words. It may even as in irony convey a meaning opposite to the words" (85). A classic example of this is seen in "After Apple-Picking" (included in *North of Boston*) and the masterful way that the overall effect of the poem's line structure, meter, and word sound elicit a feeling, an experi-ence, of weary drowsiness in the reader. Or we might think of "Stopping by the Woods on a Snowy Evening," where the speaker's impatient horse "gives his harness bells a shake / To ask if there is some mistake," eliciting a sense of impatience and urgency disrupting the speaker's dark medita-tion, an urgency that stands in tension with the plodding repetition of the last two lines: "And miles to go before I sleep. / And miles to go before I sleep" (Frost 1964, 15–16). The sound of sense, the tune of these dra-matic tones, as Tom Vander Ven (1973) argues, provides a poem with "the fundamental emotional energy of human nature... without it poetry does not matter" (244).

Why this makes poetry "matter" for Frost, as Vander Ven (1973) notes, is because the sound of sense is related to Frost's notion of the performa-tive communication, or "recognition" (250). In Frost's 1914 letter to Bartlett, he comments, "In literature it is our business... never to tell... [people] something they don't know, but something they know and hadn't thought of saying. It must be something they recognize" (Anderson 82). This notion is somewhat echoed by Dylan in *Chronicles* when he comments on the difficulty of writing effective "protest" songs: "Protest songs are difficult to write without making them come off preachy and one-dimensional. You have to show people a side of themselves that they didn't know was there" (2004, 54). As Vander Ven further explains, "Recognition functions not merely as a sharing of ideas between poet and reader, but as a sharing of voice tones, a dramatic bond. The burden of communication is, as it must be, a shared burden" (250). What makes Dylan's restless epitaphs so effective and felt, what makes them matter, is precisely the dramatic bond and shared burden they expose, the listener's active role in the drama of the narrative, the process of identifying with common archetypal human experience.

ARCHETYPE RULES OF POETIC SONGWRITING

In *Dylan's Visions of Sin*, Christopher Ricks (2003) tackles the ambiguity of categorization we saw demonstrated in Dylan's 1965 interviews. He argues, echoing Frost's comments on meter and rhythm, that Dylan "is in the business... of playing time against his rhyming. The cadences, the voicing, the rhythmical draping and shaping don't... make a song superior to a poem, but they do change the hiding-places of its power" (19). Indeed, Dylan is working in a different medium than poetry, but the mechanics are essentially the same, especially if we think of the mechanics from Frost's perspective. One might imagine that if Frost was questioned as to the primary importance of actual words or the way the words sound, or for that matter, if his "message" was the most important he may just respond as Dylan did in 1965: "The whole thing while it's happening. The whole total sound [sense] of the words" (Dylan 2006, 74).

The function of this brief look at Eliot's concept of "historical sense" and Frost's notion of "sound of sense" is not to suggest that Dylan is a poet merely by comparison, but rather to provide a sounding board to understand how he approaches songwriting with very poetic concerns in mind. As we have seen, the way that Dylan views history and folk tradition can be viewed in terms similar to Eliot's "historical sense." And if we consider Dylan's comments on some specific songwriters who influenced his craft we can note similar concerns we see in Frost's views on the mechanics of poetry and how they elicit an overall effect other than the sum of their parts. As Dylan comments in *Chronicles*, "You want to write songs that are bigger than life. You want to say something about strange things that have happened to you... You have to know and understand something and then go past the vernacular. The chilling precision that these old-timers used in coming up with their songs was no small thing" (2004, 51). Precision and recognition: the two keys to catching that fair eternal form.

Clearly, Woody Guthrie had a lasting influence on Dylan, as had Elvis Presley, Buddy Holly, Little Richard, Odetta Holmes, Lead Belly, Johnny Cash, and many other songwriters/performers. And, of course, the old folk songs he immersed himself in provided an early framework for his songs. As he notes, when recording some of his earliest songs for Lou

Levy, he had been mostly interested in the traditional folk songs and used the structure of those songs to serve as the framework for his own: "I could make things up on the spot all based on folk music structure" (2004, 228). Keys to understanding how Dylan progressed from writing some good, but mostly derivative, folk songs to compositions like "North Country Blues" and "Ballad of Hollis Brown" that resonate with these old songs but also assert their own authenticity can be found in his comments on the songwriting qualities of Hank Williams, Bertolt Brecht, and Robert Johnson.

Before Dylan left Hibbing, Hank Williams was on his radar; he had heard him on the radio and "Even at a young age [he] fully identified with [him]" (Dylan 2004, 96). The way he explains this identification speaks to Frost's "sound of sense" and "recognition": "I didn't have to experience anything that Hank did to know what he was singing about. I'd never seen a robin weep, but could imagine it and it made me sad. When he sang 'the news is out all over town,' I knew what news that was even though I didn't know" (96). Williams's songs connected Dylan to a resonant emotional energy, allowing him to inhabit a space other than the present.

Also key in his assessment of Williams is his attention to the structure of his songs, which, for Dylan, represented the "archetype rules of poetic songwriting. The architectural forms are like marble pillars and they had to be there. Even his words—all of his syllables are divided up so they make perfect mathematical sense. You can learn a lot about the structure of songwriting by listening to his records" (Dylan 2004, 96). Dylan's reference to the mechanics of the songs, the importance of syllables (or the "mathematics" of metrical structure), stresses the relationship between Williams's song composition and poetic composition. Dylan had thus internalized these archetypal rules of poetic songwriting by the time he began composing his own songs. But if Dylan was to carve out his own space as a poetic songwriter he would need to not simply imitate the traditional structure but also reorder it, speak to his present.

Dylan sensed that what he wanted to accomplish in his songs went beyond just recreating the pattern and mood of the archetypal rules. These rules were merely a point of departure. While discussing Williams in *Chronicles*, Dylan makes note of Robert Shelton's review of his April 1963 Town Hall concert. According to Shelton (1997), "Dylan broke all past songwriting and performing rules... Not every line seemed finished and polished, yet there was a sense of structure" (165). Notably, this is the first concert in which Dylan emerges as a distinct performer, breaking from folk tradition in the mode of archeological reconstruction to performing his own works imbued with folk sense. As Dylan comments, "The rules... were Hank's rules, but it wasn't like I ever meant to break them. It's just that what I was trying to express was beyond the circle" (2004, 97). This idea of expressing something beyond the closed system indicates a dimension of his craft that went beyond mechanics.

During the spring of 1963 Dylan saw a performance of Bertolt Brecht's work in Greenwich Village. The effect of this performance, as he notes in *Chronicles*, was immense: "My little shack in the universe was about to expand into some glorious cathedral, at least in songwriting terms" (2004, 272). Brecht's "Pirate Jenny," in particular, impressed Dylan, especially in the way it impacted the audience: "when the performance reached its climactic end the entire audience was stunned, sat back and clutched their collective solar plexus. I knew why it did, too. The audience was the 'gentlemen' in the song" (275). Brecht's song is a direct address to the audience ("gentlemen") through the persona of Pirate Jenny who is disguised as a servant and suffering the abuse and sneers of the "gentlemen." All the while, pirate ships are approaching the town, and when they arrive it will be Jenny who chooses who will die.

Dylan was so taken by the song that he began "taking [it] apart... trying to find out what made it tick, why it was so effective," focusing on "the form, the free verse association, the structure and disregard for the known certainty of melodic patterns to make it seriously matter, give it its cutting edge" (2004, 275). It would appear that Dylan, thinking in terms of Frost, was trying to figure out how the "tune" of the song, "its resilience and outrageous power," arose from dramatic tension in its form and structure and how he could manipulate these elements in his own work (276). Again, like in his Williams discussion, he comments on wanting to go beyond the circle, something an understanding of the song's innerworkings could help him achieve: "I could see that the type of songs I was leaning towards singing didn't exist and I began playing with the form, trying to grasp it—trying to make a song that transcended the information in it, the character and plot" (276). It is not surprising that Dylan would be drawn to these qualities in "Pirate Jenny." It seems as though he was unconsciously moving in this direction already.

We can find this approach to a song's form and structure (already) in "The Ballad of Hollis Brown" (written about five months earlier). The listener is immediately drawn into the perspective of song narration via shift in point of view from third- to second-person between the first and second verse which in turn resonates in the present reception as if the revenant of Hollis Brown is performing his desperate act in front of us. We suddenly come to feel that his gun is in our hand: "Your brain is a-bleedin'/ And your legs can't seem to stand / Your eyes fix on the shotgun / That you're holdin' in your hand." And "North Country Blues," most likely written after Dylan had seen the "Pirate Jenny" performance, likewise functions as a direct address (the only Dylan song that does so through a female persona) to the audience, drawing us into this confined, decaying north country room as the speaker unwinds her memories while we gaze out of the window with her.

In Dylan's reflections on Williams and Brecht we see him constantly focusing on the need to understand archetypal and mechanical patterns as integral to breaking out of a confined form/tradition, and trying to understand the accumulative effects of the songs' individual parts that make this possible. We see him focusing on the same aspects of Robert Johnson's work as well. When John Hammond gave Dylan an early pressing of Robert Johnson's posthumous *King of the Delta Blues* (1961), Dylan listened to it intently. Every time he listened, "it felt like a ghost had come into the room. The songs were layered with a startling economy of lines. Johnson masked the presence of more than twenty men. I fixated on every song and wondered how Johnson did it" (Dylan 2004, 283–4). How did Johnson break out of standard songwriting techniques using the traditional elements of the blues? How did the songs create a presence, a ghost, and not just one ghost, but a presence of more than twenty men, a presence that taps into a universal sense? And what is more, how did Johnson make his audience feel the resonance of this (absent) presence?: "Johnson's words made my nerves quiver like piano wires. They were so elemental in meaning and feeling and gave you so much of the inside picture.... all the songs had some weird personal resonance.... I could feel it in my bones" (284). Of course, Dylan wanted to figure out how Johnson accomplished this, as he did when he heard Williams and Brecht: "I copied Johnson's words on scraps of paper so I could more closely examine the lyrics and patterns, the construction of his old-style lines and the free association that he used, the sparkling allegories, big-ass truths wrapped in the hard shell of nonsensical abstraction ... I didn't have any of these dreams or thoughts but I was going to acquire them" (285). Once acquiring this "sense," the next step was to figure out how to make use of the craft/ sense he gleaned from listening to Johnson, Brecht, and Williams in his own work.

RESTLESS EPITAPHS: "NORTH COUNTRY BLUES" AND "BALLAD OF HOLLIS BROWN"

Epitaphs speak volumes beyond their pithy punctuation on a life when one tunes into their resonance. Think of Ishmael listening to Father Mapple sermonize from his ship's bow pulpit and surrounded by epitaphs of dead sailors on the church walls before shipping off with Ahab on his mad, restless hunt. Or think of the inhabitants of Edgar Lee Masters's Spoon River revenants buried under cemetery hill outlining (and probing deeper) the epitaphs on their gravestones.[4]

The ten songs on *The Times They Are a-Changin'* are oratorical, but there is a distinction to be made between the songs of public oratory ("sermonizing oratory," those that "sermonize" from the outside) and private oratory, like an epitaph that makes a public statement for the buried ("restless epitaphs," those in which an inner restlessness is expressed). The ten songs can be divided equally into these categories. The songs of sermonizing oratory (which essentially participate in the contemporary "protest" song genre) are "The Times They Are a-Changin'," "With God On Our Side," "Only a Pawn in Their Game," "When the Ship Comes In," and "The Lonesome Death of Hattie Carroll." The songs of the restless epitaph type are "Ballad of Hollis Brown," "One Too Many Mornings," "North Country Blues," "Boots of Spanish Leather," and "Restless Farewell." The songs of sermonizing are still epitaphs, to be sure, even the hopeful ones because they stamp an epitaph on older times; and they do have a restless quality in the sense that they ultimately argue that the times *need* to be changing. We may also consider that "11 Outlined Epitaphs" is calling attention to the epitaphic quality of all the songs; these liner notes are also, after all, the eleventh epitaph, the tombstone for the ten songs buried in the record grooves. But the songs I specifically categorize as restless epitaphs here speak more to isolation, as if speaking from beyond a

---

[4] Dylan seems to be playing with the latter literary allusion in "Scarlet Town," which appears on *Tempest* (2012), a song in which he implicitly returns to the notion of epitaphs: "On marble slabs and in fields of stone / You make your humble wishes known." The former literary allusion seems apropos as well, since Dylan highlighted *Moby Dick* as an influential touchstone in his Nobel Prize lecture.

figurative grave with an acute presence. The sermonizing songs report and prophesize. The restless epitaphs dramatize and make the listener a part of that drama.

It is not known exactly when Dylan penned "North Country Blues," a dramatic narrative resonating with the historical rise and decline of the iron ore country of his youth, but it was probably soon after he had spent time back in Minnesota. On July 26, 1963, he would debut the song at the Newport Folk Festival. As Clinton Heylin (2009) notes, "a trip home seemingly inculcated him with nostalgia for his 'younger days'... The sight of his hometown gripped by irreversible decline... prompting one of his most effective ballads" (148). As David Pichaske (2010) notes, employment in the area had declined by 4000 jobs between 1958 and 1964, and "by the end of the fifties, Hibbing was the dying town Dylan describes in '11 Outlined Epitaphs'" (23–4). When Dylan performed the song at Newport amidst the old and new guard of traditional folk performers, introducing it as a song about "an iron ore town," he was speaking to the contemporary situation in Hibbing and perhaps implicitly expressing the consequences of not "running" before it is too late. But the song also comes off as tragically (and doubly) timeless: (1) it could have been written about any mining town at any time and (2) it offers us the sense of time standing still, grinding down the lives of the isolated and trapped inhabitants.

Speaking to Robert Shelton in 1966, Dylan comments, "Anytime I'm singing about people, and if the songs are dreamed, it's like my voice is coming out of their dream" (Dylan 2006, 88). Evoking the dream quality of song again in *Chronicles*, Dylan (2004) notes that "A song is like a dream, and you try to make it come true. They're like strange countries you have to enter" (165). Implicitly, Dylan seems to be arguing that to inhabit a song, and more pointedly, a character in the song, one must do so by filtering another consciousness, a sense, and make it present, make it "come true." In "North Country Blues" we see him filtering the consciousness of a woman born, raised, and growing old in an iron ore town that has seen a cycle of growth and decline over the years mirroring her own life of loss and gain, now watching everything slip away. As impersonal as the narrative is from Dylan's perspective (as performer), there is clearly a personal presence that resonates with his own witnessing of this cycle in Hibbing. As Pichaske (2010) notes, small details in the song have biographical resonance for Dylan, "like the move during prosperous times from the wrong side of town (the south side, where the speaker was born, and where Echo [Dylan's high school girlfriend] lived) to the more upscale north end of town" where the speaker's children are born and Dylan's family lived (26).[5] In "11 Outlined Epitaphs" we can see a similar divide between old, decaying north Hibbing, where Dylan's mother was born, and new south Hibbing, where Dylan was brought up. The combination of these two details, however, points to a feeling of decline and isolation creeping in from the old north ruins and the "wrong side of town" to the south. This feeling of being boxed in by decay is central to the nameless speaker's consciousness.

As noted, this is the only Dylan song presented entirely through a female persona, and while this is not a tale of revenge like we see in "Pirate Jenny," there seems to be a distinct correlation. Not only is she speaking to us, while probing the past, as if we are presently sitting in the room with her (signaled by the traditional folk ballad phrase, "Come gather 'round friends / And I'll tell you a tale")[6]; structurally speaking, her narrative has a central focus that ties the entire dramatic situation together amid the cycle of boom and bust years. In "Pirate Jenny," Brecht breaks from Jenny's audience address to the harbor as the black freighter approaches. In "North Country Blues," the central motif is a window. In general, we can imagine the speaker gazing out of the window as she tells her tale, and we can see a reflection of the town and her own fate in the first verse as she mentions "the cardboard filled windows" in town, suggesting both abandonment/loss and a kind of entombment.

The window serves as a still point in her boom/bust world (essentially representing the passage and cycles of time). Time is always passing, giving, and taking, while her life remains framed by a confining past. Thus we join her as opportunities, "when the red iron ore pits ran aplenty," seem to be closing for good in the first verse—a fact that is signaled by windows filled with cardboard. Likewise, in the second verse, the implicit suggestion of prosperity signaled in her children being born in the north end of town, instead of the south end, is undercut by loss: we see this most obviously in the last verse when she notes that her children will leave as soon as they are grown, but more immediately in the second verse as she

---

[5] The north end of town where Dylan's family lived is not to be confused with old north Hibbing, the site from which the mining company moved many of the buildings and left the ghost of ruins Dylan references in "11 Outlined Epitaphs."

[6] As, inexplicably, the lyrics to "North Country Blues" do not appear on Bobdylan.com, these lines (and those that follow) are quoted from the most recent volume of *The Lyrics: 1961–2012*, pp. 88–89.

recounts her "wee hours of youth" when her mother died and her brother is left to take care of her. Already implicit in the second verse is that fact that her father abandoned the family (or died in the mine), but the cycle of gain and loss is made explicit in the third verse's tragic shift from prosperity "as the years passed the door" with "the drag lines an' the shovels... a-humming" to the moment her brother "Failed to come home / Same as [her] father before him." And onward the pattern goes after "a long winter's wait, / From the window [she] watched" and marries another miner during prosperous years who will also leave her after she has born three children and the mine is shut down. From that point the stillness and decay creep in: "the air, it felt frozen... /... the red iron rotted / ... the room smelled heavy from drinking / Where the sad silent song / Made the hour twice as long / As I waited for the sun to go sinking." And as she watched the sun go down, she "lived by the window / As [her husband] talked to himself, / the silence of tongues it was building."

This endless cycle grinding out the individual, restlessness turned to resignation, is punctuated by Dylan's musical accompaniment: two chords swinging to and fro (C minor and A#, capo on the third fret, sounding in the key of C minor) sounding the dramatic, restless tension as the narrative swings between hope/boom and despair/bust.[7] Similarly, Dylan's use of accompaniment to dramatize the arc of narrative in "Ballad of Hollis Brown" (originally titled "The Rise and Fall of Hollis Brown" in its first publication in *Broadside* #21 [February 1963], and presented as "a true story") achieves a similar effect. Although in the former it is more of a tense lulling into submission, swinging back and forth like a trapeze artist until all momentum ceases and the woman is left framed and trapped in that window, soon to be covered over. In "Hollis Brown," the accompaniment is a relentless drone (punctuated by a double-dropped D guitar tuning) made of one chord (D# minor, capo on the first fret, establishing the key of D# minor) with interspersed bass notes seeming to be a constant rhythmical pounding in Hollis Brown's head.[8] It is no wonder Dylan

[7] This music formation hints at the possibility of resolution with the ghost of the fifth note of the C minor scale (G) and hints at the resolution of this ghostly G with the D (fifth note of the G scale) ringing in the A#. These ghosts of resolution drive the restlessness of the composition.

[8] Double-dropped D tuning involves tuning the first (high E) and sixth string (low E) down a whole step to D, which becomes a D# when the capo is added to the first fret. The intermittent bass notes move from momentary resolution to a depressed tone, a tension that signifies a constant thinking. The bass notes move ceaselessly between the A# fifth note of

dropped "the rise and fall" from the original title: when we are introduced to Hollis Brown in the first verse there is nothing left but the fall, like a trapeze artist whose motion has already stopped and who is starting to feel the twitch of muscles and sweat gather on his hands as he is about to lose his grip.

Musically, as noted in the original *Broadside* publication of the song, the tune is "much like" the traditional murder ballad "Pretty Polly." Early performances of "Hollis Brown" (written in September 1962) before Dylan recorded it for *The Times* certainly make this noticeable, especially when compared to his own performances of "Pretty Polly" in 1962. In performances of "Pretty Polly" Dylan seems to be paying very much attention to the dramatic tension in the song and trying to punctuate it with droning bass notes, intermittent foot-pounding and dynamic vocal delivery. "Hollis Brown" has a similar feel to it as Dylan was tapping into the "folk sense" of the song during this time, and he even includes a few harmonica interjections. By the time he recorded it for *The Times* much of the external effort to punctuate the dramatic tension seems to have dropped away and the song's tragedy and revenance come of its own accord—with Dylan performing it through impersonal narration.

A North Dakota farmer at the end of his metaphorical rope as his family succumbs to sickness and his land to disease and drought decides to end his life along with his wife and five children. He uses the seven shotgun shells he bought with the last of his money. As Greil Marcus (2015) comments, this is the kind of story we might find collected in Michael Lesy's *Wisconsin Death Trip*, a narrative collage of news stories and photographs from Black River Falls, Wisconsin, and surrounding areas at the end of nineteenth century (33–4). Indeed, as I have noted in a previous work, there is a news item included in the book that particularly resonates with Hollis Brown's story.[9] On September 24, 1891, the *Badger State Banner* reported the following: "Poverty and no work caused August Schultz of Appleton to shoot himself in the head while sitting in his little home with

---

the scale, the resolution, and the minor third note of the scale, F#, mimicking an unquiet mind, unable to settle, and building mental instability and final dramatic rupture. Special thanks to Dr. Michael Jones and his input on this matter and the previous footnote.

[9] Cf. I discuss this news item in relation to "Hollis Brown" in the "Greetings from the Old, Weird America" section in chapter 3 of *Lead Belly, Woody Guthrie, Bob Dylan and American Folk Outlaw Performance*.

his wife and 5 children" (Lesy 1973, 9/24/91).[10] Perhaps Dylan even ran across a similar story while pouring over those old newspapers at the New York Public Library or sifting through the eclectic archives at the Folklore Center. But as is the case with "North Country Blues," the song may resonate with the past, but it also seems entirely present.

One technical choice Dylan makes in "Hollis Brown" to emphasize an immediate presence, even more so than in "North Country Blues," is to employ a shifting narrative perspective. As Dylan (2004) notes in *Chronicles*, during his college days in Minneapolis he learned a folk song called "Old Greybeard," which "is sung in first, second and third person" (240). He further comments on the effect this attention to perspective achieves in the folk ballads he was learning: "Lyrically they worked on some kind of supernatural level and they made their own sense. You didn't have to make your own sense out of it.... I was beginning to feel like a character from within these songs, even beginning to think like one" (240). Speaking of the presence of the characters in the songs, he comments, "when they spoke in the songs they entered your life" (240). In "Hollis Brown," through Dylan's use of third- and second-person perspective in the narrative, Hollis Brown not only enters our life, but we also enter his.

In a sense, this eleven-verse song (a tragically restless epitaph) is outlined/framed by the first and last verse in third-person perspective, which are essentially epitaphs on Hollis Brown's life in themselves. In the first, we are introduced to Hollis Brown and his isolation is immediately implicated by the fact that he "lived on the outside of town" with his family and decaying cabin. And, of course, he is introduced in the past tense. In the last verse, it is as if Brown and his family become one more anonymous victim in the endless cycle of poverty grinding people out of existence. It is no longer Hollis Brown's farm. It is just a South Dakota farm where seven nameless people lay dead.

What makes the song particularly effective is the shift to second person in the intermediary verses, which not only puts the listener in the place of Hollis Brown, making it personal, but also creates a dramatic tension in relation to the droning accompaniment and impersonal, emotionless vocal delivery. There is also a tension between past and present in verses two through five, as if the narrative is pulling us into the past in order to make

---

[10] Michael Lesy's *Wisconsin Death Trip* was published without page numbers. For citation purposes the date of the news story is given.

it present and more intensely felt. For instance, in the second verse, Hollis Brown/You "looked for work and money / And you walked a ragged mile," and this past failure punctuates the restless helplessness of the present (which physically and psychologically increases as the narrative progresses) where "Your children are so hungry / That they don't know how to smile." In verses three and four we remain in the present as the family assaults "you" with their desperate gaze and your flour and mare are physically infested by rats and disease ("bad blood"), respectively. In verse five we move beyond the physical decay that is creeping in to spiritual hopelessness: "You prayed to the Lord above / Oh please send you a friend." Here again we experience a past action that fails, punctuated by the present moment of (y)our empty pockets.

From this point on the song remains painfully in the present as we accompany Hollis Brown in the increasing physical and mental decay made even more resonant by the relentless musical accompaniment and the effective use of repeating lines. And here we should note that when Dylan published the song in *Broadside* the verses followed a standard three-line AAB blues structure, but as performed and later published in official lyrics collections the verses became six lines. This shift in form points to Dylan making use of structure to further take advantage of dramatic effect. Instead of one line repeating we now have two lines that repeat. This effects a more incessant pounding. Even the "mathematical" syllable counts of the lines resonate with the overall narrative where, in general, the lines vacillate between six (seventeen lines) and seven (thirty-nine lines) syllables. The majority of lines running seven syllables fittingly correlates with the seven people who will die (along with the seven shotgun shells and seven breezes blowing), and perhaps the shift to six syllables reflects the recurring sense of loss and decay. Lines that mark an increase of mental and physical pressure on "you" run to eight syllables (seven lines). The only lines that deviate from this are the first and third lines (which consist, only, of three syllables), "Hollis Brown," and one line in the second to last verse (which is five syllables), "seven shots ring out." Essentially, these are the lines that signal the end of Hollis Brown, and Dylan seems to purposely play with the suggestion that these lines together come out to eight syllables (i.e., "Hollis Brown"/"seven shots ring out"), finally pushing Hollis Brown over the edge.

We may think of Yeats's widening gyre, and perhaps that widening cone is a model for civilization's decay, but in "Hollis Brown" it is not a widening that leads to things falling apart, but rather the scavenger circling closer as the body and mind lose their grip and are pierced with physical disease/rot and collapsing mental stability to pick at the bones.

Echoing some of Dylan's commentary on folk sense, Greil Marcus (2015) comments on the element of inflection, the particularly in-tune resonance with folk sense/tradition, in "Hollis Brown"; Marcus's comment thus speaks directly to the quality of revenance we have been considering in his early narratives: "there is a language in the American folk song that, as people speak the same phrases as everyone else, seduces or compels them to add their own shadings, their own cues, elisions, emphases, stresses... so that any statement can appear at once as commonplace and individual... A language in which there is, at the source, no original—and if there is no original, there is no copy" (24–5). What Marcus ultimately highlights about "Hollis Brown" (I would also include "North Country Blues") is the process by which "Dylan was able to make the song sing as if it were not his" (37). The various parts of this process are tied to the three perspectives from which we might evaluate the song: "Bob Dylan's song; the folk song; and his song that sounds like a folk song, authorless, written by history and weather, no original and no copy" (Marcus 48). In terms of revenance, the result of these three parts becoming something more than their sum, we can view these parts as the present (Dylan's song), the resonant (his song that sounds like a folk song), and the revenant (the folk song).

FAREWELL

In a February 1964 performance of "Restless Farewell" (originally titled "Bob Dylan's Restless Epitaph"), the last song Dylan wrote and recorded for *The Times*, in the Canadian TV show *Quest*, Dylan closes out the half-hour show alone in what appears to be an isolated cabin in a northern logging camp: "Oh, ev'ry thought that's strung a knot in my mind, / I might go insane if it couldn't be sprung." A restless thought indeed, punctuated by his isolation, and bearing a tragic resonance with Hollis Brown's decline and end. The show began with Dylan surrounded by loggers going about their various leisure activities with a slight air of melancholy and Dylan performing "The Times They Are a-Changin'." There is an ominous moment as he nears the end of this sermonizing oratorical song of hope. Behind him we see a man whose arm has been amputated, a hook now in its place.

These two songs also open and close *The Times*, and if we reflect on the dramatic space Dylan inhabits in this TV show and its resonance with the dramatic space/narrative arc of the album, we can certainly sense the tension between the songs of sermonizing oratory (i.e., "protest songs") and the songs that serve as restless epitaphs. With the specter of the amputee in the background we are also reminded of the ruins of old north Hibbing with its old school amputated. In hindsight, we can now recognize this moment in Dylan's career as a restless moment where isolation and confinement within a certain genre or classification as either poet or songwriter threaten to amputate his creative impulses, just as he had felt that remaining in Hibbing would isolate him. Unlike the subjects of those restless epitaphs "North Country Blues" and "Ballad of Hollis Brown," he broke a cycle that might have swallowed him whole.

REFERENCES

Anderson, Margaret Bartlett. 1963. *Robert Frost and John Bartlett: The Record of a Friendship*. New York: Holt, Rinehart and Winston.

Dylan, Bob. 1963. The Rise and Fall of Hollis Brown. *Broadside Magazine*, February: 7.

———. 1964. 11 Outlined Epitaphs (liner notes). *The Times They Are a-Changin'*. Columbia: Vinyl Record.

———. 1985a. *Biograph*. New York: Columbia.

———. 1985b. *Lyrics, 1962–1985*. New York: Knopf.

———. 2004. *Chronicles, Volume One*. New York: Simon and Schuster.

———. 2006. *Bob Dylan: The Essential Interviews*. Edited by Jonathan Cott. New York: Wenner Books.

———. 2016. *The Lyrics: 1961–2012*. New York: Simon and Schuster.

Eliot, T.S. 1950. Tradition and the Individual Talent. In *Selected Essays*. San Diego: Harcourt, Brace and Company.

Ferlinghetti, Lawrence. 1958. *A Coney Island of the Mind*. Cambridge: New Directions.

Frost, Robert. 1964. *The Complete Poems of Robert Frost*. New York: Holt, Rinehart and Winston.

———. 1966. *Interviews with Robert Frost*. Edited by Edward Connery Lathem. New York: Holt, Rinehart and Winston.

Goldsmith, Thomas. 2018. 2 UNC Students Snuck Backstage at the 1965 Dylan and Baez Show in Raleigh and Left with an Interview of a Lifetime. *News & Observer*, March 20, 2018.

Heylin, Clinton. 2009. *Revolution in the Air: The Songs of Bob Dylan 1957–1973*. Chicago: Chicago Review Press.

Lesy, Michael. 1973. *Wisconsin Death Trip*. New York: Pantheon.

Marcus, Greil. 2015. *Three Songs, Three Singers, Three Nations*. Cambridge, MA: Harvard University Press.

Ochs, Phil. 1965. An Interview with Phil Ochs. *Broadside Magazine*, October 15: 2–6.

Pichaske, David. 2010. *Song of the North Country: A Midwest Framework to the Songs of Bob Dylan*. New York: Continuum.

Ricks, Christopher. 2003. *Dylan's Visions of Sin*. New York: Viking.

Route TV. 2016. Bob Dylan San Francisco Press Conference 1965. YouTube Video, 51:04, September 20, 2016.

Shelton, Robert. 1997. *No Direction Home: The Life and Music of Bob Dylan*. Boston: Da Capo.

Vander Ven, Tom. 1973. Robert Frost's Dramatic Principle of 'Oversound'. *American Literature* 45 (2): 238–251.

CHAPTER 3

Dylan's Deixis

Charles O. Hartman

When Bob Dylan was awarded the Nobel Prize in Literature, reaction was predictably mixed. *The New York Times* summarized the debate in its story on October 13, 2016: "Bob Dylan Wins Nobel Prize, Redefining Boundaries of Literature." Instead of prolonging disputes over "poem" and "song," however—disputes that seem fossilized and unresolvable—we might more usefully ask what Dylan's song lyrics have in common with the traditions and concerns of poetry in the usual, narrow sense. One connection can be found in the core but easily overlooked operation of language called *deixis*. This essay offers some examples of how Dylan uses deixis to create character and setting, draws parallels with how poets use it, and points out the ethical work that these manipulations enable.

In the circumstance that linguists call deixis, language acknowledges its yearning for the world.[1] When we converse, the mechanism seems straightforward because the chief deictic categories—person, place, and time—are

---

[1] Among those who have occasion to speak this word, there seems to be difference about its first vowel; it rhymes with either "makes us" or "likes us," apparently with an American preference for the latter and British for the former. It derives from a Greek word meaning "reference" or "pointing." The *OED* says it entered English as a noun in 1949, though the adjective "deictic" goes back to technical texts in philosophy and rhetoric as early as 1828.

C. O. Hartman (✉)
Connecticut College, New London, CT, USA

© The Author(s) 2019
N. Otiono, J. Toth (eds.), *Polyvocal Bob Dylan*,
Palgrave Studies in Music and Literature,
https://doi.org/10.1007/978-3-030-17042-4_3

all conveniently embodied in the speaker: *I am here now.* If we were face to face, you would know what I mean. Your ability to verify my statement through your senses would make my statement deictic: words like "I" take on referential meaning within the context of a situation shared by speaker and listener.

Writing mystifies the game, since there may be little information about whom "I" refers to, and whenever or wherever "now" and "here" are, they are rarely the here and now of the reader. What David Crystal (2006) says in *How Language Works*, that "writing avoids words where the mean-ing relies on the situation (*deictic* expressions...)" (150), is manifestly untrue, but the norm he enunciates highlights enigmas about writing/reading. This is the ordinary mystery on display when we read the opening line of Robert Browning's best-known dramatic monologue: "That's my last Duchess painted on the wall" ([1842] 2005). We readers, looking at a page, can't see the painting, but we promptly conceive someone who is being shown it, someone who is already acutely conscious of what we grasp indirectly: that only a Duke could be speaking of "my last Duchess." We construe both "That's" and "my" as deictic terms, and mentally con-struct the situation they entail.

Bob Dylan's songs seem to thrive on our need to interpret, the diffi-culty of interpreting, and our skill at it. Famously, they invite exegesis on a maximum range of scales. The deictic categories offer especially funda-mental examples. Before we sort through the sometimes-fugitive opera-tions of deixis in his songs, however, it may be useful to pause for a moment over another poem; the steadiness of print makes it easier to observe our process of determining whether deixis is in play or not, and how.

Gwendolyn Brooks's "Sadie and Maud" (1963)—a poem almost as familiar from anthologies as Browning's—begins with the line, "Maud went to college." Unlike "I" and "you," the third person is not typically deictic; *you* and *I* must be present for context to define those pronouns, but we can talk about *her* and *him* behind their backs. The exception occurs when names or nouns or pronouns are used demonstratively: "Chester (over there) sings well." In Brooks's written line there is no fin-ger to point and no person to point to. (Though "go" often stands in deictic contrast to "come"—away from here, toward here—"go to col-lege" is a fixed phrase; "I *went* to college *here*" makes sense.) Yet Maud is at least notionally pointed to as an example. Going to college is a good thing to do—for the individual, for the family, and indeed, particularly in Brooks's early twentieth century, for "the race." This judgment seems confirmed by the contrast that is promised by the title and presented in the second line: "Sadie stayed at home" (2).

Brooks's language here seems almost the opposite of deictic; rather than speaking within a situation, she creates a showcase. This accords with the storytelling, ballad-like tone of the poem. Stories live in elsewhere: "Once upon a time" is not now; the story unfolds most freely "in a galaxy far, far away"—and most tellingly with regard to our own ostensibly different world. Brooks's opening lines establish a narrative of two sisters that presents itself as detached and objective, though it seems weighted against Sadie, who, as we will hear, "bore two babies / Under her maiden name" (9–10). We are encouraged to side with "Maud and Ma and Papa" (11) who "Nearly died of shame" (12). The phrase used to describe Sadie's out-of-wedlock pregnancies—the most genteel circumlocution available—seems theirs. Yet much of the poem's attention focuses on Sadie, who "scraped life / With a fine-tooth comb" (2–3): grudging praise but vivid. In the end, after Sadie's death,

> When Sadie said her last so-long
> Her girls struck out from home.
> (Sadie had left as heritage
> Her fine-tooth comb.)
> (13–16)

The daughters' departure is predictable, though the presumably uncomfortable household of six (until the parents' unmentioned death) has apparently held together long enough for the "girls" to be capable of fending for themselves.

The poem's final stanza readies the case for final reckoning. It begins again with Maud, and reminds us of her favored status: "Maud, who went to college" (17). The following line—"Is a thin, brown mouse" (18)—though we may be startled by the bitterness of its scorn, does not surprise us, because Sadie, "one of the livingest chits / In all the land" (7–8), has been accumulating admiration throughout the telling, in spite of the others' "shame." But whose admiration? The poem's ending shocks us by answering this question. Maud (the "thin, brown mouse") "Is living all alone / In this old house" (19–20). The demonstrative "this" can only be deictic; the house can only be the one in which the family has lived and died; and the speaker, delivering a verdict in Sadie's favor, can only be Maud. By using deictic language of place ("this ... house") Brooks creates a deixis of person: Maud turns suddenly into the poem's implicit "I."

The astonishment of Brooks's last line rests on her outmaneuvering our assumption that written language will be cut off from deixis. In this regard, what is the status of song? Though singing recuperates language from the silence of the page, it does not return us to the clarities of speech. If someone in my presence says "I want you," and if I don't believe I'm being addressed, then I am overhearing a conversation, and I expect to see a person there to play the role of "you." (Never mind the perplexities wrought by cellphones.) Yet if someone onstage alone sings "I Want You" (Dylan 1966) we are not puzzled by the absence of a visible "you." We know perfectly well that songs exemplify what Barbara Herrnstein Smith (1978) calls "fictive discourse" (14ff.). In a poem *or* a song, we perceive that we must figure out the who, where, and when that in normal speech situations we simply presume. In a fiction, any deictic context is deduced, not known directly.

It seems important to add—if only to set the point aside in focusing on Dylan's lyrics—that live performance entails and generates its own deixis, distinct from any deixis contained within the fiction of the song itself. The singer before us visibly and audibly embodies the lyrics' "I," who at the same time he visibly is not (e.g., "I Am a Lonesome Hobo" [1967]). In the case of Dylan, the "I" in or behind the songs has been long and notably revisited and revised; he has performed "Like a Rolling Stone" (1965) and some others over 2000 times, often at first unrecognizably. We in the audience are not the "you" of the lyrics (e.g., in "I Want You"), but we are absorbingly addressed, and we know that we are necessary to the performance. The here and now of his performance are motivated and made vivid by our ritual presence, an effect all the stronger for the frequently glaring contrast with any setting conjured by the song (for instance, "Desolation Row" [1965]). We are sitting in the same deictic space with the singer, yet this space moves from performance to performance, though the venues are usually quite similar. The intensity of this mutual presence is presumably what Dylan desires enough to keep performing, around the world, dozens or hundreds of times every year. He doesn't need the money. As audiences and critics have long noted, these presences are at best simulated in recordings—though Dylan has long striven to keep his recordings as raw as possible, always seeking the feel of live performance.

The first stanza of "I Shall Be Free No. 10" (1964) begins with archetypal here-I-am-singing-in-front-of-you deixis. (Interestingly, this is a song that Dylan has never performed live.) It combines this emphasis on the present self with the everyman modesty befitting songs in the Woody

Guthrie tradition. But Dylan, as slyly as Guthrie himself might have done, pushes *both* pretenses to the point of parody:

> I'm just average, common too
> I'm just like him, the same as you
> I'm everybody's brother and son
> I ain't different from anyone

Obviously, then, "It ain't no use a-talkin' to me / It's just the same as talkin' to you."

Within a fictive discourse, however, deictic language gains leverage by entailing our deft constructive assistance; we excel at deducing whatever places, times, and persons the fiction requires. True, it is possible to forget that not only the "you" of a song but the deictic "I" is, no matter how apparently or ostensibly similar to the writer or singer, a fiction. An early reviewer of *John Wesley Harding* felt compelled to point out that the "I" of "I Am a Lonesome Hobo" "cannot be Dylan: lonesome the young millionaire may be, but a hobo, no." (Charles E. Fager 1968, 821). Subtler versions of the confusion Fager is fending off abound—internet comments on song lyrics are rife with them—but as long as we keep our heads level, we are expert in navigating the framing strategies of verbal art.

The deixis of person, if only as a fictive gesture, cannot be completely absent from any discourse that contains a first-person pronoun. Yet in "Tomorrow Is a Long Time" ([1963] 1971), the deixis seems irrelevant, or at least impossible to pin down, because every self-statement of the "I" is negative: "I can't see my reflection in the water ... Or remember the sound of my own name." Similar kinds of slippage or indeterminacy occur in many of Dylan's songs. The discourse of "Blowin' in the Wind" (1962) is deictically anchored only by the address "my friend," and by the self that is implicit in asking questions. The remembered "Girl from the North Country" (1963) is not a party to the conversation, which is instead directed to a faceless "you" ("If you're travelin' to the North Country fair") like the "you" in "If You See Her, Say Hello" (1975). In "Walls of Red Wing" ([1963] 1991), which is about a juvenile detention center, deixis is oblique—its anchor is "I remember," modulating to "some of us"—but crucial to the ethos of the song, the ground of its authenticity as a protest song. So clearly do we understand this "I" as recounting the experience of an inmate that we may hardly notice the shift to second person: "Oh it's all afternoon / You remember your hometown." Logically this should be confusing, but in conversation we negotiate the same shift all the time. In "Seven Curses" ([1963] 1991), in classic third-person ballad style, only the voicing of the curses at the end feels deictically laden with an unstated but formidable "I." On the other hand, what holds our attention in "North Country Blues" (1964) is a story that progressively defines its "I": a woman at the disintegrating center of a mining family. "Just Like a Woman" (1966)—which I have discussed elsewhere at some length (Hartman 2015)—works in a similar manner. To see this, we need only note its shift, halfway through, from third person—at least the apparent third person of "Baby's got new clothes" and "Baby can't be blessed"— to second person: "your long-time curse hurts." The transition to the direct address of complaint and plea drives the song's increasing emotional intensity.

In many songs, one of our primary listening tasks is to work out exactly who "I" and "you" are. This is most evident in pop songs of the 1950s and 1960s, though the task is not difficult when the cast of characters, exactly two in number, are identified with their presentation of standard roles: rejecting, being rejected, desiring, missing, threatening. This is context or background for many of Dylan's own more complex love songs. "Buckets of Rain" (1975) mimics, though it does not typify, the standard love-song pattern, in that it seems largely devoted to characterizing the poles of the axis of its discourse: "You got all the love, honey baby, I can stand." This is not "I Want to Hold Your Hand," but Dylan counts on our knowing the conventions of pop song that he is subverting. Despite the epic scope that lifts "Sad-Eyed Lady of the Lowlands" (1966) out of any Top-40 ambit, the adoration and anguish manifest throughout its eleven minutes are emotional materials that countless other love songs seem to wish they could give such clear voice to.

Yet often, in Dylan's work, the relation between "I" and "you" is more mysterious, and these riddles are inseparable from the song's moral point. "Sweetheart Like You" (1983) seems to begin affably enough—"By the way, that's a cute hat / And your smile's so hard to resist"—but the refrain is hardly seductive: "What's a sweetheart like you / Doing in a dump like this?" By the first bridge, the fictive speaker and his interlocutor are enmeshed in a bewilderingly venomous bargain: "You could be known as the most beautiful woman / Who ever crawled across cut glass to make a deal." (As is true of many of Dylan's songs, it is horrifying to imagine being on the receiving end of these lines, though to imagine uttering them may be exhilarating.) Whether we know anything about the "you" by the end of the song is debatable—she almost disappears from the last stanza, which turns toward corruption on a public and historical scale—but we know a great deal, though nothing simple, about the attitudes of the "I." "Idiot Wind" (1975), well known as a portrait of Dylan's deteriorating marriage, presents an even more confounded connection between two people who can neither escape nor embrace each other. The refrain that begins as invective—"Idiot wind, blowing every time you move your teeth / You're an idiot, babe, / It's a wonder that you still know how to breathe"—in the end turns into sorry commiseration: "Idiot wind, blowing through the dust upon our shelves / We're idiots, babe, / It's a wonder we can even feed ourselves."

Even an apparently straightforward song of transitory romance such as "One of Us Must Know (Sooner or Later)" (1966) gives us more hints about the "Us" than we can ever quite make cohere. We intuit that the underlying tone of baffled complaint in the singer's voice reflects his own doubt:

> Sooner or later, one of us must know
> You just did what you're [or "you were"?] supposed to do
> Sooner or later, one of us must know
> That I really did try to get close to you

It is not easy to say whether we, or she, should believe him, or whether he himself knows.

Sometimes Dylan's strategic sense of deictic choice seems to be unstable, most famously in his vacillation between versions of "Tangled Up in Blue" that center on "I" (1975) and others that use "he" for the same role (e.g., the original recording from the *Blood on the Tracks* sessions released on *Bootleg Series, Vol. 1–3* [1991]). In other cases the obscurity of the context seems to be the very point. "What Was It You Wanted" (1989) presents as directly dramatic an exchange as any song without explicit dialogue. (Dialogue is fairly rare in songs, for obvious yet interesting reasons—lyric and dramatic poetry are distinct on various grounds—though "Tin Angel" [2012] contains stretches of stichomythia and "Isis" [1976] depends and ends on a laconic four-line exchange that seals our comprehension of the characters' marriage.) Yet the song's title and signature line—"What was it you wanted?" (which is repeated several times in each stanza)—represent a refusal to acknowledge the claims of deixis. To ask this question once is to invite a request; to ask it repeatedly is to reject any interchange at all.

Indeed, the song, which two-thirds of the way through has asked, "Are you the same person / That was here before" and "Who are you anyway," ends with the line, "Are you talking to me?" We are hearing half of a dialogue conducted at profound, even paranoid cross-purposes. This is familiar territory for Dylan; though the lyrics of "I Don't Believe You (She Acts Like We Never Have Met)" (1964) are cast in third person, the title summarily challenges what the language-philosopher Paul Grice (1989) called "the Cooperative Principle" and the resulting "maxims" of conversation.

In "Up to Me" ([1975] 1985), we know that the urgency of "at least I heard your bluebird sing" is not ornithological. The stanzas of this great, rejected song shuffle the "I" and "you" cards into telling glimpses. The title phrase, in the sense *incumbent upon*, is an American colloquialism from poker, and the first stanza makes the contest explicit: "somebody had to show their hand," and since "you're long gone, / I guess it must be up to me." The second stanza is all "I" with no "you," but in the next two, the speaker assumes the mantle of the "Somebody" who must "find your trail" and "unlock your heart." The "officers' club" stanza shows the protagonists divided by jealousy, just as the "you" had "betrayed me with your touch" a stanza before. This is how what is "up to me" becomes the "get[ting] free" that one of the two of them must do. The task that is "up to me" evolves: to save "you" by taking down your wanted poster; to "make me move" (which sounds also like "a move"); "to tell the tale" and "cross the line" and "cry some tears"; finally, "to hit the road"; and postfinally, to "play that tune," which is presumably *this* tune.

The "I" and "you" in "Don't Think Twice, It's All Right" (1963), though they mutually define each other, emphatically do not share a deictic space: compare "your rooster" and "your window" to "down the road," "that long, lonesome road." The rupture of deixis-as-joint-presence establishes the song's longing. Deixis, then, not only traffics in locative and interpersonal information, but exerts emotional and ethical force. The breach between her who remains and him who leaves seems unhappy but simple. But the song is affecting because he can't leave badly enough alone: "Still I wish there was something you would do or say / To try and make me change my mind and stay / We never did too much talking anyway."

Later in his career Dylan acts out this quandary of irresolution most thoroughly in "Abandoned Love." (The song was written for *Desire* [1976], but—like "Up to Me"—inexplicably omitted from the album; a rehearsal take was released on *Biograph* [1985], and a unique live coffee-house recording is known from a few weeks earlier in July [1975].) The *narrative* of "Abandoned Love" goes nowhere—*can* go nowhere—but its *plot* is articulated by the five occurrences of the word "love." In the first four it is a verb, but "I love you" is perplexed by a series of reservations: "I love you still"; "I love to see you dress before the mirror"; "as long as I love you I'm not free"; "I love you but you're strange." The song's last line appears to triumph over love by reducing it to a noun: "Let me feel your love one more time before I abandon it." As for his love, we may doubt that even the blow of this final line kills it; the song ends "before" he achieves his abandonment.

Person is the most basic and pervasive deictic category; most songs—by Dylan as by any modern composer—center on an "I," but this person's location in space and time may be peripheral to the lyric utterance. Time-deictic expressions are occasionally used emphatically by songs. Two examples not by Dylan that spring to mind are Paul McCartney's "Yesterday" (1965)—which is very different from Jerome Kern's "Yesterdays"—and Ed McCurdy's "Last Night I Had the Strangest Dream." More generally, a majority of songs, including many of Dylan's, lean into a deictic present simply through choice of tense. If the past tense announces story, the present announces lyric. (George T. Wright [1974] elucidates this dynamic.) Dylan's "One Too Many Mornings" (1964) begins, "Down the street the dogs are barking and the day is getting dark." All the rest of the song's statements, whether observations like that one ("I gaze back to the street / The sidewalk and the sign") or general-izations like the one containing the title ("I'm just one too many morn-ings / And a thousand miles behind"), grow out of the present ground prepared by the first line. Of course deixis of time is thoroughly entangled with deixis of space, as it usually is in our experience.

An interesting reversal of this process of unfolding time, but one that finally focuses just as sharply on the present, occurs in "Love Is Just a Four-Letter Word" (1967), which was recorded by Joan Baez on *Any Day Now* (1968). The song begins with an incident in the past ("Seems like only yesterday..."), but through its remaining stanzas works up to a "now I understand" which, as the inexorable chronicle helps us understand, is possible only because the speaker has lived the whole gamut of experiences that rotate all of the title's facets into view. Conversely, in "Long Ago, Far Away" ([1962] 2010), deixis is explicitly but ironically negated—these bad things (the Holocaust, the Crucifixion, etc.) don't happen anymore—

so as to make us home in on the unstated "now," which turns out unhappily to be our own. Again the effect is much different from either Jerome Kern and Ira Gershwin's "Long Ago (and Far Away)" or James Taylor's "Long Ago and Far Away," both of which follow the phrase's lure into nostalgia.

Some of Dylan's early songs seem fascinated by the deixis of time and space, and make deixis of person a kind of secondary effect. "Walkin' Down the Line" ([1963] 1991) gives us almost nothing *but* the here and now under our noses: "I got my walkin' shoes"; "I see the morning light." This "I" seems defined—seems to define himself—exclusively by his existential condition. On the other hand, if *I am here* is *ur*-deixis, what is *I was here*? This is the stance Dylan explores in "Long Time Gone" ([1963] 2010)—though he did not invent the stance, as other uses of the title phrase suggest: "I'm just a long time coming and I'll be a long time gone" echoes through titles and lyrics by Richard Fariña, Sam Cooke, David Crosby, and many others. The attitude is a staple of American folk sensibility, combining prophetic presence with a kind of self-elegy.

Although the most basic vehicles of deixis are pronouns ("I," "you"), demonstratives ("this house"), and adverbs ("here," "now"), in storytelling deixis can permeate the language less obviously. In "Subterranean Homesick Blues" (1965), our sense of immediacy depends on a deictic "the": "Johnny's in *the* basement / Mixing up *the* medicine / I'm on *the* pavement / Thinkin' 'bout *the* government." We are readily persuaded to pretend that we know which basement and medicine, and the pretense endorses a feeling that we're standing next to him on the pavement. Hugh Kenner (1972) pointed out the same phenomenon in William Carlos Williams's "Poem (As the cat)":

> cat.
> A "noun." And what happens if we affix the article is highly mysterious:
>> the cat—
> for the grammarians' distinction—definite article for the particular, indefinite for the general—is meant to operate between speakers, live persons in a real place who already know, because they are talking about it, which cat is "the cat": "Have you put out the cat?" But typed on a sheet of paper as if to designate some one cat though we cannot identify him, the article performs in pure abstraction a gesture of as-if-specifying: something operative not in the kitchen or the garden but in a language field. (397)

Thus within a fiction deixis may create not only the persons but the place and time. In the great opening stanza of "Visions of Johanna" (*Blonde on Blonde*, 1966), we are placed in the song's physical world by the line "Lights flicker from the opposite loft." Here "opposite" functions as a deictic word: we cannot know its referent directly, so we are motivated to fabricate it, an effort that recruits us to the scene and its making. Again the present tense aids our participation; "lights flicker" invites us to watch them. Although in a line like "Down the street the dogs are barking" we are prepared for the prepositional phrase to act deictically, we are startled when the same effect is produced even more strongly by an adjective like "opposite," in which Dylan discovers a precise urban meaning: *across the street at the same elevation.*

There seems to be no standard term for the operation, in a fictive discourse, of this force that conjures our transported attendance. As Walter Jackson Bate (1963) notes, Keats, in his marginalia to *Paradise Lost*, used the term "stationing" to praise an aspect of Milton's imagery in which Keats emphasized the absence of movement; his own appositive term is "statuary" (246). We might employ "positioning" as a complementary term, one that will emphasize, rather than the absence of motion, the poem's (or poet's) ability to place us not just before a scene but within one. Positioning is quite different from the reified "setting" proper to landscape painting (the intellectual backdrop of Keats's notion of "stationing") and prose fiction. In that line from "Visions of Johanna," Dylan *positions us* within the scene, so that we seem to know what we will see if we turn in any direction, and what we will hear: "In this room the heat pipes just cough / The country music station plays soft." (A comparison with Virtual Reality is tempting but premature.)

This positioning—though it is practiced upon us more than it is a part of our own practice—is related to the principle of *compositio loci* (i.e., Composition of Place), a stage of meditation recommended by St. Ignatius of Loyola. Louis Martz pointed out in *The Poetry of Meditation* (1954) that the Ignatian *Spiritual Exercises* (1548) underlay English poetic procedures in the late sixteenth and early seventeenth centuries. The tradition continues, for instance, in James Wright's meditative lyric, "Lying in a Hammock at William Duffy's Farm in Pine Island, Minnesota" (1963). The whole poem—from its extravagant, memorializing title onward—is an exercise in imaginative deixis: the (imaginary) deixis of a place the poet at once commemorates, remembers, and makes us register as if we had been there and perhaps been him. "Over my head," the poem begins, and it proceeds to inventory the speaker's mindfully absorbed surroundings. When he says "Down the ravine behind the empty house," we know that "behind" means not *beyond the back of the house, on the side away from its mailbox and front porch,* but rather *on the other side of the house from me*: the speaker's point of view is rigidly adhered to throughout the poem. What happens behind the house, which he cannot see but only hear, is absurdly but precisely that "the cowbells follow one another."

Though in Ignatian religious practice "composition of place" can be elaborately ritualized, as it is also in Wright's poem ("To my right / In a field of sunlight between two pines / The droppings of last year's horses / Blaze up into golden stones"), poems and songs often rely on the modest power of "grammar words"—articles, prepositions, conjunctions, and such—to provide us with a sense of being positioned in relation to a scene. We have already seen how "the" can act deictically. Dylan controls the trajectory of meaning in "Desolation Row" (1965) through little shifts in the prepositions that govern the title line at the end of every stanza. At the beginning, "Lady and I" look out "from Desolation Row"—language that stresses their perspective as denizens. The next two stanzas survey the vibrant, ominous panoply of characters and events "on" this urban scene. Then Ophelia peeks longingly "into" it, since outside is only her "lifelessness." The sixth stanza brings us back inside, but lists the news you can hear about Dr. Filth's world "If you lean your head out far enough from" one of our windows. The next stanzas try on the point of view of the outside enforcers ("They," "the superhuman crew," "insurance men") who keep the allegedly fortunate citizens of the outer world from "going to" or "escaping to" or "think[ing] too much about" this place whose attractions Ophelia and Casanova intuit. The final stanza introduces a "you"— oh dear, is it us?—prone to inane communications, and refuses any further "letters" not mailed "from" within what is clearly the direst and hippest place to be.

Although earlier I suggested that in speech deixis works straightforwardly, even as simple a mediation as the telephone produces puzzles like "I'm coming home." (Only "I'm going home"—leaving the place where I am now—makes immediate, uncomplicated deictic sense.) It turns out that many non-fictive communications, spoken and written, depend on our ability to distinguish actual deictic point of view from some projected version of it. Hence the notion of a *deictic center*. On the transatlantic phone, if I say "I'm going to London next week" I keep my New York deictic center; by instead saying "I'm coming to London next week," I shift the center to my interlocutor, as a kind of courtesy. A shifting deictic center can effect surprisingly compelling imaginative transformations.

We can see such a transformation at work in Philip Levine's "For the Poets of Chile" (1976). The poem begins with the deictic line "Today I called for you" (1). But the "you" is not "the Poets" but "my death, like a cup / of creamy milk" (2–3)—though the poet's death is at issue only in his dream, provoked by distant news of "the thousands" (7) imprisoned and tortured "in the *futbol* stadium / of Santiago de Chile" (8–9). Levine is toying, seriously, with a standard tactic of political poetry, and forcing us to notice the phoniness of the North American poet's too-easy identification. The opening gesture, which tries to assert itself as one of solidarity, degenerates into one of self-congratulatory appropriation. The speaker is sympathetic, but safe: "calling" out vacuously for his own deliverance by death, he is at liberty to "[wake] / myself to the empty / beer can, the cup / of ashes" (25–7).

After this splendid false start, the poem redeems itself slowly by piecing together what "must" be happening in Chile, specifically to the young daughter of Victor Jara after her father's execution. Amid the ingenious jumble of our language, Levine has picked out the power of "must" to denote not coercion but imaginative necessity: "A year passes, two, / and still someone must / stand at the window ... Someone / must remember it over / and over..." (30–45). At the end, though, the girl and her mother truly "must / drink" (72–3) their milk alone. But their glasses of milk recall the poet's dreamed death cup at the beginning, and meanwhile "the floors / and cupboards cry out / like dreamers" (63–5)—like the dreamer whose poem now embraces them all. Before our eyes, yet as if behind its own back, the poem enacts a shift of deictic center from the poet's domestic "study" (21) to the daughter's grief-stricken "house" (62) and so transmutes the mere solicitude of the opening into a fictive but persuasive union.

Similarly, Dylan's "Mama You Been on My Mind" ([1964] 1991) dwells in the distance between what is here, "the crossroads I'm standing at," and what will happen in tomorrow's elsewhere when "you look inside your mirror." The difficult freedom to shift from one center to the other authenticates his protestations that "Where you been don't bother me" and "I don't even mind who you'll be waking with tomorrow." The song makes an urgent claim for the deictic imagination, the space-and-time-defying effort to occupy another person's literal and spiritual point of view: "I'd just be curious to know if you can see yourself as clear / As someone who has had you on his mind." The claim is remarkable. Whether these lines act out empathy or arrogance is not finally decidable, though any listener may take them one way or the other; the mechanism is the same, just as "I Want You" is both generous and imperious.

So although in most songs an "I" longs for a "you"—as "Boots of Spanish Leather" (1964) glumly anticipates—deixis can also, arduously, run both ways. It would be difficult to find a nicer convolution of deixis than the song title "I'm Not There." (Sometimes the title is given as "I'm Not There (1956)." No one seems to know why.) Famously, we don't even know what the lyrics of this song *are*. Online attempts at transcription disagree strikingly, and the relevant page on bobdylan.com is spookily, fittingly blank. This quality of articulated absence presumably encouraged Todd Haynes to adopt it as the title for his great non-biopic of six Dylans; the *I'm Not There* soundtrack was the first legally sanctioned distribution of Dylan's unique 1967 recording. Yet we catch enough of the words to comprehend the drama, which is played out by the singer's vacillation between the deictic center of his own point of view and the one he projects onto a woman who wishes he were where she is.

REFERENCES

Baez, Joan. 1968. *Any Day Now*. Vanguard. Vinyl record.

Bate, Walter Jackson. 1963. *John Keats*. Cambridge, MA: Harvard University Press.

Brooks, Gwendolyn. 1963. Sadie and Maud. In *Selected Poems*, 8. New York: Harper & Row.

Browning, Robert. 2005 (1842). My Last Duchess. In *The Major Works*, ed. Adam Roberts, 101–102. Oxford: Oxford University Press.

Crystal, David. 2006. *How Language Works: How Babies Babble, Words Change Meaning, and Languages Live or Die*. Woodstock, NY: Overlook Press.

Fager, Charles E. 1968. Cryptic Simplicity. *Christian Century* 85 (25): 821.

Grice, Paul. 1989. Logic and Conversation. In *Studies in the Ways of Words*, 22–40. Cambridge, MA: Harvard University Press.

Hartman, Charles O. 2015. Dylan's Bridges. *New Literary History* 46 (4): 737–757.

Kenner, Hugh. 1972. *The Pound Era*. Berkeley: University of California Press.

Levine, Philip. 1976. *The Names of the Lost*. New York: Alfred A. Knopf.

Martz, Louis. 1954. *The Poetry of Meditation: A Study in English Religious Literature of the Seventeenth Century*. New Haven, CT: Yale University Press.

Sisario, Ben, Alexandra Alter, and Sewell Chan. 2016. Bob Dylan Wins Nobel Prize, Redefining Boundaries of Literature. *New York Times*, October 13, 2016.

Smith, Barbara Herrnstein. 1978. *On the Margins of Discourse: The Relation of Literature to Language*. Chicago: University of Chicago Press.

Wright, George T. 1974. The Lyric Present: Simple Present Verbs in Lyric Poetry. *PMLA* 89 (3): 563–579.

Wright, James. 1963. Lying in a Hammock at William Duffy's Farm in Pine Island, Minnesota. In *The Branch Will Not Break*, 16. Middletown, CT: Wesleyan University Press.

CHAPTER 4

Not Just Literature: Exploring the Performative Dimensions of Bob Dylan's Work

Keith Nainby

The task is to find an account of communication that erases neither the curious fact of otherness at its core nor the possibility of doing things with words.
(John Durham Peters, *Speaking into the Air*)

Not a word was spoke between us, there was little risk involved
(Bob Dylan, "Shelter from the Storm")

And to [When I] think of how she left that night, it still brings me a chill
(Dylan, "If You See Her Say Hello")

The Final epigraph is one example among many in which I hear on a given reference recording lyrics that differ from the "official" version as published on bobdylan.com, a version which Dylan has modified over time and that can often therefore differ when compared with lyrics as printed on albums at the time of their release or as they are audibly sung.

K. Nainby (✉)
California State University, Stanislaus, Turlock, CA, USA

© The Author(s) 2019
N. Otiono, J. Toth (eds.), *Polyvocal Bob Dylan*,
Palgrave Studies in Music and Literature,
https://doi.org/10.1007/978-3-030-17042-4_4

The word "chill" offers interesting oral/aural qualities that lend themselves to the possibility of doing disparately poetic things with words: The opening, unvoiced "ch" with its dry, fricative press of sibilant breath near to a hiss can chill us. Its bloodless, cool sound can chime with onomatopoeia given the word's meaning—a sense clinched if its singer snaps the remaining short "i" vowel sound off with a clean, brittle edge and lets the final voiced "l" decay rapidly in volume and weaken in articulation. Bob Dylan does just this in the version of "If You See Her, Say Hello" (1975) that he performs on *The Bootleg Series, Vol. 1–3*, highlighting the cold distance from a former lover that the song laments. But if the same word is voiced with its singer leaning heavily on the vowel and milking the liquid "l" for its warm, vibrating quality over an extended time, we can hear a more complicated sense: We can hear a suggestion of how a chill can linger, can decay, moving over time from bitingly frosty to less keenly felt to, finally at the moment of utterance, perhaps a paradoxical kindling of longed-for connection—the chill transformed to a thrill, betraying the complicated emotions of the one singing. This is the performance Dylan gives us on the version of this song on *Blood on the Tracks*. The word "chill" in this performance ends not merely in a line but in a stanza, lending further weight to the work that duration can do to the memory of "how she left that night" and echoing the ambivalent stance toward lost love and the past that makes this song compelling. When we consider these two distinct approaches to reliving the narrator's remembered feeling of a chill, we can recognize the scope of poetic possibility within Dylan's oeuvre. In his work, poetry depends not merely on the words themselves but on how they are engaged through his performing artistry as a vocalist.

My purpose in this chapter is to explore the connection between Dylan's vocal performances and his texts, focusing on how this connection generates meanings for the listener. As I do so, I strive to attend to the ways that Dylan's vocal performances not merely inflect but deflect. As both John Durham Peters (1999) and Dylan (1975) suggest in the epigraphs above, regarding moments when words are spoken between people: Language fixes meanings but also obfuscates them, bringing us together in a shared realm of understanding while throwing our alienation from one another into relief. This paradox is Durham Peters's central insight as a philosopher of communication, and I consider it an insight of Dylan the artist as enacted in his richly textured performances of his songs.

One trace of this insight rests in the second quote among the epigraphs above, from "Shelter from the Storm" (1975): "Not a word was spoke between us, there was little risk involved." The implication is that when words are spoken between at least two people, there is the potential for great risk. This view, that verbal articulation involves great risk, is shared by Elaine Scarry (1985), who holds that "the story of *expressing* physical pain eventually opens into the wider frame of *invention* [...] we make ourselves (and the original interior facts of sentience) available to one another through verbal and material artifacts, as [...] derealization of artifacts may assist in taking away another person's visibility" (22, emphasis in original). In developing this argument, Scarry links (1) human efforts to bridge across the differences among our felt experiences of our separate bodies, which we do through sharing symbolic invention with one another, to (2) the ultimate impossibility of fully sustaining such bridges. Even though the aim for shared sentience will always be dashed, those moments when we are denied the chance to strive for this aim (in Scarry's analysis, situations of extreme political violence such as torture and lengthy imprisonment) are the least humanizing of all. Again we have a paradox, the one implied in "Shelter from the Storm": we must seek shelter with, and in, one another in order to be fully human—yet to do so is also to risk our own humanity, because in the seeking we come to know that we will inevitably remain cut off from one another as well.

I attribute to an artist named "Bob Dylan" this insight that communication both conjoins and confounds. But this claim needs some further clarification given the concerns regarding performance authenticity and analysis of popular music that scholars have raised. Peter Kivy (1995) holds that any particular musical performance can be described according to the authenticity of the performance along four dimensions: first, with respect to the original composer's intent; second, with respect to the historical performance context of the original work; third, with respect to the performer's expressive palette; and fourth, with respect to the audience's reception of the work. My interest in this chapter lies with the third and fourth dimensions: How do listeners engaging Dylan's sung performances (part of his "expressive palette" or, if you like, "expressive palate") make meaning based on the choices he employs—specifically, his vocal choices? I aim to pin down no particular intention to Dylan the composer nor to Dylan the performer, but to consider how Dylan as a performer of his own compositions offers us, through patterned vocal choices, a wealth of poetic treasures whose depths we listeners can plumb to our delight. I attempt throughout the chapter to further contextualize my claims about vocal choices by considering: (1) the sense of the words as I hear them sung; (2) the images and themes in the songs themselves; and (3) occasionally, these elements' relation to Dylan's media/star image as an exceptionally popular, influential and valorized musical artist.

Dylan's body of work has historically been treated by scholars in one of the three distinct ways: as poetry (Herdman 1981; Day 1988; Gibbens 2001; Scobie 2003; Ricks 2004), as the musicological product of a set of specific song traditions (Marcus 1997; Harvey 2001; Lloyd 2014) or as a textualization of his image as a cultural icon (Marqusee 2005; Marshall 2007; Boucher and Browning 2009; Wilentz 2010). One scholar who combines these three lenses is Michael Gray (2000). Gray, Paul Williams (1996, 2004, 2005a, b), Betsy Bowden (2001) and David Yaffe (2011) each take up in their own ways the question of how Dylan, as performing artist, offers a profusion of meanings through his oral/aural choices. Bowden puts the matter most closely to how I also understand it:

> But it was not Dylan's lyrics alone, nor his guitar and harmonica, that sent our parents clutching their ears and climbing their respective suburban walls in the sixties. It was that voice—that whining, grating, snarling voice that can drip scorn or comfort, can stretch or snap off words in disregard of their meaning or in fulfillment of it, can say for the listener what she has not quite yet said for herself. (3)

Alas, though Bowden's excellent book-length study of Dylan's vocal performances was published in 1982 (its later revision did not include research on additional songs), in the third of a century since then few scholars have returned to an analysis of these vocal performances. Williams comes closest through attending carefully to the aural and sensual experiences of Dylan's concerts, but his focus is much more strongly on the qualities of the total live performance as experienced by the audience across particular Dylan tours; he treats vocal choices in some passages, as I note below, but these are not his primary concern. Yaffe's focus on Dylan's singing voice is perhaps the most sustained; but he is primarily interested in mapping Dylan's range of personal and public locations within his cultural landscape. In this chapter, my central purpose is to trace the aural forms of

Dylan's vocal choices and some of their impact on how we might take up those songs' particular meanings.[1]

One author who can help us articulate what's at stake when poetic language like Dylan's breathes through the audible voice of the recorded performing artist and is engaged by audience members is, as I note above, Durham Peters (1999). He offers a compelling synthesis of significant conceptions of communication, as distinct from conceptions of language, writing or persuasion. In that synthesis Durham Peters describes two key conceptions of communication: One devotes pragmatic attention to how we make meanings and sustain communities through interactions that accumulate over time and in particular spaces. The other devotes metaphysical attention to how meanings are deferred and human contact mystified through our attempts to come to know through systems of language (see pp. 16–22). These two views of communication—(1) meanings shaped in *context* and (2) meanings clouded in *contact*—are each embodied in Dylan's assuredly Laureate-worthy poetics throughout his full body of recorded work. I suggest that Dylan's vocal performances make these two types of aesthetic moves on us, his listeners, as he moves through the songs—stretching images by his stretching of vowels, inspiring through his respirating, condensing language poetically while condensing syllables and words, attacking sensory recall in attacking the eruption of consonants.

Varying Vowels

"One of Us Must Know (Sooner or Later)" (1966) is a song with a title linking duration of experience to epistemological outcomes. The ending phrase of one line from this song is about the narrator's decision whether to leave with the song's second-person addressee or with someone else, and Dylan sings it—"I didn't realize how young you weeeeeeeeere"—over several beats of music. He thereby thickens the ironic barb directed by the narrator at a (presumably by now uncomfortably older, less naïve, less gossip-inducing) past lover. Dylan leans on the vowel to lengthen the time of our listening and enact through performance what both this line and the

---

[1] In large part, then, I am animated by Philip Auslander's (2004) contention that a given performer who develops a performing persona within a given cultural and music industry context, and who uses that persona to create a particular character in a particular performative act such as a recording of a song, must rely on a range of musical expressions in order to ultimately communicate any of these performance elements to an audience.

song's title insist: that when we take time, time takes us and changes us by changing how and what we know about ourselves, our relationships, and our responsibility for one another. This is one instance of vocal performance working with a listener over the fabric of the music's measuring of time—in a way distinct from how printed lines of text work with a reader—to shape possible resonances of meaning in context. But meanings are also clouded by listener-performer contact in this same instance, as the second-person narrative mode suggests a double irony: Can a listener addressed by "how young you were," who presumably has always known her or his own age, be drawn into the narrator's surprise and effort to make retrospective sense by the lengthening of "were?" Or is the narrator's performance instead here an inevitable failure of contact (one more time), a failure enacted by the choice of second-person address and by a reproducing of his own confusion, the very lack of past knowledge he laments, as he sings the song now with its lengthened verb? One epistemological implication here about what "one of us must know" is that chronological age is as irrelevantly yoked to genuine experience of youth as musical beat and syllabic sound are irreverently uncoupled in Dylan's performance.

In "Lily, Rosemary and the Jack of Hearts" (1975), Dylan also uses the vowel lengthening maneuver, as he indeed does frequently in his recorded work, in these same two complex ways at once: He sings, "The door to the dressing room burst open and a cold revolver cliiiiiiiiicked," the vowel again stretching over several musical beats. As Ricks (2004) observes, this vocal choice enacts the experience a person frozen in fear might have, the moment of the trigger being pulled seeming in its terror to stand outside time. In this respect it might serve to share, from singer to listener, a felt experience, a textured moment of embodiment. But this song is relentless in its elision of actors and roles from start to finish; surely a song unfolding in this complex way will not allow singer and listener to rest easy ourselves. By its end (when one character hangs for another's murder, the weapon not a revolver but a penknife) we do not learn clearly who pulled this trigger nor at whom it was aimed. Our desire for narrative closure is not all that is thwarted, however; as Scarry (1985) suggests, to enter into shared sentient contact with another is never a simple choice but one always fraught with the risk of confronting our own enduring difference from one another. We are entailed ethically the moment we take aim at any listener, for each of us through the act of articulation becomes responsible for navigating the ultimately unnavigable, the space from one body to another. The elongated vowel here might remind us that when we are holding the gun, the impact of our action may "click" for us only as it draws us, in that infinite agentic moment, into eternal ethical contact with the intended targets.

Elongated vocal technique also works poetically in Dylan's performances to draw our attention to the sensory and temporal experience that music provides, an effect importantly different from how a poet might use phonemes or syntax to elongate experience given the necessity of time's passing within a song. Also, in 1975 but first officially released in 1991, "Golden Loom" (1991) contains end rhymes that consistently land on images that engage the senses. Interestingly, in a pair of cases of nouns that might seem semantically like images directly and bluntly indexing the senses, "light" and "taste," Dylan comes off these end rhymes quickly, keeping the vowel sounds in each monosyllabic word brief; but in more oblique, finely threaded images which bring to our memory more delicate sensations (and which Dylan pairs with active verbs that recall how we might come upon these sensations in the world), he luxuriates in the central vowels: we "drink the wiiiiine"; "wildflowers bloooooom"; "I lift your veil" (as "vayayaal"); "you're gone and then all I seem to recall is the smell of perfuuuuuume." The song's subject, also oblique, appears to be a distantly remembered and mysterious wedding ritual, though the narrator's use of present rather than past tense suggests this "memory" may instead be a dream. Assuredly, the song centers on longing for lost and achingly thinly felt connection, whether real or dreamt. Dylan's vocal performance reminds us that wine lingers on the tongue, that flowers and veils leave the traces of their remembered softness on the skin even after they are no longer touched, that the smell of these flowers and of perfume can root itself for a long while in our noses. His oral performance, capturing the feeling of delicate filaments of sense beyond the visual and aural (taste, touch, smell), has much in common with an intriguing writing practice Scarry (1999) describes, in which authors deliberately juxtapose their more finely wrought, gossamer-like imagery of ephemeral objects with their weighty etchings of sharp-edged, voluminous architecture, landscape or still life in order to lend the weighty elements a greater sense of realness and gravity through contrast. I find that Dylan does the converse in "Golden Loom," giving us casual sketches of the "stars," "boats," "trees," "feet" and "cars" in this dream world that we might expect to hear in a popular song (well, perhaps not "feet") so that we might feel the ache the narrator feels for the bride who is now gone—an excellent example of how, in Dylan's mouth, we can hear language conjoining by necessarily confounding.

Constriction of vowels within a single syllable, too, plays its role in Dylan's performance choices. In "Lonesome Day Blues" (2001), Dylan twice sings the word "whispering" as a two-syllable word, "whispr'n," a common enough elision in everyday language and in song. But what makes this choice compelling is how, with it, Dylan tightens his grip on the meaning of both the word "whispering" itself (a sound deliberately harder for our ears to hold because of the way a speaker articulates it) and the marvelous twist at the end of the stanza in which he deploys the sound:

> Last night the wind was whisperin', I was trying to make out what it was
> Last night the wind was whisperin' something—I was trying to make out what it was
> I tell myself something's comin'
> But it never does

As Ricks (1984) observes, one of Dylan's poetic devices involves enlivening hoary clichés (365). Here, the similarly hoary warning "something's coming" is enlivened as Dylan sets us up to expect something will indeed come, the music telling us something's coming even as the narrator tells himself the same thing. This telling is a product of the rhythm the song has already established—despite Dylan's long pause (which sets up the twist). We know that "something's comin'" cannot be the end of the verbal structure; there are too many measures in the song left. Time and expectation are inextricable here, and the singer is playing with our expectations of vowel length, phrase length and narrative revelation. And what comes (or, more precisely, what *never* comes in this clever turn of phrase) turns the warning on its head; we're left grasping to hear in Dylan's constriction, in this lyric, the reminder that Scarry (1985) and Durham Peters (1999) also give us: that expectations, like dreamt lovers, like younger past lovers at whom we might sneer, like mysterious interlocutors at whom we might aim our weapons or our warnings, will sometimes withdraw into nothingness despite our efforts at vigilant communion.

Reshaping in Respirating

Another song from 1975, "Idiot Wind," exemplifies both Dylan's vowel stretching and his use of breath as a performer. In the song's refrain he repeatedly sings the title adjective as "eeedeeot," enacting the poor articulation named by the word itself. He simultaneously grits his own teeth in a performative move resonant with the assonance at the heart of the refrain's end rhymes of "teeth" and "breathe," spitting out the closing "th" fricatives with what sounds like an audibly clenched jaw embodying the very recalcitrance this narrator has the temerity to call out in the addressee. Yet this wind he creates through clenching also clenches him tightly to the second-person addressee—a wind far too clever to be merely idiotic, because it blows through the song as the singer blows his voice on the recording through a varied line concerning complex and tenuous human contact. The contact of this breath/wind sensuously marks vibrant skin or its lack—skin being the one organ that can feel breath's repeated flow on its surface. Each time the refrain starts anew, such contact (or its lack) is evoked: it blows first by hinting at both kiss and bite "every time you move your mouth," then with a gesture toward softly silken life blooming in the face of death "through the flowers of your tomb," then with a macabre scalping of its narrator that still prompts a vigorous thrash of geometric knowledge ("like a circle around my skull") and finally embracing an image of snug yet temporary warm conjoining "through the buttons of our coats." This final refrain thus closes by at last admitting of both narrator and addressee at once: "We are eeedeeots." Dylan's figuring of breath here thus ultimately draws narrator and addressee together, in shared sentience of this wind—and, at the same time, stops the flow of the song on an image not of mutual understanding but mutual misunderstanding, an image at the heart of the hair-raising paradox of communication.

In "Soon After Midnight" (2012), we can hear Dylan again breathe poetic life into a simple phrase, this time "she's passing by," which he sings with an audible inhale, pause and exhale between the second and third words: "she's passing...by." Is he also bidding her farewell by using the space in the phrase to contextualize "by" as both sustained vector of movement and oral wave? Is he gesturing to us, as he does so often in his later work, reminding us that his sense of his own nearing end is abbreviating his syntactic vim, challenging his ability to sustain the breath he needs to move through phrases? Is "she" the one whose life is at stake, the one who risks her own death as a character by coldly moving out of range of the narrator's breath? Once more here we have an image of "coming together" prompting a paired image of "unbecoming" in Dylan's poetic performance.

Dylan explores the relationship between breath for singing and breath for life quite often in his work from 1997 forward, using his breathing in

close-miked studio recordings[2] to allow us to hear him aspirate consonants, take in short bursts of breath between words and dwindle in articulation and volume as a given breath leaves his lungs. One of the best
examples of Dylan's creative use of nuances in breathing, from start to
finish on a single track, is "Spirit on the Water" (2006). Each of the three
"breath as limited life force" performance choices I describe above (aspirated consonants, short bursts of breath and phrases that exhaust breath)
is audible at multiple points on this recording, and these breathing choices
suck us into a sound world of delicate instrumentation and a lyrical world
in which the narrator addresses a murky love who is called both "spirit"
and "baby" in the first stanza—and therefore associated with the end of
life and its beginning. Indeed, each verse includes an image of either temporal or physical spans, spans that are consistently framed as both too
distant to reach and too near to ignore. Though I typically hear Dylan's
"breath as limited life force" style of vocal performances, given their burgeoning on works of the last twenty years, as connected to his sense of his
own mortality as a person past middle age, the complex dialectic throughout "Spirit on the Water" reminds us that the three vocal choices I note
here (aspirated consonants, short bursts of breath and phrases that exhaust
breath) are also qualities of young speakers. Thus, Dylan suggests that we
learn and relearn to use our voices just as he has done throughout his
diverse career, reshaping ourselves each time we reach out to others by—
to use Durham Peters's (1999) phrase—"speaking into the air."

CONVIVIAL CONDENSING

Meanings complicated by context and confounded by contact move
throughout Dylan's recordings via his very common vocal device of condensing entire syllables and, thereby, turning elaborated syntax into something more poetically vibrant. His approach to vocal performance as a

---

[2] The specific musical means of expression on which I focus throughout this chapter is
Dylan's vocal choices on a series of studio recordings, because studio conditions allow us to
hear precise choices such as those audible in close-miking. Dylan's live recordings have been,
as is well known, both extensively bootlegged by unlicensed recorders and distributors and,
especially recently through such releases as the 36-disc *The 1966 Live Recordings*, made copi-
ously available for sale through Dylan's official record companies (now Sony). However, in
this chapter I address studio recordings exclusively because I find the vocal choices more
crisply describable and because I hope readers will find them easier to trace as a lens through
which to engage my claims.

significant dimension of his poetic efforts is apt in two ways: First, Dylan is a unique type of poet (especially among Nobel laureates) whose work has been initially accessed in its primary form not as printed word but as oral performance. Second, the fact that Dylan's reputation rests first and foremost on oral performance is significant in light of Dylan's repeated deflection of the label "poet" and its associated academic cachet. This thread of deflection began ironically in 1964 with the winking line "Yippee! I'm a poet, I know it / Hope I don't blow it" in "I Shall Be Free No. 10" (1964); continued in 1965 with the sardonic rhyming of "old folks home and the college" with "your useless and pointless knowledge" in "Tombstone Blues" (1965); in 1970 with his derisive distancing of his own alienated affective experience from the grandiose pomp into which he was thrown, upon receiving an honorary degree from Princeton, in "Day of the Locusts" (1970); in his career-spanning series of acknowledgments in interviews of *performances* (on record and on stage) rather than writing as the primary force driving his work[3]; and most recently echoing quite loudly in his absence at the scheduled Nobel Prize award ceremony in December 2016. (He eventually accepted the award at a private ceremony in April of 2017.)

A prime example of Dylan's vocally directed poetics stretches across two songs—one from his middle period, "Tangled Up in Blue" (1975) and one from his early work, "I Shall Be Free" (1963). In both recordings Dylan sings "I was" as "I'sa."[4] In "Tangled Up in Blue" the coupling runs like this: "Later on when the crowd thinned out / I'sa just about to do the same." The homophony here of "I's"—as in "I was" and "eyes"—is telling; the issue of sight is rooted in this verse's context of a "topless place" with its fulsomely bodied crowd about to "thin out" in front of our watchful narrator. This homophony of "I'sa" and "eyes" resonates again in his interlocutor's taking up in the very next line of a position at the "back o' my chair" that forecloses his chance to look at her then and there. In "I

---

[3] Some examples: "Oh, I think of myself more as a song and dance man" (from the famous 1965 press conference [Dylan 2006, 62]); "I began writing because I was singing" (from a 1985 interview for *SPIN* [Dylan 2004, 222]); "I found out I could do it effortlessly—that I could sing night after night after night and never get tired" (from a 2001 interview for *Rolling Stone* [Dylan 2006, 422]).

[4] The printed lyrics of "Tangled Up in Blue" and "I Shall Be Free" as published on the official Bob Dylan website differ from the audible vocal sounds I describe here, which reflect instead what I hear on the studio recordings *Blood on the Tracks* and *The Freewheelin' Bob Dylan*, respectively.

Shall Be Free" Dylan sings "Took me a woman late last night / I'sa three-fourths drunk she looked alright / Till she started peelin off her onion gook / Took off her wig says 'How do I look?' / I'sa high-flyin... barenaked... / out tha window." He also condenses the space between words poetically in this verse, rushing both times through the phrase "off her" to slyly remind us of the sexual invitation ("offer") suggested by these removals. The first "I'sa" here again chimes with the "eyes" the narrator has clouded with booze and the eyes we need to imagine exactly what "onion gook" layering might have been necessary for this woman to create a desired "look." But both here and in "Tangled Up in Blue" the condensing of "I was" into "I'sa" works to confound verb tense and ontology: "I was" rings instead in our ears with an ending "a," as tales of the narrator's past metonymically link to an article that names him as an object of his own observation in the present and thereby distances himself from himself and from us—as "a" one who may yet thin out, "a" one who may yet defenestrate himself in shock, a narrator on whom we cannot depend to stay thickly grounded in predictable relation to us, his listeners. In his vocal condensing on these phrases, then, Dylan suggests that the paradox of articulation—its capacity to both conjoin and confound—works not only in our efforts to relate to one another but also to our efforts to relate to ourselves.

TACTICS OF ATTACK

Dylan's use of vocal attack—the rate at which he breathes sound into the microphone and the rate at which he allows that sound to decay—throughout his recorded work reminds us that his early huffing as a harmonica-saddled folk singer has poetic echoes in his creative use of his singing voice. Decay works interestingly in the line "I can survive and I can endure / And I don't even think about her" from "Most of the Time" (1989)—though the effect is clearer in Dylan's singing in the performance of this song on Disc One of *Tell Tale Signs*, a compilation released as *The Bootleg Series, Vol. 8*. Paul Williams (2005b) writes persuasively about Dylan's use of breath in this song (in its *Oh Mercy* version), but I find that the qualities of decay and attack in Dylan's voice are choices worth distinguishing from his use of breath and from his condensation of entire syllables. We can hear these qualities as consonants are begun and rounded off. The rhyming words "endure" and "her" at the ends of these phrases audibly decay; Dylan refuses to round the words off. Instead he squares their sound with the song's theme about a desiccated relationship that the speaker keeps trying to cast aside but just cannot. This is a poetic insight we can hear in his weak voicing of the halting promise to "endure" even as the sound of the word itself cannot, and an insight we can hear in the pained-sounding closing of his lips as if in a defense against the simple pronoun "her."

The rapid decay at the end of nearly every line of "Floater (Too Much to Ask)" (2001) resonates with the lyrics and with the sunny, gentle, mid-tempo swaying music to conjure a sense of a summer day in the south spent on a rickety porch—perhaps by some old codger reflecting on both his own past and on what he witnesses around him. But this is not the "exhausted-breath" Dylan, whose vocal choices I described in the "Reshaping in Respirating" section; in "Floater," the singer retains what sounds like a powerful force of breath, and he controls the decay of his voice. This works especially well in complicating meaning in lines such as "But old, young, age don't carry weight / It doesn't matter in the end," the voice suggesting that the line is not merely about the universality of mortality (as the words alone might indicate) but about the narrator's unwillingness to be defined in a limited way by his age. Likewise, the voice that sings "Try to bully ya—strong-arm ya—inspire you with fear / It has the opposite effect" suggests that one way to live within the ambiguity the text allows (is the "opposite effect" to cause one to shrink with "fear?" To "inspire" one with rage? With self-assurance?) is to consider that the narrator withdraws his breath of his own volition and that we, the second-person addressee, also have the existential responsibility to be inspired or fearful only as we so choose. This playful narrator, then, performs this text in a way that reminds us of the paradox and risk of articulate contact as surely as the mysterious pistol-wielder in "Lily, Rosemary and the Jack of Hearts."

This vocal device of rapid decay works in the other direction, rapid attack, as well: Returning to "I Shall Be Free," when the narrator responds to President Kennedy's telephoned question about how to "make the country grow," he sings the second and third names in his list of foreign movie star sex symbols—Anita Ekberg, Sophia Loren—by exploding onto the first syllable of each last name, raising his volume and broadening the fullness of his vocal timbre very sharply and abruptly as he intones "EKberg" and "LOren." By these names, after Bridgette Bardot has already glided past our ears, Dylan has planted the seed of synecdoche: He is coyly suggesting that "grow" (when referring to a population) might signal not only the migration across borders of European women to the

United States (presumably to Hollywood), nor only the procreative impulse presumably impelled among at least some listeners by looking at these women, but also the phallic tumescence of a reproductive organ on a path to being productive of new citizens—a conception that swells with the abrupt, exhilarated explosions of his singing of the initial syllables of their names.

Returning to where this chapter began, and by way of conclusion: "Shelter from the Storm" tells us that "Not a word was spoke between us, there was little risk involved." Dylan's creative uses of his voice in how he stretches vowels, how he breathes, how he condenses syllables and how he attacks words reminds us that there is indeed great risk in speaking words. His performances show that when we speak words we create fresh meanings within the contexts in which we speak, and that in this way words always join us to one another but also stand between us, keeping us at some distance from one another—a poetic parallel to the philosophical conceptions Durham Peters traces. Dylan's poetry is thus worthy of Nobel recognition and worthy of intensive study—at least in significant part as performance.

Dylan's extant body of work thus highlights his unique approach to the recording process. For Dylan, songs are living, and only ever fully present in the moment of expression, or in the always shifting space between performer and audience. He consistently uses the studio recording process as a means to explore a single song in a variety of performance contexts, sometimes capturing the fresh energy of a song in a small number of takes (even when these are not sonically "ideal") and other times using different assemblages of artistic materials (both his songwriting texts and the available musical resources) to bring a song to life in multiple forms. This is illustrated quite clearly in his working methods during both the New York City and the Minneapolis sessions for *Blood on the Tracks*,[5] in which several of the songs were tried in robust takes in a variety of arrangements—from solo voice/guitar, to just bass added to this instrumentation, to just organ and bass added, to a full band also including piano, drums and additional guitar. Songs from early in these sessions even featured audible clacking from the buttons on Dylan's jacket but were completed and recorded given the full performance commitment associated with the takes.

[5] The various outtakes from these sessions are now available as *More Blood, More Tracks* (2018)—Vol. 14 of the ongoing Bootleg Series.

This studio aesthetic fits with Dylan's widely noted lack of interest in using modern multitrack recording techniques to assemble, from multiple takes or parts, a definitive version of a song that would be released on a particular permanent medium. As he claims in a 1978 interview, "I'm a live performer and want to play onstage for the people and not make records that may sound really good" (2004, 166). He has consistently marked himself as a live performer first and a songwriter second. In a 1985 interview, Dylan (2006) elaborates on this priority: "I began writing because I was singing. I think that's an important thing. I started writing because things were changing all the time and a certain song needed to be written. I started writing them because I wanted to sing them. If they had been written, I wouldn't have started to write them" (312). Dylan's studio processes parallel this series of avowals, reflecting his interest in songs as opportunities for performance rather than as textual objects designed for permanence.

Musicians who have worked with Dylan also describe his commitment to performative exploration of songs in the studio. Marcus (2005) notes that Al Kooper, whose organ playing is aurally prominent in the sound world of "Like a Rolling Stone," was not an organist but a guitar player professionally, and was expected to be only an observer rather than a player on the studio sessions for *Highway 61 Revisited* (104, 111). Irwin (2008) quotes Harvey Brooks, a bass player on this same album, who recalls that "Bob worked really spontaneously and fast and we didn't spend a lot of time looking for the perfect notes, it just had to feel right" (163–4). Gill and Odegard (2004) report that Tom McFaul, a member of the band Deliverance that backed Dylan on the initial *Blood on the Tracks* sessions in New York in September 1974, maintains that "each take was a performance. Dylan played and sang as if it were a live gig, rather than a recording session" (74). Ramone, also interviewed by Gill and Odegard, describes the outcome of this performance practice:

> not because you're trying to be a perfectionist, but more because of the way it formed itself when the bass player played the right notes—because there's no information on paper, the bass player kept his eyes peeled on Dylan's hands all the time. And sometimes, Bob might go straight into a second verse with no amount of bars that were typical of how music was written, which gives you this incredible, shocking change. That's an interaction you can feel on the record. (78)

The recording strategies audible in Dylan's archive reveal his commitment to performative repertoire, to songs as opportunities to live in and through musical actions in the moment of creation and recreation.

Importantly for such a scholarly endeavor, Dylan's massive recorded corpus gives us the opportunity to access an extraordinarily rich archive of performed texts. Dylan's own actions as copyright owner significantly augment this access—to extensively documented studio sessions as well as many hundreds of hours of live concert recordings—through releases such as *The Official Bootleg Series* and *The Complete 1966 Live Recordings*. Diana Taylor (2003) describes how performances that are alive and engaged with community memory and identity development in specific cultural places and times, which she calls "repertoire," can become documented in more permanent forms using relevant technologies and then become an "archive" with its own status within a given culture. She argues that repertoire and archive can be brought into dialogue with one another as a vital way of making sense of cultural locations and trajectories. I hope that Dylan's repertoire—in the form of his ongoing performances, the memory of his performances among his listeners, and his long history of troubling his own relationships to the evolving contexts in which he worked—might in future research be brought into dialectical tension with the vast archive of his recorded work, helping us better understand how "Bob Dylan" (the cultural, political and musical figure) is woven into the fabric of our contemporary society. In this chapter, one small step in that direction, I find that his vocal performance choices are an integral element of his poetic treatment of human relationships, relationships he frames as troublesome and beautiful because they are fraught with the paradox at the heart of communication: that in drawing closer to one another we inevitably find ourselves enriched by contact yet hollowed by confusion.

REFERENCES

Auslander, Philip. 2004. Performance Analysis and Popular Music: A Manifesto. *Contemporary Theatre Review* 14 (1): 1–13.

Boucher, David, and Gary Browning. 2009. *The Political Art of Bob Dylan*. 2nd ed. Exeter: Imprint Academic.

Bowden, Betsy. 2001. *Performed Literature: Words and Music by Bob Dylan*. 2nd ed. Lanham, MD: University Press of America.

Day, Aidan. 1988. *Jokerman: Reading the Lyrics of Bob Dylan*. Oxford: Basil Blackwell.

Dylan, Bob. 2004. *Younger Than That Now: The Collected Interviews with Bob Dylan*. New York: Thunder's Mouth Press.

————. 2006. *Bob Dylan: The Essential Interviews*. Edited by Jonathan Cott. New York: Wenner Books.

Gibbens, John. 2001. *The Nightingale's Code: A Poetic Study of Bob Dylan*. London: Touched Press.

Gill, Andy, and Kevin Odegard. 2004. *A Simple Twist of Fate: Bob Dylan and the Making of Blood on the Tracks*. Cambridge, MA: Da Capo Press.

Gray, Michael. 2000. *Song and Dance Man III*. London: Cassell.

Harvey, Todd. 2001. *The Formative Dylan: Transmission and Stylistic Influences 1961–1963*. Lanham, MD: Scarecrow Press.

Herdman, John. 1981. *Voice Without Restraint: Bob Dylan's Lyrics and Their Background*. New York: Delilah Books.

Irwin, Colin. 2008. *Bob Dylan: Highway 61 Revisited*. New York: Billboard.

Kivy, Peter. 1995. *Authenticities: Philosophical Reflections on Musical Performance*. Ithaca, NY: Cornell University Press.

Lloyd, Brian. 2014. The Form is the Message: Bob Dylan and the 1960s. *Rock Music Studies* 1 (1): 58–76.

Marcus, Greil. 1997. *The Old, Weird America: The World of Bob Dylan's Basement Tapes*. New York: Picador.

————. 2005. *Like a Rolling Stone*. New York: Public Affairs.

Marqusee, Mike. 2005. *Wicked Messenger: Bob Dylan and the 1960s*. New York: Seven Stories Press.

Marshall, Lee. 2007. *Bob Dylan: The Never Ending Star*. Cambridge: Polity Press.

Peters, John Durham. 1999. *Speaking into the Air: A History of the Idea of Communication*. Chicago: The University of Chicago Press.

Ricks, Christopher. 1984. *The Force of Poetry*. Oxford: Clarendon Press.

————. 2004. *Dylan's Visions of Sin*. New York: HarperCollins.

Scarry, Elaine. 1985. *The Body in Pain: The Making and Unmaking of the World*. New York: Oxford University Press.

————. 1999. *Dreaming By the Book*. Princeton, NJ: Princeton University Press.

Scobie, Stephen. 2003. *Alias Bob Dylan: Revisited*. Calgary: Red Deer Press.

Taylor, Diana. 2003. *The Archive and the Repertoire: Performing Cultural Memory in the Americas*. Durham, NC: Duke University Press.

Wilentz, Sean. 2010. *Bob Dylan in America*. New York: Doubleday.

Williams, Paul. 1996. *Bob Dylan: Watching the River Flow: Observations on His Art-In-Progress*. London: Omnibus Press.

————. 2004. *Bob Dylan: Performing Artist 1960–1973: The Early Years*. London: Omnibus Press.

————. 2005a. *Bob Dylan: Performing Artist 1974–1986: The Middle Years*. London: Omnibus Press.

————. 2005b. *Bob Dylan: Performing Artist 1986–1990 & Beyond: Mind Out of Time*. London: Omnibus Press.

Yaffe, David. 2011. *Bob Dylan: Like a Complete Unknown*. New Haven, CT: Yale University Press.

CHAPTER 5

The Complexities of Freedom and Dylan's Liberation of the Listener

Astrid Franke

It has become almost a cliché to speak of Dylan as a man wearing many masks, a "Jokerman," a man continuously reinventing himself and his songs. And indeed, even though reinvention and masking are embraced by a host of other performers (Madonna or even Bruce Springsteen may come to mind) and poets (such as Eliot, Auden, or Lowell), none of them are or can be as radical and thorough in the reworking of their creations: The poets change only the content and style of their writings, the musicians change only their performing selves. Dylan, however, does all of the above and in addition continues to present songs he wrote half a century ago in perpetually new ways. An example is provided by Sonja Dierks (2007) who has worked through 18 versions of "A Hard Rain' A-Gonna Fall" (1963) and found none to be like any other. His oeuvre then presents a particular challenge for all efforts to assess it as a whole—to formulate an underlying continuity that makes it Dylan's.

To assess this difficulty, it is worthwhile to think a bit more about the many voices of Dylan, both metaphorically and literally. In an interview with the German magazine *Der Spiegel* in 2001 Dylan commented on his

A. Franke (✉)
University of Tübingen, Tübingen, Germany

© The Author(s) 2019
N. Otiono, J. Toth (eds.), *Polyvocal Bob Dylan*,
Palgrave Studies in Music and Literature,
https://doi.org/10.1007/978-3-030-17042-4_5

role as producer of *"Love and Theft"* (2001) by saying that no album before has ever produced his voice as he wanted it:

> Whosoever controlled the recordings for my previous albums said to themselves: OK, this is a Dylan-album and these are Dylan-songs. That is, they never reacted to the way my voice or my songs actually sounded at the time, they just realized their own idea of what Bob Dylan's voice must sound like.[1]

That Dylan cares so much for the right sound of his voice is not really surprising for those who recognize the craftsmanship of his musical production.[2] But it is, at least initially, surprising as he has done so many songs in so many different voices. Apparently, for Dylan, a song needs a certain voice *at a certain moment,* and it is really important that this voice is adequately captured. But there is apparently not only one "correct" voice (and musical arrangement) for that song but, through time, numerous "correct" voices and arrangements, and if that is true through time then can one exclude that it might also be true *in* time, that is, at a given moment for different listeners? For if, in history, collective experiences as that of the counterculture and its aftermath or the end of the cold war change and thus change the perception and meaning of a song, might it not be the case that even at one and the same moment in history different people actually "hear" something different in one and the same song or even hear that song differently?

Obviously, this is a complex problem of aesthetic theory and it is not only posed by Dylan and not only by song. But the problem achieves a certain urgency in his art because of the tensions still produced when a song is presented in a new way, potentially covering or even destroying "one's own" previous favorite version of that song. And of course, this experience captures *en miniature* the tensions that arose when Dylan converted from folk singer to rock star or from rock star to born-again Christian. How, then, is it possible to understand the power of Dylan's songs and (to borrow Jane Tomkins' phrasing [1985]) the "cultural work" they perform when taking the concept of polyvocality into account?

---

[1] My translation of the German translation of what Dylan said in the interview: "Wer auch immer die Aufnahmen zu meinen bisherigen Platten kontrollierte, sagte sich: Okay, dies ist eine Bob-Dylan-Platte, und das sind Bob-Dylan-Lieder. Das heißt, sie reagierten nie darauf, wie meine Stimme zu dem Zeitpunkt tatsächlich klang oder die Songs sondern sie verwirklichten nur ihre Idee, wie Bob Dylans Stimme zu klingen hat."

[2] For more on the importance of form in Dylan's work see Brian D. Lloyd (2014).

One intriguing suggestion has come from the German philosopher Axel Honneth (2007). In an essay entitled "Entanglements of Freedom,"[3] he suggests that in the polyvocality of his oeuvre, Dylan has expressed the experience of three contradictory sensitivities that accompany the realization of individual freedom: the freedom to reinvent oneself anew which might lead to a feeling of emptiness, the freedom from past social ties which may involve painful denials of childhood memories, and the longing for a freedom to merge with something or someone without losing oneself, as in love or religion. The overwhelming confusion of emotions, desires, and ideas is perhaps a defining experience of our epoch since the end of World War II, as two or three generations by now have been able to experiment with their individual lives to an extent that was previously only rarely possible.

Honneth bases his argument on a central tenet of John Dewey's aesthetic theory, namely that aesthetic experience is perhaps the only way to access the fullness of "an experience" (Dewey 1934, 35). Experience, according to Dewey, arises in situations where our common knowledge and habits do not suffice to establish the detachment needed to master them; instead, we are surprised by the confusing simultaneity of feelings, desires, fears, intentions, and ideas. Affect and cognition still form a unit we cannot dissolve and this may happen over a short while, as when passing the New York skyline on a boat, but it may also be true for longer periods of time when we are caught in circumstances in such a way that we do not find a way out of our confusion. At the end of his essay, Honneth acknowledges a problem with both Dewey and his own adoption of it, namely that it always supposes a historical antecedent to aesthetic experience when, in the case of the music of the 1960s, that music is so much part of the historical experience. The rise of rock music is perhaps the most prominent reminder that art does not just give expression to something prior to it but shapes an experience in the first place.

In the following, I would like to complement Honneth's argument in two ways. I want to provide his discussion on the entanglements the pursuit of individual freedom will run into with traditions in American culture to show that Dylan's interweaving of the three strands does not only grow out of an experience of a particular generation. Rather, his art projects an experience that grows out of the collective historical experiences of

---

[3] My translation of "Verwicklungen von Freiheit: Boy Dylan and his Time" which is the title of Honneth's article. All quotations from this article are my own translation.

especially immigrants and African Americans. Secondly, I want to show that literal and metaphorical polyvocality is a way to include the freedom of the recipients of art, who may be free for different aesthetic experiences only to the extent that they free themselves from previous ones. My assumption is that we are socialized into hearing, just as we are socialized into seeing or reading, so that the ways in which groups of people hear and experience the performance of songs can be understood via cultural studies and history. What we hear is not independent of previous (listening) experiences, both individually and, more importantly, collectively. Thus, what we hear may have become a habit that needs to be broken in order to really appreciate a song. To make this argument, I will have to outline Honneth's thesis and complement it with regard to cultural traditions. The second step then expands on the idea of freedom by examining songs that sound different and *are* different in different contexts and thereby acquire cultural significance *in the moment*. In particular, I will discuss songs from Dylan's gospel phase and his Sinatra phase.

AXEL HONNETH AND THE COMPLEXITIES OF FREEDOM

The easiest, most intuitive connection to be made between Dylan's songs and the idea of individual freedom is in his insistence on individual self-determination, his refusal to be bound by the expectation of his social environment (e.g., personal background or audience). This may be found in numerous texts where it may acquire an explicitly political dimension ("Maggie's farm" [1965]) and where, on a micro level, it is signaled by the surprising absence of the pronoun "we"—even in the so-called protest songs such as "The Lonesome Death of Hattie Carrol" (1964), "Only a Pawn in Their Game" (1964), or "Masters of War" (1963); it can be found in musical styles rejecting older versions of songs including his own and in gestures and postures of youthful protest against an adult world of conformity through dress, hairstyle, or manners; in a nasal, sometimes metallic and perhaps arrogant voice expressing rejection, sarcasm, or defiance; and finally, of course, in the insistence on change—the continuing reinvention of the persona of the singer, beginning with the symbolic gesture of renaming himself. While Elizabeth Brake (2006) associates this stance with the term "negative freedom" by Isaiah Berlin (1970, 81),[4]

---

[4] Berlin conceptualizes "negative liberty" as the freedom from external interference and constraint.

Honneth reminds us of the "existentialist motif of a choice of self, the Sartrean pathos of permanently reinventing oneself anew" (2007, 20–1). Both therefore point to the potential emptiness or even loss of self that may result from sheer negation. But Honneth is not primarily interested in the philosophical roots and discussions of this kind of individual freedom. Rather, his argument is a cultural and historical one. When Dylan used this posture in his (re-)turn to rock music, and thus rejected some of his fans' expectations, it functioned as a reminder of the precursors to the counterculture that celebrated him: the anti-war movement and the white support for the civil rights movement built upon the radical, perhaps exaggerated, gestures of rebellion against conformity we may associate with the Beat Generation, with Jazz and Rock 'n' Roll, and, indeed, with an existentialist stance popularized by authors such as Salinger, Bellow, Auden, Baraka, and Mailer.[5] Thus the tensions surfacing on Dylan's famous first "electric" tour of England are tensions actually inherent in the social and political culture of the 1960s: its beginnings, one might argue, actually lay in the emergence of rebellious youth made possible by the beginning prosperity of the post-war era. After two decades of subordinating individual needs to the common good for economic, political, and military reasons, the 1940s and 1950s marked the beginning of what Alan Petigny (2009) called a "permissive society," and the pathos and exasperation of somewhat puerile male voices (such as we get in Salinger's *Catcher in the Rye* or Kerouac's *On the Road*) were a necessary counterforce to the danger that the conformist pressures would be kept up by cold war politics. But this prehistory of grand individual gestures of rebellion and alienation is pushed aside in the (primarily white) folk scene of the early 1960s. In as much as social movements rely on collective action, activists often exert a certain pressure on conformity, and this includes forms of political and also artistic expression—in the 1960s, politicized folk songs as well as gospel and spirituals, especially in the form of single voices accompanied by guitar or banjo, counted as authentic and more adequate expressions of resistance against various forms of injustice than rock 'n' roll and electric amplification. Dylan's insistence on the identity of his folk and rock persona and on bringing together these two major forms of musical expression served as a reminder of a past devoted to radical self-expression and a search for autonomy which stood in an uneasy relation to the needs of collective action.

[5] As George Cotkin (2002) puts it, "Nearly everyone, it seemed, coming of age in 1950s and 1960s America danced to the song of French existentialism" (1).

So far, these tensions experienced by the youth of the 1960s can be found on both sides of the Atlantic; thus the interpretation of cultural history offered by Honneth is backed up primarily by European sources. Matters in the U.S. are complicated by the significance of African Americans to (and their role in) political, cultural, and artistic developments at the time. While the politicized folk in the vein of Guthrie, Seeger, and Baez had its most audible roots in an Anglo-Scottish-Irish tradition, the "soundtracks of the Civil Rights Movement" (Rabaka 2016, 13) are largely African-American with a long history of songs and music about (a lack of) freedom and the struggles connected to it: its genres are spirituals or gospels, hymns, worksongs, and the blues. Here, individual freedom is inevitably tied to collective freedom, memories of past struggles, and visions of possible achievements in the future. Freedom is framed as deliverance and often carries religious connotations, just as religious topoi in slave songs covertly expressed a desire for freedom. I will come back to the simultaneity of literal and spiritual meanings of freedom or love; before that, however, Honneth discusses a second aspect of the search for individual freedom that seems to contradict the first:

> For someone ready to leave the past behind, Dylan evokes it surprisingly often in a melancholy, even gentle fashion. He certainly does not idealize the past, but he does not cut off ties to "the world of fathers and mothers" either. (Honneth 2007, 22)

The tension between ties to the past and the wish to break free can be found in many songs, among them "Desolation Row." While the end, according to Honneth, aggressively rejects an apparent routine ("don't send me no more letters, no"), the beginning evokes bizarre images of the past of the kind one finds in childhood memories: "postcards of a hanging" and a circus in town. The album is tellingly called *Bringing It All Back Home* (1965), and while one may not recognize a home in any of the songs and thus wonder where the homesickness of "Subterranean Homesick Blues" may come from, many of the surreal images in several songs on that album are suffused with a certain nostalgia, often tied to a child-like perspective, as in "On the Road Again": "Your grandpa's cane / It turns into a sword / Your grandma prays to pictures / That are pasted on a board." One may also find that sentiment in Dylan's work at large. What may come to mind is the album *Christmas in the Heart* (2009)—with its raucous and hilarious version of the children's song "Must be

Santa" among traditional Christmas songs—and then, indeed, his latest *Triplicate* (2017), which covers a number of songs originally made famous by Frank Sinatra. Given the nature of these songs, it is the voice that expresses the relation to the past: somewhat broken but still strong, melancholic but not nostalgic, more or less ironic but nevertheless respectful.[6]

In the context of American culture, this complex "structure of feeling"—the impetus to start anew, to leave the past behind in the effort to make oneself while, at the same time, inadvertently remembering one's past as something that cannot and perhaps should not be forgotten because it is so much part of oneself—is a central issue in immigrant literature and in African American literature, albeit in contrasting ways. In immigrant novels such as Mary Antin's *Promised Land* (1912), Abraham Cahan's *The Rise of David Levinsky* (1917), or Jade Snow Wong's *Fifth Chinese Daughter* (1950) the abstract problem of the limits of individual freedom for human beings who are necessarily social beings becomes a lived experience in generational conflicts, the loss of home, and sometimes the impossibility to return that marks (im-)migration. This is surely why, in "I Pity the Poor Immigrant" (1967), Dylan suggests that one can only "pity the poor immigrant / who wishes he would have stayed home." This immigrant lives not the American Dream but an American nightmare of successive failures. The loss of home is not compensated for by freedom and wealth, and thus the immigrant who now wishes to revise a past decision is cursed in several parallel constructions: "Who passionately hates his life / And likewise, fears his death[,]" or "Who eats but is not satisfied, / Who hears but does not see."

While the iconic immigrant cannot return home, a different but related dilemma is often portrayed in African American novels, poems, and songs: here we find the same desire to break out, go north, get rid of the "old negro" and invent oneself anew. Again and again, however, this turns out to be impossible—not only because of skin color but, as novels of passing emphasize, because "race" includes the collective experience of oppression and thus a collective past that cannot easily be shed. And so the narratives of novels such as Claude McKay's *Home to Harlem* (1927) or Ralph Ellison's *Invisible Man* (1952), and songs, notably the Blues, often have a circular structure; they portray attempts to get away from racism and the past, start anew, find some luck (and some love), but they end up arriving back at the same old disappointing story again and again.

---

[6] The official music videos support this relation to the past visually through soft brownish colors, vaguely vintage clothing and hairstyles, and a record as a dated musical medium.

Because of its unique history of immigration and slavery, the complex emotional and intellectual consequences of the pursuit of individual freedom resonate much more strongly in American culture than in many European ones. Novels, poems, movies, songs, and many American family histories—a continuum of lived and aesthetic experience—abound of the structures of feeling conveyed in the songs mentioned above. It is thus not only the specific experience of a generation coming of age in the 1960s that lies behind Dylan's songs, but a mixture of traditions likewise preoccupied with the philosophical problems of individual freedom. These songs were thus particularly prepared to both express and shape the experience of a generation caught between the desires for individualization and the desire for community.

A third strand of musical expression concerns the longing for a kind of freedom that may be found in love or religion—in the merging of one's personality with that of another being without feeling bound by a kind of submission. Because, in the state of being in love, our interests seem to coincide and consequently there is no power struggle, we rightly cherish and celebrate this relation of lovers as exceptional. Being in love, it is possible to feel a twoness that is not a constraint to one's self but an extension of it. True, many of Dylan's love songs express disappointment, the pain of separation, the resentment, contempt, or even hatred for a former lover—but even in this negative fashion, Honneth argues, one may find a longing for the enriching experience of merging with someone. This common experience is both worldly and spiritual in that its kernel may seem banal—any teenager may know it—and yet its significance is spiritual, too. Nowhere is this dual nature of the desire to merge both physically and spiritually more obvious than in Dylan's many songs to women-angels or covenant women. These mystical creatures—sisters, wives, lovers—who seem to still both spiritual and physical desires, are explicitly addressed in the gospels. But, as Heinrich Detering (2007) has pointed out, the "covenant women" or precious angels are part of a continuous theme and can be found in "Isis," "Oh Sister," "Sara," or "Shelter from the Storm," to name but a few. These songs stand in sharp contrast to the existentialist pathos described earlier: one cannot, at the same time, cut all ties to others and claim one's right to be entirely self-determining and then long to form a mutually binding contract and pledge to belong—or admit "I want you" (1966). The contrast is underlined by another quality of the voice, the melodies, and the instrumentation: the voice in these songs can lose its metallic edge and be soft, smooth, lyrical, and loving, or even "crooning," with mostly guitar or piano accompanying it gently.

What is striking in Dylan's songs over the years is not only the presence of three contrasting moods and a resulting contrast of different feelings, Honneth argues—in a way, this is quite common in popular music. Taken separately, love and desire (on the one hand) and youthful rebellion (on the other) might in fact be the most frequent themes of rock music. But in Dylan's songs, these different impulses often collide, suggesting an entanglement that leaves no way out, no compromise, no solution. The result is being stuck in a state of confusion, trying to escape and sorting out contradictory wishes. Meanwhile, time passes and things change. Perhaps this captures the experience of a generation coming of age in the 1960s and 1970s with its undoubtedly large step forward in granting individual freedoms on a new scale and to new groups. But it seems limiting to assert a pre-existing collective experience, to be transformed and re-presented in art, when the music itself was so much part of that same experience that it clearly shaped it, too. Here, it seems more helpful to think of the songs as creating something new by putting several strands of what one may want to call "vernacular philosophy" together—the implied experiences of the pursuit of freedom to be found in immigrant literature and African American culture. These traditions form a rich soil to negotiate the tensions between radical self-determination and self-fashioning on the one hand and one's inevitable social interdependence and the forces of the past in the present on the other—in a sense, these are variations of the tensions in a country that has been founded on the promise of freedom and simultaneously on the enslavement and exploitation of black people. It is precisely by making something new out of the diverse materials available that art can be an expression of something that was not realized fully before the artwork was created.

So far, the combination of different voices with instrumentation and texts serves to highlight the tensions between different experiences, both individual and collective, in pursuing freedom. The result has been for numerous people to appropriate both singer and songs as "theirs," as their spokesperson who presumably expressed what they felt rather than offering them an aesthetic experience they had *not* had before. While this appropriation may happen to any artist, it is particularly inappropriate to a singer because it creates a kind of timeless listening habit by which people refuse to relate to every performance anew and thus desensitize themselves to how time passes. Altering his performances, I believe, Dylan attempts to free the songs themselves of their past and thus urges his old fans (and also his critics) to discover the songs anew, freeing them, too, of their listening habits.

THE TIMES THEY ARE A-CHANGIN'—HOW ABOUT THE AUDIENCE?

Two points in Dylan's musical development are frequently mentioned to document his changes and the reactions of the audiences to them: the juxtaposition of (and in a way return from) the 'folk' paradigm to rock, marked by a change of instrumentation in 1965/66, and the change from the by-then accepted version of rock music to gospels in 1979. The disappointed and often outright hostile reaction of the audience is well documented, especially in the earlier case; in hindsight, it is quite amazing how much a musical style could mean to people—the Astor riots in 1849 in New York over the way to play Hamlet may come to mind as a similar instance of artistic style signifying larger cultural shifts. Various critics have by now pointed out that the ruptures seemed sharper than they really were as there are musical and thematic continuities in both instances. It is as though the early audiences simply did not hear the significance of religion and the musical roots of his songs in Blues and Rock. As Brian Lloyd (2014) puts it, "Much of the deaf-earedness that from the start has characterized the media's perception of Dylan might have been avoided if observers had taken him at his word when he said, several times, that he was more of a blues or rockabilly performer than a folk singer" (62). Perhaps we are all selectively deaf to parts of a song without malice or any kind of personal intention—we are socialized into listening as much as we are socialized into reading and even seeing.

"The Times They Are a-Changin'" (1964) might be a case in point. For a few years now, there have been many detailed analyses of this song—along with "Blowin' in the Wind" (1963), "Only a Pawn in their Game," and "The Lonesome Death of Hattie Carroll"—to persuade us that these songs were never simply or only protest songs. Christopher Ricks has unpacked the complex poetic means of every line of the song (2005, 258–71); we understand now how the performances are hardly meant to induce "sing-a-longs" (though when Peter, Paul and Mary performed "Blowin' in the Wind" on the March on Washington, their slow regular pace makes people hold hands and sway), and the reduced resonance of the voice may support the transcendence of the moment—the timelessness or mythical time of the changes both "Blowin'" and "Times" talk about and support through biblical imagery such as rising waters or sinking like a stone (Ette 2007, 34–5). What these interpretations drive at is the timelessness of the song, even at their first occurrences. To counter the limiting frame of the "protest singer" they emphasize how song and performance transcend a particular politicized moment in history. However, attributing timelessness to a particular voice is also an imposed framework and may become a listening habit that, in turn, denies the experiences of some people who heard the song in 1964.

For if one has been socialized into associating that nasal voice with a left-wing songwriting tradition and its political work, the song as performed with that nasal voice would appear timely and highly topical. Listened to in this way, the refusal to resonate through sound, timbre, or vibrato is connected to the desire to 'resonate' solely through words that describe the injustices now. For those engaged in the civil rights movement or even just observing the glacial speed of changing civil rights legislation, specific lines (in "Times")—for example, "Come senators, congressmen / please heed the call / Don't stand in the doorway / Don't block up the hall"—had a resonance of their own, directly connected to the political developments in the U.S. Beyond the continuation of the politicized folk tradition, the particular edge of the voice then signaled to many their own frustration, anger, and a latent threat. In a way, "The Lonesome Death of Hattie Carrol," "Blowin' in the Wind," and "The Times They Are a-Changin'" are dramatizations of the state of impatient waiting—variations of the (biblical) question Martin Luther King would ask on the March from Selma to Montgomery: "How long will it take?"

In 2010, when Dylan performed "The Times They Are a-Changin'" at the White House to remember the civil rights movement, he could have tried to imitate his 1960s sound. That would have reified the song into a "thing" that serves as a leftover of an artistic and historical process—akin, perhaps, to Marcel Duchamp's "Fountain," a signed urinal turned upside down that serves as a reminder of a happening, that is, an action and event. The attempted repetition of a song as sung before can, of course, create a moving experience: like a smell, a song has the power to evoke past moments in all their emotional complexities. But in the White House the song sounded very different: the voice Dylan uses is raspy and not angry; it starts each stanza in a curiously mechanical rhythm which, perhaps, signals impatience, but loosens up as the stanza progresses, and the instrumentation of piano, guitar, and bass underlines the overall gentleness of the delivery[7]: it is not so much a threat as a satisfying statement, perhaps

---

[7]A recording can be listened to on http://www.pbs.org/video/in-performance-at-the-white-house-bob-dylan/.

even a promise. And again the "now" of the performance may guide what people hear—a black president in the audience is as much a result as a promise of change that will continue. It is possible to hear this when listening to the song for the first time or by re-listening and comparing it to remembered earlier versions. In both cases, we understand that the emphasis is not on the song but on the singing, that is, the performance, which is in time. The version stands on its own without the need to reject the previous version: performances can do what is difficult to do in life, namely to acknowledge and even accept and embrace the past with an act that creates something new. For the listener, this requires distancing oneself from the memory of previous versions and from habitual listening so as to be free to grasp the being-in-time of a song.

Many aspects of Dylan's behavior at concerts might be regarded as offering every member of the audience individually as much freedom as possible to listen themselves: the refusal to talk much and warm up the audience, to create a collective mood, a "we-feeling" as a soil to receive the songs. That is, he rigorously denies himself the power he has to shape and frame the listening experience. Even the preaching and the gospels can be reappraised in this way: in 1979, Grail Marcus (2010) found the gospel songs "monolithic" (96), while Ron Rosenbaum (2001) called them "humorlessly preachy" (236); Stephen Scobie (2004) describes them as "rigid, [and] dogmatically based" (168) and John Hughes (2013), though acknowledging their lyrical beauty, fails to hear their irony or humor and puzzles over the "un-ironic, incongruous grafting of the erotic into the biblical" (210)—in, for instance, "Do Right to Me Baby (Do Unto Others)" (1979), "Precious Angel" (1980), and "Covenant Woman" (1980). Surely, the way we hear gospel music partly depends on our familiarity with the genre and our own religiosity. In the late 1970s it was also colored for many by the "rise of the new Christian Right" with its many evangelical groups, megachurches, and televangelists (Hadden and Shupe 1988, 38). But as the debate on the Christian Right and its political influence has somewhat subsided we may (now) hear different aspects in these songs: the desire for the kind of freedom to be found in love and religion as outlined above, and, as noted, the tendency to address this desire to women (just as the opposite desire to break free is also often addressed to women); a number of open acknowledgments of the African American contribution to American religion and music; the continuation of social critique in, say, "Gotta Serve Somebody" (1979)—such as the alignment of business and crime in "business man or high-degree thief" or the conjunction of military and financial power through rhyme in the lines

"You might own guns and you might even own tanks / You might be somebody's landlord, you might even own banks." More importantly, without the urgency to oppose a religiously based right-wing backlash, many only now feel free to detect instances of humor as a mode of not taking oneself entirely seriously, as when (in "Do Right to Me Baby" [1979]) "Don't want to amuse nobody, don't want to be amused" is added to the well-known maxim of "Ya got to do onto others / like you have them [...] do unto you." Humor does not contradict sincerity but it does suggest a certain distance of parts of the personality and from that distance might arise the freedom to take a different position at a different time. One can certainly hear the gospel songs as expressions of sincere religiosity and conversion, but one may also read the lines above as signaling that this might be sincere now, but not necessarily forever.

If there is a commitment in Dylan's oeuvre, it is one to process and the freedom to change, countering ossifying habits, which tend to seal us from new experiences. In life as in philosophy, insisting on the possibility and freedom to change sometimes stands in an uneasy relation to commitments, both to people and to causes—both of which may also provide us with deeply satisfying and meaningful experiences. But with regard to art, the willingness or refusal to engage a piece of literature or music again can tell us much about ourselves; at the same time, it may also illuminate the social conditioning of reception. Rereading a book after ten years and being struck by how different the aesthetic experience can be alerts us to the fact that the aesthetic experience even of the same book is an experience in time, not determined but also not independent of our dispositions at that moment. A song sung differently over the course of years is a singer's acknowledgment of that phenomenon and challenges us to recognize how much we sometimes prefer to be stuck in something familiar. It is a gift to a culture to have a singer around for so long that he can make us realize the patterns in which we listen to him (and presumably every other song, too). Ultimately, Dylan's performances of his songs not only make us experience the conundrums of freedom, but try to liberate our listening habits, too.

References

Berlin, Isaiah. 1970. Two Concepts of Liberty. In *Four Essays on Liberty*, ed. Berlin Isaiah, 118–172. Oxford: Oxford University Press.

Brake, Elizabeth. 2006. 'To Live Outside the Law, You Must be Honest:' Freedom in Dylan's Lyrics. In *Dylan and Philosophy. It's All Right Ma (I'm Only Thinking)*, ed. Peter Vernezze and Carl J. Porter, 78–89. Chicago: Open Court.

Cotkin, George. 2002. *Existential America*. Johns Hopkins University Press.

Detering, Heinrich. 2007. 'I Believe in You.' Dylan und die Religion. In *Bob Dylan. Ein Kongreß*, ed. Axel Honneth, Peter Kemper, and Richard Klein, 92–119. Frankfurt: Suhrkamp.

Dewey, John. 1934. *Art as Experience*. New York: Perigee Books.

Dierks, Sonja. 2007. Dylans Stimme—am Beispiel von 'A Hard Rain's Gonna Fall. In *Bob Dylan. Ein Kongreß*, ed. Axel Honneth, Peter Kemper, and Richard Klein, 143–159. Frankfurt: Suhrkamp.

Dylan, Bob. 2001. Interview mit Bob Dylan: 'Ich finde Farben scheußlich.' *Der Spiegel Online*, September 10, 2010. Accessed May 11, 2018. http://www.spiegel.de/spiegel/print/d-20074578.html

Ette, Wolfgang. 2007. Zeit bei Bob Dylan: Vom Frühwerk bis zur Gospelphase. In *Bob Dylan. Ein Kongreß*, ed. Axel Honneth, Peter Kemper, and Richard Klein, 29–49. Frankfurt: Suhrkamp.

Hadden, Jeffrey K., and Anson Shupe. 1988. *Televangelism: Power & Politics on God's Frontier*. New York: Henry, Holt and Company.

Honneth, Axel. 2007. Verwicklungen von Freiheit: Bob Dylan und seine Zeit. In *Bob Dylan. Ein Kongreß*, ed. Axel Honneth, Peter Kemper, and Richard Klein, 15–28. Frankfurt: Suhrkamp.

Hughes, John. 2013. Ain't gonna Go to Hell for Anybody': Dylan's Christian Years. *Popular Music History* 8 (2): 205–221.

Lloyd, Brian D. 2014. The Form is the Message: Bob Dylan and the 1960s. *Rock Music Studies* 1 (1): 58–76.

Marcus, Grail. 2010. *Bob Dylan: Writings 1968–2010*. New York: Public Affairs.

Petigny, Alan. 2009. *The Permissive Society: America, 1941–1965*. Cambridge: Cambridge University Press.

Rabaka, Reiland. 2016. *Civil Rights Music: The Soundtracks of the Civil Rights Movement*. Lanham, MD: Lexington Books.

Ricks, Christopher. 2005. *Dylan's Visions of Sin*. London: Ecco.

Rosenbaum, Ron. 2001 (1979). Born-again Bob: Four Theories. In *The Bob Dylan Companion*, ed. Elizabeth Thomson and David Gutman, 233–337. New York: Da Capo.

Scobie, Stephen. 2004. *Alias Bob Dylan: Revisited*. Calgary: Red Deer Press.

Tomkins, Jane. 1985. *The Cultural Work of American Fiction 1780–1860*. Oxford: Oxford University Press.

PART II

Performance and Literature

"Blowin' in the Wind": Bob Dylan, Sam Shepard and the Question of American Identity

Katherine Weiss

In 1975 Bob Dylan invited Sam Shepard, the young playwright who had won several Obies and who had met with success in the London theater scene, to go on tour with him in order to write scenes for a film of the tour (i.e., the Rolling Thunder Revue). While Shepard's film was never produced,[1] Shepard published his thoughts of the Rolling Thunder Revue in *The Rolling Thunder Logbook* (2004), a collage of images and short reflexive texts, which charts the playwright's interest in Dylan. As Shepard recounts in the *Logbook*, both men strive to reimagine American history and both question what it is to be American. Furthermore, the connection formed between Dylan and Shepard during the tour led to "Brownsville Girl," which Dylan and Shepard began co-writing in 1984 and which

---

[1] *Renaldo and Clara* (1978), a four-hour film which includes footage of the tour, was written and directed by Dylan. This film stars Dylan, Joan Baez, Harry Dean Stanton (who played the father in the film adaptation of Shepard's 1981 play *Fool for Love*) and Sam Shepard.

K. Weiss (✉)
East Tennessee State University, Johnson City, TN, USA

© The Author(s) 2019
N. Otiono, J. Toth (eds.), *Polyvocal Bob Dylan*,
Palgrave Studies in Music and Literature,
https://doi.org/10.1007/978-3-030-17042-4_6

Dylan recorded for *Knocked Out Loaded* (1986), as well as Shepard's one-act play, *True Dylan* (1987). In the play, Shepard depicts both Dylan and himself as being preoccupied with icons such as James Dean—icons that for them are central to American identity. Iconic images of America, too, appear feverishly in both Dylan and Shepard's works and these images speak to their explorations around identity. Through Shepard's words in *The Rolling Thunder Logbook*, the lyrics to "Brownsville Girl," *True Dylan*, and Shepard's collaborative revision (with T-Bone Burnett) of his musical play, *The Tooth of Crime* (1972), this chapter explores the manner in which Dylan and Shepard reflect upon the fluidity of American identity and the need for and destabilization of the myths that help to form what it means to be American.

COWBOY MOUTHS, MASKS AND *THE ROLLING THUNDER LOGBOOK*

After the tour, and along with the publication of *The Rolling Thunder Logbook*, Shepard continued to work with Patti Smith and T-Bone Burnett. (Both had been on the legendary tour.) Shepard and Smith were friends from before the tour. They had already worked together on Shepard's *Cowboy Mouth*, written and staged in 1971. In this strange one-act play, Shepard's central characters are reminiscent of a 1970s Bonny and Clyde. Cavale, "a chick who looks like a crow" (145), has kidnapped Slim, "a cat who looks like a coyote" (145), to turn him into a rock-and-roll star, "but," as Shepard notes, "they fall in love" (147). With these vivid character descriptions, it should be no surprise that Smith and Shepard co-starred as the lovers in the American debut of the play. Central to the play is Cavale's description of what a rock-and-roll star is. She says that he must be a "saint" with a "cowboy mouth"; "what Dylan seemed to be for a while. A sort of god in our image ... ya know?" (156). Despite Cavale's disenchantment with Dylan (whether it is Cavale's, Smith's or the playwright's is not clear), four years later, when Shepard finally meets Dylan on the Rolling Thunder Revue, he portrays the rock-and-roll legend as that god-like figure, noting (after seeing Dylan lying across "a metal folding chair") that he looks "like he's practicing a levitation trick, both ragged cowboy boots popped up on a metal desk" (Shepard 2004, 15).

Shepard's fascination with the image of the rock-and-roll cowboy stems from his love for America and his status as the "rock 'n' roll cowboy mouth"[2]—an image of the American loner, speaking the raw truth about his nation and his generation. It is this image that attracted Dylan to Shepard. Despite Shepard's portrait of the rock-and-roll icon, Dylan recognized that Shepard is not advocating for hero-worship. Instead, "he questions the assumption of personal heroes like Dylan" (Bottoms 1998, 9), insisting that the image and the music Dylan has invented comes out of hard work. Throughout the *Rolling Thunder Logbook* Shepard sees in Dylan a kindred spirit. Shepard records the Rolling Thunder Revue, depicting it as a folkloric and epic journey. Even before leaving New York City, Shepard contemplates his identity through the image of cowboys riding toward an adventure: "I'm wondering about cowboys. About the state of cowboys. About 'real life' and 'fantasy.' About making yourself up from everything that's ever touched you. From Pecos Bill to the Rolling Thunder Revue" (2004, 17). The Rolling Thunder Revue sends Shepard on a meditation of the "early-day American heroes" (76). He speculates that the stories we hold on to, stories of Buffalo Bill and Jesse James, for example, are "tall tales" (76). "Bragging" is the curse of these fictions. Despite his admiration for the musician, Shepard, here, appears concerned that the film and *Logbook* will be a work of bravado, transforming Dylan into an American hero.

Other times, Shepard (2004) contemplates that "Dylan has invented himself. He's made himself up from scratch. That is, from the things he had around him and inside him" (98). But the mystery is not solved. Shepard comes back to the philosophical question of who Dylan is repeatedly and (yet) repeatedly finds himself no closer to unraveling the mystery. To perpetuate the mystery, Dylan arrives on stage one night with a "rubber Dylan mask" (108)—a scene which can be viewed in the film *Renaldo and Clara*. He is a folk hero who remade himself, turning his Jewish heritage into that of the voice of American mythology. In his memoirs, *Chronicles*, Dylan (2004), aware that America was changing rapidly, recalls that he needed "some kind of new template, some philosophical identity that wouldn't burn out" (73). He went through several names before "Bobby Zimmerman was killed in 1964 on the Bass Lake run" (79). The name he stuck with, he insists, was not inspired by Dylan Thomas but rather Matt Dillon of *Gunsmoke*: "Then sometime later, unexpectedly, I'd

---

[2] I'm using this term to allude to both Shepard's 1971 play *Cowboy Mouth* and his 1972 play *The Tooth of Crime*. Both feature musician-types and in both violence and survival make up a large part of the characters' struggles.

seen some poems by Dylan Thomas" (78). *I'm Not There*, Todd Haynes's 2007 film about Dylan's life, visually proves this very point. Six actors, varying in age, race, nationality and gender, depict different stages of Dylan's life, ultimately leaving the viewer without any sense of who Dylan was or is. Dylan proves, according to Greil Marcus (1997), that "One could make oneself up, ... but only if, whatever one's sources, the purest clay was always evident, real American red earth" (19–20). The construct of Dylan's identity, according to Marcus and Shepard, originates from both internal and external sources. Regardless of the fabric making up his masks, Marcus notes that something essential exists underneath the mask—that pure and authentic being Marcus likens to clay. For Shepard, too, land, and especially the American West, is essential to the myths that underlie American identity as it is central to the heroic cowboys/outlaws that Dylan and Shepard are inspired by and strive to revise.

What Shepard neglects to share in the *Logbook* is his own invented self. Shepard, a cowboy playwright who until his recent death continued to woo cosmopolitan theater-goers, is less daring than Dylan, however. Sam's full name is Samuel Shepard Rogers III. Until his flight to New York City, Shepard was known as Steve Rogers—a name that Shepard thought was "corny" (Shepard 1988, 71) because of its associations with Roy Rogers. He shed his father's name both to steer away from associations with the "King of Cowboys" and to distance himself from his father, a violent alcoholic. Despite changing his name and moving away from his family home in California, Shepard remained haunted by the old man who appears in many of his plays. With his new identity, Shepard also fabricated a new past for himself. He liked "to pretend he was always a bad-ass juvenile delinquent growing up," but "Steve Rogers was somewhere in between a glee-club cheerleader-type" and a "tough-talking scrapper precociously schooled in class analysis" (Shewey 1997, 21). Shepard, like Dylan, enjoyed wearing a mask; he even fondly recalled people commenting that he shared a name with the American neurosurgeon who in the fifties was accused of murdering his wife (*Sam Shepard: Stalking Himself* 1998).

The juxtaposition of Dylan in the flesh opposed to Dylan behind a mask and Dylan in photographs speaks to Shepard's concern with the "real" versus the "true," a concern evident in the *Logbook*:

> [Dylan] is known through his photographs to anyone who meets him. But faced with him in the flesh, I have a hard time shaking loose of the

photographs and just seeing him. All I'm seeing are album covers for about six minutes straight. (2004, 15)

For Shepard, though, "Dylan creates a mythic atmosphere out of the land around us. The land we walk on every day and never see until someone shows it to us" (63). Key concepts for Shepard are myths and territory. Shepard and Dylan are linked here in the way Shepard sees Dylan making the familiar sites—historical landmarks that make up the myth of America—mysterious and mythic. To this effect, Shepard writes, "If a mystery is solved, the case is dropped. In this case, in the case of Dylan, the mystery is never solved, so the case keeps on. It keeps coming up again. Over and over the years. Who is this character anyway?" (71). Shepard's use of the word "character" suggests that identity for both musician and playwright is a performative act. Along these lines, it is interesting that so many of Dylan's songs focus on an iconic individual. Dylan retells the stories of outlaws, such as with "John Wesley Harding" (1967) and "Hurricane" (1976), men who are central to American identity in that they challenge institutions that threaten individuality.

Fascinated with the historical narratives that define what it means to be American, Shepard ruminates on the historic places the Rolling Thunder Revue toured—places that Dylan was drawn to. Shepard speaks to a sense of historical urgency while also questioning the truth of historical accounts when he recalls Dylan and other members of the tour at Plymouth Rock, at the last Shaker village and on the Mayflower (the latter of which is photographed and included in the *Logbook*). The image of Dylan on the Mayflower with Bob Neuwirth, Roger McGuinn, Ramblin' Jack Elliott and others, for Shepard, resembles the "painting of *Washington Crossing the Delaware*" (36). In New England, he finds that "[e]verywhere replicas of history are being sold" (46). The historic stops and Dylan's playful reenactment of the past, for Shepard, becomes a symbol of rediscovery of what it means to be American in the highly charged Vietnam War era.[3] The reproductions of history, for Shepard, touch on his anti-capitalist ideas that are anything but anti-American—as we see in his 2004 play, *The God of Hell*. In Shepard's play, the miniature American flags serve as a

---

[3] Shepard moved to London in 1971 to escape the Vietnam War. Despite fleeing the painful unrest in America during this time, Shepard's thoughts turned to his homeland. Prior to his move to England, his plays were deracinated. Once in London plays, such as *The Tooth of Crime* (1972) and *Geography of a Horse Dreamer* (1974), bare the mark of his nationality.

visual representation of the government agent who has invaded the farm house. In the *Logbook*, however, the replicas speak to the way Shepard sees the journey as crucial to American history and identity much like songs that are recorded and repeated. These key moments in the *Logbook* are interspersed with the turmoil of contemporary American injustice—which is most notably evident in Shepard's entry regarding the benefit concert for Hurricane Carter, which became an opportunity for Dylan to reshape American justice.[4] From the onset of the Rolling Thunder Revue, Shepard transforms Dylan into an American icon, an icon of justice.

In Shepard's account of Dylan's involvement with the benefit concert for the release of Hurricane Carter, he does not blindly praise Dylan's efforts. Shepard uses this opportunity to further expose America's problematic obsession with myths and icons. Bitterly, Shepard reveals that in America "Nothing's important or has any value until it's blown up in 'bigger than life' proportions" (2004, 163). He continues:

> I keep coming back to the idea that it's a black man that the concert's being given for. A benefit for a black convict initiated by a white singer with black support. It's too sticky to figure out. Ali's been trying to trump up support for Carter for quite a while. Before Dylan even. But it took Dylan to get this whole thing together. (164)

For Shepard there is an irony in both the grandeur of the event and of the race politics that perpetuate it. The benefit becomes an Epcot Center of "justice" and in this display Dylan becomes a mythic hero of sorts. It is Dylan's image, not the cause, that becomes important.[5] While Shepard at times is also drawn in by Dylan's presence, here he recognizes the tragedy of it. The American people and legal system will not take note of its wrongs when a black man, even one as prominent and celebrated as Mohammed Ali, speaks, but when Dylan, a white folk singer and cultural icon, takes the stage, all listen. In all fairness, the public's draw to Dylan, rather than Ali, is not merely racially motivated. Dylan, unlike Ali, conjures up images that remind the public of a very particular American dream. Dylan sings of cowboys from the old West (white men living on the fringes of the law)

---

[4] See Damian Carpenter's (2017) work on Dylan's performance of the honest outlaw (195–206) especially.

[5] This is not to say that Dylan took the cause lightly. Marcus (1997) explains that Dylan understood "moral, generational, and racial divisions" as rooted in "Americans defining themselves not as who they were but as who they were not" (8).

and of modern times (men of color who have been marginalized by the law), who, when trying to take a stand, are brought down in the process.[6] Dylan and Shepard, here, destabilize the myth of the lone hero, focusing instead on causes that go beyond the individual. Their idea of the West is not one that privileges whiteness or individual bravado despite Hollywood's reliance on white actors. Rather, it speaks to the need to oppose injustice, especially when that injustice is sanctioned by the government. The government, as Shepard urges, not cowboys, was responsible for the atrocities against North American indigenous peoples (Shepard 1988, 78).

"Brownsville Girl" and the Mythic West

It took a decade for the two iconic writers to collaborate again; this time co-writing the song "Brownsville Girl." This song explores American identity and myth through American icons torn down by the death of the Wild West—a death brought on by increasing modernization. Both Dylan and Shepard have an affinity for classic Hollywood Westerns. In *Still on the Road*, Clinton Heylin (2010) quotes Dylan as praising John Ford's films and elaborating on Hollywood:

> I think America has produced the greatest films ever. No other country has ever come close. The great movies that came out of America in the studio system ... were heroic and visionary, and inspired people in a way that no other country has ever done. If film is the ultimate art form, then you'll need to look no further than those films. (288)

Along with "Brownsville Girl"—his 1986 song drawing on Henry King's 1950 movie, *The Gunfighter*—Dylan wrote (eighteen years earlier) "John Wesley Harding" (1968), which portrays the outlaw Hardin as a good man who "trav'led with a gun in ev'ry hand" but "was never known / To hurt an honest man." Dylan and Shepard, neither of whom financially depends on acting, have chosen to appear in Westerns. In Uli Edel's *Purgatory* (a 1999 film about violent outlaws who, in a purgatorial otherworld, have the opportunity to gain redemption by keeping peace there), Shepard plays Sheriff Forrest, formerly Wild Bill Hickcock. Two years

---

[6] The lyrics of "John Wesley Harding" depict another story of injustice. Here, a man who always lent a "helping hand" and never made a "foolish move" winds up the victim of a younger gunman's desire for fame.

prior to the Rolling Thunder Revue, Dylan was cast as the character Alias in (and then composed the score for) Sam Peckinpah's *Pat Garrett and Billy the Kid* (1973). Like many of Peckinpah's films, *Pat Garrett and Billy the Kid* deals with the encroaching modern world which threatens to corrupt and even destroy the West. In this film, the law, rather than the outlaw, is corrupt. Billy dies because (as he reveals early on in the film) the world is changing, but he will not. *Purgatory* and *Pat Garrett and Billy the Kid*, along with *The Gunfighter* and "John Wesley Harding," mythologize American identity and the West.

In the melancholic "Brownsville Girl," Dylan and Shepard are united in that they are both survivors of the modernization of the music and literary worlds they work in. In "Brownsville Girl," Dylan and Shepard speak to their listeners as icons who, despite the changes that have occurred since the 1970s, encompass the American zeitgeist. In a haunting, disenchanted voice, Dylan speaks as a survivor who remakes the world and himself continually in "Brownsville Girl." Here, he and Shepard contribute to the destabilization of the iconic Western by creating a modern tale of the American West.

In a 1986 interview with *Rolling Stone* magazine Shepard described "Brownsville Girl" in the following way:

> It has to do with a guy standing on [*sic*] line and waiting to see an old Gregory Peck movie that he can't quite remember—only pieces of it, and then this whole memory thing happens, unfolding before his very eyes. He starts speaking internally to a woman he'd been hanging out with, recalling their meetings and reliving the whole journey they'd gone on—and then it returns to the guy, who's still standing on [*sic*] line in the rain. (Shepard 1986, 198)

Shepard's account of the song may seem oversimplified, as de Castro (1997) argues. However, in his typical conversational style, Shepard does not eliminate the underlying theme. "Brownsville Girl," which Shepard's understated account of it reveals, is explicit in its depiction of the iconic hero's isolation, disappointment and demise. Dylan's storytelling vocals add to the protagonist's struggle to remember the plot of the Gregory Peck film, *The Gunfighter*, which opens with a lone cowboy "riding 'cross the desert" and ends with his being "shot down by a hungry kid trying to make a name for himself." Jimmy Ringo, Peck's character, who was based on John Wesley Hardin, is a gunfighter whose fame haunts and traps him.

Like so many of the Westerns that speak to Shepard, *The Gunfighter* is atypical of its genre; there is very little action in the film as Ringo finds himself waiting in a bar, hoping to see the mother of his child so that they may begin a new, quiet life together.

Drawing on *The Gunfighter*, Dylan and Shepard question the validity of a "true West," a concept that Shepard grappled with most notably in his 1980 play *True West*. Throughout *True West*, a play set in the kitchen alcove of a suburban home in Los Angeles, two brothers, both working on film scripts, are brought to the point where they no longer believe that anything around them is "real." Austin cries out to his brother, "There's nothing real down here, Lee. Least of all me" (49). The antagonistic brother, Lee, who is working on a ridiculously stupid Western, moreover, recalls that the last real Western was *Lonely Are the Brave*, a 1962 film that questions whether there ever was such a thing as the West. Jack Burns, a romantic cowboy played by Kirk Douglas, is warned by his unrequited love that the West he lives in doesn't exist. "Perhaps it never did," she laments. For Shepard, the words "true" and "real" are always in quotation marks and are not synonymous with one another. The call of the coyotes and the violence that erupts among the brothers are the "true" West in Shepard's play. The highways and Hollywood promises—Los Angeles of the 1980s—are the reality they live in, but it is not the "true" West. It has no ties to nature and is not interested in survival or justice. Shepard is hyper-aware of the myths we have created—myths of heroic battles for territory. And, although he finds himself at times attracted to these myths, his attraction is always critically hesitant. What draws Dylan and Shepard to *The Gunfighter*, then, is not only Ringo's tragic death—the death of a star—but also the way in which Ringo, while dying, creates a myth that the "hungry kid," who shot him down, must live by. Instead of letting the town hang Hunt Bromley for shooting Ringo in the back, Dylan, echoing the dialogue of the film, sings (while ostensibly quoting Ringo), "Turn him loose, let him go, let him say he outdrew me fair and square."

In fact, Shepard reveals a nostalgic side of himself when he defends the cowboy image as Shepard and Dylan align this image with the "honest outlaw" (Carpenter 2017, 195). As Carpenter argues, there is a tension between the individual and the community in regards to one's moral obligation to oppose empty morality or social codes in Dylan.[7] He continues

---

[7] Damian Carpenter's (2017) chapter on Dylan is essential reading for anyone interested in Dylan and the outlaw.

that the "key to understanding Dylan and the honest outlaw he presents is to partake in the struggle to recognize the 'godawful truth' below the surface of cultural myths, a struggle that finds its clearest expression when there is nothing left to lose" (210). Along these lines, Peck, for the musician and playwright, denotes American heroism as seen in all his roles, the most famous of which is Atticus Finch, the father in the 1962 film adaptation of *To Kill a Mockingbird*. The line in "Brownsville Girl," "when I saw you break down in front of the judge and cry real tears," is (according to Heylin [2010]) a direct reference to the film in which Atticus, the Alabama lawyer, defends a black man on trial for raping a poor white woman. Merging the two Peck roles, that of Atticus (the upstanding, good man who does not seek recognition or fame for defending a black man in the segregated South) and the gunfighter (an outlaw looking to begin again), Dylan and Shepard revision the American hero as a man who searches for justice and truth in spite of the costs that the hero pays.

"Brownsville Girl" and the American Dream

Along with questioning the historical myths that shape America and its people, Dylan and Shepard tackle the myth we call the American dream; in "Brownsville Girl" this is done through a comparison between old Western romances and the modern-day romances along the border towns of Texas. Each time Dylan, the songster, recalls the film, he is reminded of the Brownsville girl whose "memory ... keeps callin' after [him] like a rollin' train." The reason this particular woman haunts the protagonist is, of course, love, or more specifically, a lost love. Ringo from *The Gunfighter* risks death to convey his love to Peggy—a love that was lost as Peggy left Ringo—but a love that for Ringo represents the dream of settling down with a family and living off the land. Unlike Ringo who dies before his dream is realized, Dylan and Shepard's protagonist is haunted by his failure and fear. While love is tied to the American dream and redemption, the narrator often fears that very dream because family, as witnessed in Shepard's plays, is also a source of violence. Afraid, the protagonist in "Brownsville Girl" rationalizes his choices: "Way down in Mexico you went out to find a doctor and you never came back / I would have gone on after you but I didn't feel like letting my head get blown off."

The reason the Brownsville girl crosses into Mexico to find a doctor is never explicit; however, through Shepard's canon we may discern the significance of her travels to Mexico. Throughout Shepard's plays and short stories, Mexico is a place of danger and restoration. In Shepard's *True West*, for example, Austin recalls that his father hitchhiked to Mexico in order to have his teeth extracted. He did not have enough money to have the procedure done in America. The description of him, however, is one that makes us question the safety of the journey and the dental treatment he receives. Austin reveals that his father winds up alone and destitute in Mexico with his gums sewn up. His destitute state and extracted teeth make for pathetic images of a dying father. In the short story "Opuestos" (1996) the narrator travels to Mexico for the day to watch cock fights. He tries to convince his significant other to join him, but she fears the dangers lurking on the other side of the border. And, in his 2004 play, *The Late Henry Moss*, a Mexican neighbor (Esteban) brings soup to nourish the alcoholic father Henry's hangovers whereas Henry's girlfriend Conchalla, a mysterious Mexican-Indian woman, kills a fish and then brings it back to life. At the play's conclusion, Conchalla takes Henry back to the time he abandoned his family—a journey that allows him to rest in peace. Keeping in mind these and other examples from Shepard, it is possible that the Brownsville girl seeks an abortion—a medical procedure that refuses the American dream. She rejects family—that very institution that Ringo, the gunfighter, sought out when returning to reunite with his family. With this said and in exploring Shepard's work in which Mexico is an imagined space, which is violent and uncivilized, the Brownsville girl flees into Mexico to escape modern domesticity and, possibly, to do so she seeks to have an abortion to destroy any possibility for renewal. This reading points to the protagonist's lack of courage. He must live with the fact that he did not go with her to Mexico.[8] In addition to fearing death, he fears a life without the comforts of home, no matter how corrupt America, according to Ruby, who lives on the "wreckin' lot" with her absent lover Henry Porter, is becoming. And, he fears family life. Afraid, he allows her and the potential dream she offers him to disappear.[9]

Shepard's motif of the bitter disappointment ripe in America resonates throughout "Brownsville Girl." Not only is the protagonist "broken-hearted,"

---

[8] Brownsville, Texas (also known as Little Mexico), is a US-Mexican border city. It is not uncommon for residents in Brownsville to travel into Matamoros, Mexico, despite the dangers, to obtain inexpensive pharmaceuticals and medical treatments.

[9] Shepard is in love with the myth of the American family, but repeatedly reveals that family life is plagued with the same type of violence which America was founded on. For an excellent discussion of the American dream, family and violence, see Shepard's interview (2002b) with Matthew Roudané.

but Ruby also reveals her crushed dreams. She says, "Welcome to the land of the living dead... / ...Even the swap meets around here are getting corrupt." Disappointed by her zombie-like life and the corruption in her world, Ruby gently scolds the protagonist and his girl: "Ruby just smiled and said, 'Ah, you know some babies never learn.'" Here, Dylan and Shepard reveal that modern America is corrupt. We need only to think of the unjust arrest and retrials of Hurricane Carter. Even though Dylan announced the court's decision to acquit Carter at the end of the concert (*Logbook* 2004, 170), Carter was retried and sentenced before he was finally released in 1988. But as "Brownsville Girl" reveals, the corruption in the modern world is buttressed by the very myths that Americans love— myths of younger generations usurping their forefathers.[10] Ringo is both the corrupted and corrupter of his world. On the one hand, Hunt Bromley, representing a younger generation that will do anything, even shoot a man from behind to make a name for himself, brings Ringo down. On the other hand, Ringo sustains the corruption of the modern world by allowing the young gunfighter to go on living; Ringo perpetuates the mythology of the Wild West, of a young man who was able to take on a giant.

Film icons, according to Dylan and Shepard, have been torn down by a new type of film industry, an industry devoid of the stellar performances of Peck and his lot. Although Dylan and Shepard's own cinematic performances are nowhere near the quality of Peck's, the roles they have chosen reveal an affinity to Westerns. However, unlike the traditional Western, like those associated with Gregory Peck, Dylan and Shepard worked with directors like Sam Peckinpah and have selected roles that break down this tradition—a tradition that focuses on the individual hero. While Peck's film career died down as he aged and new faces made their way into the film industry, the Brownsville girl herself will not be replaced. She is not described as a "star," but rather we learn in the chorus that she has "teeth like pearls shining like the moon above." She is a natural satellite with the ability to show the protagonist "all around the world."

In the song's conclusion, the protagonist reveals that once he "sat through [the movie] twice" but he doesn't "remember who [he] was or where [he] was bound"; in essence, the protagonist tries to place himself in the film. Which character did he play? Where was he headed? Inevitably,

---

[10] Rather than finding an old, free democracy in American history and folklore, what Dylan discovers is that such claims are reached by mistake (Marcus 1997, 89).

he could have been Ringo, but instead he is no one. To him it "Seems like a long time ago, long before the stars were torn down." Ending again on a note of disappointment—now the stars have been torn down—Dylan and Shepard reveal that the protagonist is lost: he does not know what happened to his lover. Through the love story and the reference to the Western, Dylan and Shepard, here, reveal the difficulty of origin—the reality of the matter at hand—because memory skews everything. Myths replace facts and mask both imaginary and actual landscapes and identities. This "fact" is highlighted (more overtly) in Shepard's recollection of Dylan wearing a rubber Dylan mask: "Tonight," Shepard writes, "Dylan appears in a rubber Dylan mask that he picked up on 42nd Street. The crowd is stupefied. ... is this some kind of mammoth hoax? An imposter!" (109).[11] This mask both stood as the mythic Dylan as well as brought about confusion as to who Dylan was. Ultimately, for Shepard, the authentic, the true, that which is uncorrupted by the stories we create, is unattainable, and unknowable, even though it exists. For Dylan, as his donning of the Dylan mask suggests, the "real" or "authentic" is non-existent, a façade—identity, for Dylan, is the mask.[12]

TOOTH OF CRIME AND THE GYPSY

Dylan continually remakes the world and himself—a trait that Shepard admires with trepidation. Shepard, just two years prior to meeting Dylan, wrote *Tooth of Crime*. Four years after his collaboration on "Brownsville Girl," Shepard rewrote the play, calling it *Tooth of Crime (Second Dance)*. In this strange tale, Hoss, a rock-and-roll hero, "*turns the knife on himself*" (93) when he recognizes that he cannot keep up with the ever-changing music world represented in the arrival of a younger musician, Crow. In the play's second act, Hoss and Crow face off in a verbal and physical battle for their existence. Ultimately, it is Crow, the gypsy who freely moves in and out of identity, who survives. He rides on the wind, changing easily. Crow, like Dylan, is a wanderer. Shepard is very much aware of Dylan's invented self and his gypsy lifestyle. He writes that Dylan "seems determined to maintain a gypsy status at all costs" (130). The image of the

---

[11] Marcus (1997) recalls a similar episode in his description of Dylan's 1966 London concert. Captured partially on the Basement tapes, the London crowd violently shouted, "TRAITOR. SELL-OUT. MOTHERFUCKER. YOU'RE NOT BOB DYLAN" (7).

[12] For more on the significance of masks and Dylan, see Marcus (1997).

gypsy recalls Shepard's Crow, the rocker who will usurp Hoss in the battle that ensues in *Tooth of Crime* as well as the image of the gunfighter in Dylan and Shepard's "Brownsville Girl." Dylan has no permanent home, no single musical style. (*Blonde on Blonde* [1966], alone, testifies to Dylan's versatility.) Dylan long ago shed his birth identity. As Bob Dylan, he assumed a Welsh name that he took from an American Western. Interestingly, the name also means tide or flow. While Dylan (like Crow) is comfortable with the fluid nature of identity, Shepard's play laments the death of Hoss, the rocker who cannot change with the times, revealing Shepard's unease with change—the change that Dylan seems to embrace— even though he sees change as necessary.

For the purpose of our discussion, I will focus on act two when Crow arrives. Entering the stage, Crow sings "The Rat Age," identifying himself as a scavenger who can shift his image as is needed:

> You've changed your face you've changed your scent
> You've even changed your fingerprint
> Image is everything. (56)

Shepard asks the audience to ponder lyrics that may seem like a paradox. Often image is aligned with identity and identity too often is conceived of as fixed. For Crow, however, image is fluid; it changes as easily as a crow rides on the wind, looking for fresh kill. Crow, moreover, is identified as a gypsy—as was Dylan in the *Rolling Thunder Logbook*. A gypsy is a wanderer—a person without a home, without territory. For Shepard, home and territory are entwined with identity and image. In his plays, he depicts battles over territory as struggles to maintain an image of oneself as belonging to "civilized" America. While land may give a sense of permanence and security to the settler who displaced the indigenous population (as it seems to for Hoss), Shepard reveals this as an American myth.

Hoss attempts to take a verbal swipe at Crow, to throw him off balance with the following:

> You ripped your own self off and now all you got is yer poison to call yer gift. Yer punk chump with a sequin noseband and you'll need more than a Les Paul Gibson to bring you home. (85)

Hoss's insult reveals that he does not understand the gypsy Crow. He believes that Crow seeks a home, but Crow's response exposes just how dangerous he is:

> Home! Home? Home is where the heart is! That's easy ditty. I got no heart to tie me down. I'm everywhere at once. Ubiquitous! Omnipotent! I'll tap dance right across your sentimental rainy street every time you put your big toe in. I'll shake yer booty while you weep for the naked ancestors. I'll eat your maudlin lunch while you pay tribute to drivel and fantasy stick. I'm burnin from the inside out, Mighty Man. I got no time for retrospect. I'm in the charred zone. Gone. Blasted in oblivion. For me, this match is done dick. Dead. All you been doin is spinnin yer wheels from bell on. (85)

It is Crow's lack of home and heart that leads to the successful usurpation of Hoss. The name, Crow, although not designated as such, is reminiscent of the feathers used in traditional ceremonial clothing of and the names given to indigenous Americans. What is more, it is the bird associated with the shape-shifting trickster in many North American indigenous cultures. Shepard's audience is left to wonder whether this battle is one in which Shepard asks his white audience to rethink American myth and its privilege as Dylan did with his benefit concert for Hurricane Carter.

For Shepard, land gives us an identity, but land can be usurped; we can end up homeless, without identity. Only gypsies, individuals who embrace this landlessness, Shepard argues, truly understand. Although Shepard has categorized the play as an epic tragedy in line with *Beowolf* (*Sam Shepard: Stalking Himself* 1998), Crow's fluidity is admired, as we see when he out-moves Hoss:

> So you wanna be a rocker. Study the moves. Jerry Lee Lewis. Cop some blue suede shoes. Switch yer head like Carl Perkins. Put yer ass in a grind. Talkin sock it to it, get the image in line. Get the image in line, boy. The fantasy whine. It's all over dee street and you caint buy dee time. Caint buy dee bebop. Caint buy dee slide. Got dee fantasy blues and no place to hide. (90)

The verbal moves here contrast to Hoss's whining and drug use. Crow, confident of his image and his moves, targets Hoss's insecurity. He sees that Hoss is losing his image; he sees that despite having been a "rocker" Hoss no longer holds that honor. What Shepard does, ultimately, is rewrite American identity, revealing that the idea of a permanent home (like those longed for since the Eisenhower age), of being settled, is not the truth of who Americans are. What makes America unique is that its people are not settlers. The vast landscapes that Shepard draws on call on a gypsy-nature— a people without home—cowboys and Indians riding across the desert.

"True Dylan" and Survival

Shepard places Dylan in the same category as Crow—the victor of *Tooth of Crime* who continually remakes himself. Dylan, like Crow, is a gypsy, as Shepard highlights in the *Logbook* and as Dylan's "The Times They Are A-Changin'" (1963) testifies. As Shepard writes, "Dylan is an invention of his own mind. The point isn't to figure him out but to take him in" (98). Dylan, as Marcus (1997) reveals, has "a greater collection of masks" than most performers (220) and as such a greater chance of surviving the changing world. In *True Dylan*, Shepard portrays Dylan as elusive. The characters' names and the play's subtitle, *A One-Act Play, As It Really Happened One Afternoon in California*, assert that the play documents a real conversation during one of Dylan and Shepard's meetings. Additionally, Shepard stresses place in the opening stage directions. The shabby patio has a distant view of the Pacific Ocean, close enough for the viewers to hear the waves. The worn-out human construction set up against the magnificent view of the ocean is reminiscent of the nineteenth-century Manifest Destiny paintings hung in dingy taverns—paintings meant to inspire movement. The set reminds one, too, of the *Rolling Thunder Logbook*—which juxtaposes historical places and sparse motel rooms.

Shepard allows viewers to eavesdrop on an uncanny meeting in which two American legends discuss American music and film stars. Although set up as real, *True Dylan*, like *True West*, immediately undermines assumptions of the real despite being true. The Jimmy Yancey boogie woogie piano solo heard in unison with the ocean waves sets up two rhythms: Sam (Shepard) seeking truth; Bob (Dylan) embracing invention. Sam and Bob discuss how music has defined Bob (i.e., what he was listening to at certain times of his life). The music Bob refers to is varied in genre but all are older forms. No music from 1987, the date of the play, is ever mentioned. Bob is content with this whereas Sam seems uneasy:

> BOB: … I've always been content with the old forms. I know my place by now.
> SAM: So, you feel like you know who you are?
> BOB: Well, you always know who you are. I just don't know who I'm gonna be. (1987, 64).

In this exchange, both Sam and Bob pose existential questions. However, Sam is uncertain about the here and now whereas Bob's uncertainty lies in the future. He is content, knowing his place, but, like the ever-changing shape of a wave, understands the fluidity of identity. This extraordinary moment is saturated with references to the past. It positions Sam as the disciple, learning from Bob who will guide him through the unknown. This journey is one marked with danger, however, as the sound of a car crash and the idolization of James Dean and the spot in which he died haunts the play.

Throughout, Sam attempts to interview Bob, an act that recalls Shepard's distrust of the iconic image. He notes in *Sam Shepard: Stalking Himself* (1998) that Americans prefer to see someone on television than speak to them in person. The image, Shepard reveals, is idolized. The Sam in *True Dylan* finds that when he rewinds his tape to listen to their conversation about the lack of authenticity in James Dean's final scene in *Giant*, among other topics, there is only a Jimmy Yancey piano solo on the recorder. Only when Bob reenters does Sam discover that the recorder did not malfunction. For Bob, the presence of Jimmy Yancey's piano solo appears to be an angel that is a symbol of truth, justice and purity. For Sam it is a mystery; he remains baffled by the presence of the music. This strange occurrence reminds the viewer that, despite the set-up, we are not viewing a real story and our Bob may not be the "real" Dylan, even if he is a "true" portrait of Dylan.

Despite its interview format, the play repeatedly reminds the viewer that what they are viewing is artifice but artifice that holds the truth. Bob repeatedly avoids giving straight answers, quoting instead the Pope and Elvis. Moreover, he often uses music lyrics instead of his own words. And, most explicitly, Bob and Sam recommend "Mak[ing] it up" (Shepard 1987, 60, 66) if memory fails, or the answer is unknown. The viewer cannot be sure that the dialogue is not a fabrication. The theme of fabricating reaches its apex with the story of James Dean's last scene in *Giant*. During this short one act, the sound of a car crash, presumably Dean's, is heard three times. Bob recalls being at the same spot where Dean crashed. In speaking of the aura that he felt at the site of the crash, Bob speaks to the authenticity of his experience. This is juxtaposed to the "lie" he feels when watching Dean in *Giant*.BOB: Turns out Nick Adams, an actor at the time, who was a friend of James Dean's, he overdubbed that speech because James Dean had died by that time. (68)Ironically, Bob and Sam sound alike—their "maybes," "yeahs" and "naws" are too similar in a play that features two distinct voices (Shepard's and Dylan's). Shepard essentially dubs over Dylan, but still allows Bob to be the more prolific of the two. Bob is the one who believes in angels while Sam tries to fix meaning on magnetic strips. And, while Bob poses a dilemma when he claims that "Words have lost their meaning. Like *rebel*. Like *cause*. Like *love*. They mean a million different things" (68), his notion of "lost meaning" is that of a multitude of meaning rather than an absence of meaning. Words can mean more than one thing. It appears that there is irony in regards to the loss of meaning and Bob Dylan's shape-shifting identity. His identity is fluid, but in being multifaceted, Shepard reminds his readers that the ability of words to mean many things does not equal meaning nothing. Likewise, Dylan's many masks, Shepard suggests, point to Dylan's ability to remain relevant.

Albeit never having been performed, *True Dylan* lends itself as a footnote to the *Logbook* and "Brownsville Girl." This one act, and Shepard through it, suggests that, for icons like Dylan to remain on top, to continue shining in the chaotic world of fame, they must continue to remake themselves; they must prevent becoming static. Likewise, to be American, for Dylan and Shepard, is never to settle, never to become content and never to allow oneself to be defined. Dylan and Shepard destabilize the mythic American heroes—strong cowboys with one purpose—with shape-shifting gypsies. Ultimately, Shepard's survivors are those like Dylan—men and women who, without losing meaning, change like leaves "blowin' in the wind," sometimes simply by "fabricating" stories of their past, stories that are true and fluid because they are unreal. Dylan, for Shepard, is Crow, soaring in the wind. When he lands, he takes on a new shape—an identity that is true Dylan—a gypsy with a cowboy mouth.

REFERENCES

Bottoms, Stephen J. 1998. *The Theatre of Sam Shepard: States of Crisis.* Cambridge: Cambridge University Press.

Carpenter, Damian. 2017. *Lead Belly, Woody Guthrie, Bob Dylan and American Folk Outlaw Performance.* Abingdon: Routledge.

de Castro, Jesús Lerate. 1997. Hoss vs. Crow: A Shoot-Out between Modernism and Postmodernism in Sam Shepard's *The Tooth of Crime* (and Its Sequel in 'Brownsville Girl'). In *Letras en el espejo: Ensayos de literatura americana comparada*, ed. Alvarez Maurin et al., 125–134. León, Spain: Universidad de León.

Dylan, Bob. 2004. *Chronicles: Volume One.* New York: Simon and Schuster.

Edel, Uli, dir. 1999. *Purgatory.* Turner.

Haynes, Todd, dir. 2007. I'm Not There. Weinstein.

Heylin, Clinton. 2010. *Sill on the Road: The Songs of Bob Dylan, 1974–2006.* Chicago: Chicago Review Press.

King, Henry, dir. 1950. *The Gunfighter.* 20th Century Fox.

Marcus, Greil. 1997. *The Old, Weird America.* New York: Picador.

Peckinpah, Sam, dir. 1973. *Pat Garrett and Billy the Kid.* Warner Brothers.

Sam Shepard: Stalking Himself. 1998. Great Performances. PBS.

Shepard, Sam. 1984. *Fool for Love and Other Plays.* New York: Bantam Books.

———. 1986. The Rolling Stone Interview: Sam Shepard. By Jonathan Cott. *Rolling Stone,* December 18, 1986.

———. 1987. True Dylan: A One-Act Play as it Really Happened One Afternoon in California. *Esquire Magazine,* July 1, 1987.

———. 1988. "Sam Shepard" Geography of a Horse Dreamer. By Kevin Sessums. *Interview,* September 1988: 70–79.

———. 1996. Opuestos. In *Cruising Paradise,* 199–204. New York: Vintage.

———. 2002a. *The Late Henry Moss.* In *Three Plays: The Late Henry Moss, Eyes for Consuela, When the World was Green.* New York: Vintage.

———. 2002b. Shepard on Shepard: An Interview. By Matthew Roudané. In *The Cambridge Companion to Sam Shepard,* ed. Matthew Roudané, 64–80. Cambridge: Cambridge University Press.

———. 2004. *The Rolling Thunder Logbook.* Cambridge, MA: Da Capo.

———. 2005. *The God of Hell.* New York: Vintage.

———. 2006. *Tooth of Crime (Second Dance).* New York: Vintage.

Shewey, Don. 1997. *Sam Shepard.* New York: Da Capo.

CHAPTER 7

Bob Dylan's "Westerns": Border Crossings and the Flight from "the Domestic"

John McCombe

Bob Dylan was, in his own words, "born with the wrong name" (Dylan 2004b), and he appears to have created his own by drawing from both Dylan Thomas and TV's Marshal Matt Dillon. That a child of the Cold War-era was drawn to myths of the Old West should surprise no one, and Dylan's first half-decade as a recording artist allowed him to indulge in some fabricated biography involving travel through the border towns of the U.S. Southwest (e.g., "My Life in a Stolen Moment" [1962]) and the creation of his initial portraits of western outlaws in songs such as "John Wesley Harding" (1967).

The present chapter examines Dylan's art in the context of a gender-based, cinematic discourse involving Dylan's "westerns," placing the term in quotes because it considers the western in the broadest possible sense: on film, in narrative songs involving outlaw figures, and in the ways in which Dylan has cast himself—via interviews and in memoir—as a quasi-western hero. In particular, my focus is on the period after Dylan traveled to Durango, Mexico, in December of 1972 to score, and later be cast in, Sam Peckinpah's *Pat Garrett and Billy the Kid* (1973). In the immediate

J. McCombe (✉)
University of Dayton, Dayton, OH, USA

© The Author(s) 2019
N. Otiono, J. Toth (eds.), *Polyvocal Bob Dylan*,
Palgrave Studies in Music and Literature,
https://doi.org/10.1007/978-3-030-17042-4_7

121

aftermath of that experience, Dylan began creating his own *musical* westerns. In fact, Dylan composed enough narrative songs involving border crossings and western tropes between 1973 and 1976—songs such as "Billy" (1972), "Lily, Rosemary and the Jack of Hearts" (1975), "Romance in Durango" (1976), and "Isis" (1976)—to constitute a distinct musical genre that deserves significantly more scholarly attention. My goal is to demonstrate how Dylan's westerns regularly conform to, yet occasionally subvert, gender-based binaries that distinguish the classical Hollywood western.

Dylan's mid-1970s westerns foreground two simultaneous cultural developments: one involving Nixon-era gender dynamics in the context of second-wave feminism and the other mapping the gradual evolution of gender roles in the western film genre. At the same time that the heroes of film westerns—namely, in the "professional plot" westerns at the turn of the 1970s—acknowledged that economic destiny might no longer be under their control, Dylan's western heroes reflect the same recognition and reject an outmoded individualism in favor of a community of a masculine, professional elite. The fact that these songs filled Dylan's song catalog at a time of renewed commitment to touring—beginning in 1974 (after a hiatus of nearly eight years)—confirms that the Dylan western has much to reveal about connections between the changing economic landscapes of the film and music industries in the 1970s, as well as how integral popular music can be to conversations about masculinity, domesticity, and the western genre. If this present essay collection concerns Dylan's "transgressive artistic ingenuity,"[1] it is worth noting that one of the many tensions in Dylan's art lies in the simultaneous creation of women protagonists who display agency in Dylan's "song westerns" in conjunction with elements of Dylan's art that reinscribe predominant gender tropes that mobilized second-wave feminists in the period under consideration. In the words of Barbara O'Dair (2009) in *The Cambridge Companion to Bob Dylan*, Dylan's songs regularly express an attitude toward women that is "backward looking" with protagonists "bewildered by women who stake their claims" (86). When O'Dair proceeds to discuss a gender ideology that "depends on the Other to stay in a fixed [masculine] role" (86), Dylan's early 1970s westerns initially substantiate this claim, before the Dylan western protagonist evolves in tentatively engaging with domesticity (in various forms) with the release of *Desire* (1976). While the gender

---

[1] See Toth and Otiono's Introduction to the present collection.

dynamics of these *Desire*-era songs could hardly be described as feminist anthems, the present essay will indeed suggest a nuanced evolution in the gender ideology of Dylan's westerns between 1973 and 1976.

Early Border Crossings

On 9 August 1962, in a Manhattan courthouse, Robert Allen Zimmerman legally became Bob Dylan. And despite the spelling of his new surname, Dylan was quick to indicate to an early biographer that his inspiration was not what many assume: "Straighten out in your book that I did not take my name from Dylan Thomas" (Shelton 2003, 50). In addition, at least one figure who knew Dylan during his brief tenure in Minneapolis recalls that "He always went as Bob Dillon, not Dylan" (Barker 2004b, 46). One possible explanation for the original spelling is a connection to a popular television show that began its two-decade run in the fall of 1955: *Gunsmoke*. More than 25 years after his legal name change, Dylan suggested to one of his then-band mates, César Díaz, that his choice of name was indeed inspired by the show's protagonist: Matt Dillon (Barker 2004b, 49). To strengthen the connection, consider that, when the Zimmerman family first acquired a television set in 1952, the young Robert "preferred western adventure series. [...] He could imagine himself as Wyatt Earp. Or, even more heroically [...] that lean, laconic, fearless man of justice from Dodge City, named Matt Dillon" (Shelton 2003, 35).

Although the *Gunsmoke* Dillon is a U.S. Marshal, like many western lawmen, Dylan's namesake is quick to anger and prone to violence, but often with a reflectiveness and regret concerning his actions. As a comprehensive history of *Gunsmoke* describes him, Dillon "was witness to great injustices. He was also forced to kill in the name of a greater good, a good that must have sometimes seemed to him elusive" (Barabas and Barabas 1990, 86). Much like Dylan, Dillon was also reluctant to discuss his family history or to engage in displays of emotion—for the latter, such displays might compromise his ability to promote and/or preserve law and order in Dodge City. Later in his career, Dylan begins to identify more with the outlaw than with the lawman, but even shortly after the name change, Dylan at least imagines himself as the type of outlaw Dillon confronted each week on television (and radio) during Dylan's childhood. In "My Life in a Stolen Moment" ([1962] 2004c), one of Dylan's few actual published poems, Dylan indulges in all manner of tropes concerning the American Southwest (in general) and the western (in particular), including this evocation of imagined criminality: "Got jailed for suspicion of armed robbery / Got held for four hours on a murder rap / Got busted for looking like I do." But the poem's punchline reveals these fabrications for what they are: "An' I never done none of them things." Clearly, in the very early years of his career, Dylan is certainly interested in the outlaw, if not yet identifying with the outlaw. A willingness to transgress, while certainly imagined, is also marked by a denial: the speaker "never done none of them things."

One way, among many, in which to define the outlaw is via the process of border crossings. As bell hooks (1994) suggests, the process of crossing borders more broadly—in other words, making "elaborate shifts in location, thought, and life experience" (5)—is founded upon privilege: "structures of class privilege prevent those who are not materially privileged from having access to these forms of education for critical consciousness" (5). What hooks foregrounds is the acknowledgement that power functions across boundaries of nation, of race, and other forms of difference, including gender. The notion of border crossings, as we shall see, is central to Dylan's treatment of western themes and imagery well before he makes an explicit immersion into the western film genre via his contributions to Sam Peckinpah's *Pat Garrett and Billy the Kid*. Nearly a decade earlier, in compositions like "Just Like Tom Thumb's Blues" (1965), Dylan's speaker is confronted with the Other in the Mexican city of Juárez, and this difference manifests itself in the form of sickness, despair, political corruption, and, most notable for the purposes of the present chapter, unreliable and devouring women ("hungry women" who "make a mess outta you"). Dylan initially speaks of being "lost in the rain in Juárez" and subsequently re-crosses the border back to the U.S., since that confrontation with a radically different life experience (recalling the confrontation hooks speaks of) is simply overpowering.

Most relevant to the present chapter's argument, "Tom Thumb's Blues" actually offers a roll call of women, each one posing a threat to the song's speaker: Saint Annie seems to have been his drug buddy (or dealer), Melinda is the "goddess of gloom" who invites one to her room (at one's peril), and the gender-ambiguous Angel seems to be the cautionary tale concerning excess who inspires the retreat back across the Mexican border. Although it is difficult to date the song's composition precisely, one can assume, given its recording on 2 August 1965 (16 takes in that single day, according to Clinton Heylin [2009], 259), that Dylan put pen to paper between meeting Sara Lowndes in late 1964 (Gray 2008, 201) and the couple's wedding on 22 November 1965 (Scaduto 1973, 266). Beginning in the summer of 1964, Dylan began dividing his time between Manhattan and Woodstock, NY, usually in the company of Lowndes. And by the summer of 1966, the newlywed Dylans had permanently relocated upstate.

I invoke Dylan's biography here in discussing "Tom Thumb's Blues" for a very specific reason: classic westerns foreground the western hero's struggles with domesticity—in other words, the tensions between the hero's preferred mode of rootless individualism and the lure of community, family, and the rootedness that defines institutions (law enforcement, churches, schools, marriage, etc.). This struggle surely figures in Matt Dillon's efforts to protect Dodge City. But we see it in all manner of westerns. For example, in a "classical Hollywood western" such as *My Darling Clementine* (1946), which draws its title from the name of Wyatt Earp's white-skinned love interest, the reluctant Marshall of Tombstone rejects the desperate advances of the ostensibly brown-skinned Chihuahua (portrayed by Linda Darnell in heavy make-up). In this way, Earp rejects a form of border crossing in favor of the Boston-bred, Christian, school-marm Clementine. However, throughout the film, Earp's uneasiness with the notion of domestic entanglements registers primarily through Earp's discomfort with artifacts of ostensibly Eastern culture, such as a malfunctioning barber's chair (in Tombstone's Bon Ton Tonsorial Parlor) and his use of honeysuckle-scented cologne.

What I am proposing is that one crucial context for Dylan's later 1970s "westerns"—not simply those earlier songs, such as "Tom Thumb's Blues" that share the imagery of border crossings with westerns—is rooted in significant personal and professional changes initiated by Dylan's marriage. As Dylan (2004b) suggests in his memoir *Chronicles: Volume One*, "Having children [in 1966] changed my life and segregated me from just about everybody and everything that was going on. Outside of my family, nothing held any real interest for me and I was seeing everything through different glasses" (114). The choice of "segregated" here is noteworthy. For Dylan's generation (and beyond), the "border" this word typically signifies is one of race; after all, Dylan immerses himself in the song western less than a decade after the Civil Rights Act of 1964. But rather than racial segregation, Dylan speaks of how marriage and family can serve as a (gendered) border between his songwriting and "everything that was going on" in the tumult of the late 1960s.

Listeners can attempt to borrow Dylan's new Woodstock-era "glasses" to view post-marriage songs such as "John Wesley Harding" (1967), "Sign on the Window" (1970), and "All the Tired Horses" (1970) as preludes to the immersion in song westerns to come. "Harding" was clearly an important song to Dylan, serving as the title track to his first post-motorcycle-accident album in December 1967—recorded during that extended period of domesticity in and around Woodstock. "Harding" almost derives its name from the mythical outlaw John Wesley Hardin (Dylan adds the "g"), but rather than focus on gunfights, or the 44 men Hardin claimed to have killed, Dylan opts for romance, making claims for Harding's honesty and aid to the poor, while singing of "his lady by his side." In the words of Mike Marqusee (2003), Dylan adopts "[Director] John Ford's endorsement of legend over truth" (230).[2] For the first time in his professional life, Dylan, too, had a domestic partner, as well as two young children (and two more on the way before the end of 1969), and his "family man" period seems filled with moments of attempted reconciliation: attempts to reconcile the professional and the domestic spheres.

By the time Dylan had become a father of four in 1970, several compositions begin to foreground the challenges of any such career/domestic life balance, beginning with the curiously titled *Self Portrait* (1970) (curious because the "self-portrait" consists largely of cover songs). On the album's opening lines—in one of the few Dylan originals—Dylan sings, "All the tired horses in the sun / How'm I supposed to get any ridin' done?" Not only does the presence of horses connect to Dylan's ongoing interest in the tropes of the old west, but the ambiguity of the lines he actually sings—is it "ridin'" or "writin'"?—suggests a further linkage between the western hero and domesticity. One might suspect that Dylan was consciously obscuring his lament about a possible lack of artistic productivity, especially since the 1976 sheet music collection, *The Songs of Bob Dylan: From 1966 Through 1975*, quotes the word in question as "ridin'." Between the summer of 1966 and the dawn of the new decade, Dylan elected not to tour, which seems to have altered the way in which he composed new material. The well-known documentary *Don't Look Back* (1967) captures Dylan typing frantically in hotel rooms during his 1965 U.K. tour—often while others are talking, drinking, and playing music around him. For several years, Dylan would clearly "get his writin' done"

---

[2] Readers will no doubt recognize Marqusee's allusion here to *The Man Who Shot Liberty Valance* (1962).

under pressure—either on tour or in the studio, as Sean Wilentz (2010) recounts in his essay on the making of *Blonde on Blonde*: "Departing from his reputation for recording rapidly [while in Nashville cutting *Blonde*], Dylan kept sketching and revising in his hotel room and even in the studio" (117).

Dylan's "retirement" from the road—in actuality, a hiatus that lasted for roughly eight years—was marked by several moves, as his family expanded and his desire for privacy became more urgent. In chapter three of *Chronicles*, Dylan (2004a) recounts how the once "hospitable" (116) Woodstock quickly led him to feel like "something out of a carnival show" (118), as fans and pilgrims expected the artist to continue in his role as the "conscience of a generation" (118). Dylan's response to the pressure to continue being the type of artist he had been between 1963 and 1966 is the response of a classic western outlaw: "[W]e tried moving west" (118). Dylan's ambivalence about the ways in which the domestic can exist in tension with professional ambition registers across the *New Morning* (1970) album, as Dylan's speakers either document a lack of movement— "Ain't no reason to go anywhere" ("Time Passes Slowly")—or they embrace westward movement—"Took hold of my sweetheart and away we did drive / Straight for the hills, the black hills of Dakota" ("Day of the Locusts"). Such ambivalence about domesticity becomes most apparent in "Sign on the Window," which again looks west: "Build me a cabin in Utah / Marry me a wife, catch rainbow trout / That must be what's it's all about." In singing this verse, Dylan repeats that third line, almost as if his speaker is trying to convince himself that his plan to embrace domesticity *must* be a good idea. Interestingly, however, following the release of *New Morning*, Dylan would release no new studio album, and very little new music at all, until 1973, when a movie soundtrack not only yielded a #12 *Billboard* single ("Knockin' on Heaven's Door"), but also signaled an explicit immersion in the western genre that allowed a more intensive exploration of domesticity and its potential discontents.

ROMANCE IN DURANGO

Interviewer: "Why do some of your songs bear no relation to the titles?"
Dylan: "Give me an example."
Interviewer: "'Rainy Day Women Nos. 12 & 35'"
Dylan: "Have you ever been in North Mexico?" (qtd. in Lee 2004, 82)

The exchange above occurred at a typically surreal press conference during Dylan's spring 1966 U.K. tour. And even though Dylan was crossing many borders at the time—many of them metaphorical—he had not yet literally crossed the border into Mexico. In the spring of 1967, Dylan recorded the traditional "Hills of Mexico" as part of the famed *Basement Tapes* in upstate New York, a song which finds Dylan singing "'How do you do, young cowboy / And how'd you like to go / Spend the summer pleasantly / In the hills of Mexico." And, in a moment that connects to the earlier Dylan composition, "Just Like Tom Thumb's Blues," the speaker in the traditional song laments that when "we crossed the river, boys / Our troubles they begun." Similarly, Dylan's journey into Durango, Mexico, in late 1972 brought its own set of "troubles" (both personal and professional), initiating a series of western-themed songs in response.

As discussed earlier, migration—most often western migration—became a recurring theme in Dylan's Woodstock-era songwriting, at least when Dylan was able to overcome writer's block at a time when, in his own words, "I didn't have a whole lot of songs" (Dylan 2004a, 134). The desire to move—and move with his family in tow—motivated the temporary relocation to Durango: "I'd gotten my family out of New York, [...] there was a lot of pressure there. But even so, my wife got fed up almost immediately. She'd say to me, 'What the hell are we doing here [in Mexico]?' It was not an easy question to answer" (Dylan qtd. in Gray 2008, 540).

What (the hell) Dylan was doing in Mexico was accepting an invitation from actor Kris Kristofferson to visit the set of *Pat Garrett and Billy the Kid*. Dylan had known Kristofferson since the recording of *Blonde on Blonde*, when the aspiring songwriter was a custodian at the Columbia recording studio in Nashville. By 1972 an established musician and actor, Kristofferson promised "a ball" (Shelton 2003, 426) on set in Durango, and Dylan marked the second day of his visit by performing the song "Billy," which prompted director Sam Peckinpah to offer Dylan an acting role. (He'd already been tasked with providing songs for the film's score.[3]) Recalling the earlier "John Wesley Harding," a man who resisted chains of all varieties, the title character of "Billy" also demands freedom in the face of individuals and institutions seeking to deny it.

John Saunders (2001) is one of many scholars who discusses the "professional plot" western and how it emerged from the so-called classical

---

[3] Some of the film's incidental music was provided by Jerry Fielding (Heylin 2009, 432).

western. Peckinpah's *The Wild Bunch* (1969) provides an earlier example of a narrative—one pushed further in *Pat Garrett*—in which cynicism dominates the overall tone of the film. No longer motivated by a personal code that shapes right and wrong, the protagonist of the professional plot western is motivated by money and/or a satisfaction derived from violence. Saunders writes that, in such films, "the feminine offers no simple refuge from masculine compulsions" (86). Even though the speaker in "Billy" addresses the title character and asks him to "hang on to your woman," such a request falls on deaf ears for these professionals. Institutions no longer govern the behavior of the protagonist, and the conscious doubling of the sheriff (Pat Garrett) and the outlaw (Billy) blurs these lines in Peckinpah's later film. What diminishes the institutional power of law and marriage most of all is what Jim Kitses (2004) labels "squalid capitalism" (223), a force that renders everything before it impotent: "For men of charismatic authority and individual style, a life with honor and meaning is no longer possible, neither within the community nor on the shrinking open range" (225). Unlike Wyatt Earp in the classical *Clementine*, there is no longer even the possibility of integration into the law-abiding community.

Dylan was far from the first to explore the mythology of William "Billy the Kid" Bonney in song. Among others were Dylan's early hero Woody Guthrie ([1940] 1999), who invokes a border crossing into Juárez, and foregrounds Billy's attraction to, and attention from, "the Mexican maidens" who "liked Billy so well." However, much like the Peckinpah film on which Dylan found himself collaborating, the emphasis of Guthrie's "Billy" falls on his relationship to the man who shot the outlaw dead: Sheriff Pat Garrett. In the released film, Dylan's "Billy" is broken up and dispersed among various points in the narrative; on the soundtrack, three versions of the song appear (with one in instrumental form). Lyrically, the song borrows from ballads that pre-date Guthrie's version, but many of the lines derive from Dylan's own imaginings and reflect the ways in which Dylan's westerns, especially during the 1972–1976 era, continually return to the threat of the devouring woman in league with other, larger institutional forces that challenge the hero's autonomy. Clearly, any outlaw will find himself under siege by a sheriff or a marshal, and Dylan's Billy likewise must contend with the "lawman on [his] trail." However, equally menacing in "Billy 1" is the "sweet señorita" from the "lonesome shadows" who tries to lead Billy "into her dark hallway." Four verses later, Dylan sings of "an old whore from San Pedro" who "makes advances" on Billy's spirit and soul. In this relatively early Dylan song western, the song's speaker urges Billy to reject the "whores" and, instead, "hang on to [his] woman," perhaps as one potential form of rootedness in face of so many other forces leading him away from the domestic.

In the end, however, Billy is unable to return to any manifestation of home. So much of the narrative in "Billy 1" refers to locations in New Mexico and the Texas border, and there is little if no border crossing into Mexico (even though Dylan was in Durango filming *Pat Garrett*). But the historical Billy is, one should keep in mind, a figure who was born in New York City, and then moved to the Midwest (Dylan's own biographical journey-in-reverse), which may explain why Dylan's Billy narrative laments that his title character is "so far away from home." Even though Billy may not literally cross the border into Mexico, various forces threaten to impose those "elaborate shifts in location, thought, and life experience" that bell hooks describes. However, since Billy resists those forces so strenuously, and moves about so freely, such pressures are exerted from a distance: for example, the guns aiming at Billy are "across the river," and the business-men who offer the bounty for Billy's capture or death are located at some remove in Taos—merely dispatching Pat Garrett to do their bidding.

Ultimately, of course, the outlaw Billy cannot escape Sherriff Pat Garrett and the businessmen's bounty on his head; in this way, Billy is no different from Dylan's other significant "western" protagonists who, as the 1970s progress, reject any and all social ties and resist domestic entanglements with an even greater intensity (at least until the more complex gender dynamics of *Desire*). One example of a new, extended narrative dimension in Dylan's art appears in "Lily, Rosemary, and the Jack of Hearts" (1975), a song that Clinton Heylin (2010) claims was "inspired by Dylan's experi-ence [...] making *Pat Garrett*" (18). Dylan had been exposed to the bal-lad tradition as a teenager, and during the summer of 1968, Dylan spoke of the need to reinvent the ballad form for a generation raised on film narratives:

> When they were singing years ago, it would be as entertainment... and a fellow could sit down and sing a song for a half hour, and everybody could listen, and you could form opinions. You'd be waiting to see how it ended, what happened to this person or that person. It would be like going to a movie. But now we have movies, so why does someone want to sit around for a half hour listening to a ballad? Unless the story was of such a nature that you couldn't find it in a movie. (qtd. in McGregor 1990, 276)

The cinematic turn in Dylan's art is, of course, part and parcel of Dylan's larger efforts in the mid-1970s to inform his songwriting with influences from a range of art forms—consider, for example, how the fluidity of perspective in "Tangled Up in Blue" (1975) was once described by Dylan as a product of "my painting period" and his studies with artist Norman Raeben (qtd. in Heylin 2010, 22).

In "Lily," Dylan employs quasi-cinematic elements in unfolding his highly ambiguous narrative. For example, at one point the male protagonist, the Jack of Hearts, is confronted by "Big Jim" when "a cold revolver clicked"—a moment akin to a close-up, but with no establishing shot to reveal if the gun has actually been fired and if anyone has been shot (perhaps the gun is merely cocked?). Over the course of 16 verses, Dylan weaves an elliptical account of a robbery targeting big business, one offering a challenge to the very forces of law and order charged with protecting the interests of "squalid capitalism." As the owner of the town's diamond mine, Big Jim clearly has the most to lose in the robbery and, here, the outlaw figure appears as the Jack of Hearts, a man Big Jim recalls from "maybe down in Mexico," and a man who serves as another potential love interest to both the "fair-skinned," princess-like Lily (who is also Jim's mistress) and Rosemary, who was "tired of playing the role of Big Jim's wife," and who is eventually executed for stabbing her unfaithful husband in the back with a penknife. (Again, whether or not Rosemary actually committed the crime remains unclear.)

The list of crimes accumulates quickly in "Lily," and yet the cynicism reaches such a peak that the only person brought to justice via the gallows is the long-suffering wife, Rosemary. Since her lover Big Jim has been stabbed, and the Jack of Hearts has presumably fled from the law, Lily can merely wash the dye from her hair and "think of the Jack of Hearts." Much like Billy, the Jack of Hearts must, in the words of Stephen Scobie (2003), remain "constantly in motion and hard to pin down" (167), at least until he meets his own inevitable demise. In contrast, Lily remains behind in an empty cabaret with no lover—her only agency being those thoughts of the Jack of Hearts. Incidentally, Lily is also "thinkin' 'bout her father, who she very rarely saw," which confirms the physical and emotional separation between masculine and feminine that is related to the western tropes that Dylan so regularly employs in this era.

The world inhabited by both "Billy" and "Lily" is one marked by betrayal—one in which autonomy and independence are elusive, and deception is the only means by which to prolong one's survival. In the case of the Jack of Hearts, freedom depends upon a sacrificing woman, Rosemary, who is fearless (on the gallows, "she didn't even blink") but who also necessarily stands alone in this segregated world. When Dylan sings that "the only person on the scene missin' was the Jack of Hearts," this might suggest a crowd in attendance at the hanging. However, Rosemary ultimately dies alone, as separated from the Jack as the bank robbers were, as the latter waited "in the darkness by the riverbed [...] without the Jack of Hearts." And although, unlike Billy, the Jack of Hearts is never actually gunned down at the close of the song's narrative, Lily's earlier question to him foreshadows that inevitability: "Has your luck run out? [...] Well I guess you must have known it would someday." In games of cards, after all, "the house always wins," and "the house" is simply another manifestation of that ever-encroaching and "squalid" capitalism. The Jack of Hearts does not escape; he simply disappears because Rosemary's courage and sacrifice permit his disappearance. If the classical western is, in the words of Wendy Chapman Peek (2003), typically "a celebration of men and success" (209), then Dylan's 1973–1975 westerns, like Peckinpah's professional plot westerns, reveal such celebrations to be a lie. The big leap, however, in terms of a more complex border crossing involving enhanced feminine agency and masculine/feminine partnership would arrive with Dylan's next album: *Desire* (1976).

New Desires

In connecting *Red River* to Howard Hawks films across various genres—namely, in depicting a male protagonist with a psychological block requiring a strong feminine presence to resolve the character's emotional stasis—John Parris Springer (2005) suggests that the western is a "genre overcrowded with stalwart male characters who are often willing to underestimate or ignore the role of women and 'feminine values' in the settling of the West" (124). Ignoring or underestimating the role of women may seem an inevitability in Dylan's westerns; and yet, by 1976, Dylan songs begin to acknowledge the cost of this enforced separation from the domestic sphere. In fact, a few of the songs from *Desire* promise a union or reconciliation, often within western-themed narratives, and often co-written with playwright Jacques Levy.[4] One of the album's outlaw songs is

---

[4] Note that all but two of the songs on *Desire* are co-writes with Jacques Levy. The exceptions are "Sara" and "One More Cup of Coffee (Valley Below)." Typically, Dylan scholars

"Romance in Durango," which borrows its setting from the same Mexican city where *Pat Garrett* was filmed just a few years earlier. However, unlike Billy or the Jack of Hearts, the first-person protagonist in "Durango" keeps his love interest, Magdalena (who shares a name with a Mexican town 50 miles from the U.S. border), by his side while he serenades her with his guitar. Despite the speaker's repeated claim that God is watching over the lovers (Dylan actually sings the Spanish *"Dio nos vigila"*), the outlaw speaker is hunted down as a suspected murderer. Yet even with his dying breath, Dylan's speaker asks Magdalena to sit by him, adding "take my gun" and "Aim well my little one," offering the woman far more agency than observed in earlier Dylan westerns.

Even though not every song released on *Desire* is a western-themed narrative, a number of songs portray outlaw figures from different eras and walks of life, as well as their often-troubled connection to domesticity. For example, in "Joey," the Brooklyn-born mobster thinks first of protecting his family by turning over a table in the shootout that ultimately takes his life, and he also refuses to carry a gun in later years because he is "around too many children [and] [...] they should never know of one." Additionally, in "One More Cup of Coffee (Valley Below)," a speaker castigates his jewel-eyed lover for her lack of loyalty; the woman has grown cold to the speaker, perhaps because her "outlaw daddy" was a "wanderer by trade" who taught her "how to throw the blade." As much as Dylan's protagonists desire a connection to women, children, and home, the demands of their "outlaw" professions obviously complicate any such connection; in particular, a desire to protect children against the threat of violence necessitates that the male figure maintains a physical distance from home. In "Sara," which is, admittedly, not an outlaw ballad, Dylan nevertheless laments enforced separation from children and pleads to Sara, "Don't ever leave me, don't ever go." Of course, "Sara" refers to Sara Dylan in most unambiguous terms, and Dylan's own mid-1970s marital crisis is a crucial context for this near-obsessive exploration of masculine/feminine unions via the western genre. *Planet Waves* (1974), *Blood on the Tracks* (1975), and *Desire* all contain songs that address conflict in relationships, with the middle of these three most often tagged as best reflecting Dylan's fracturing marriage. As Robert Shelton (2003) writes, *"Blood on the Tracks* bore

---

view Levy as having collaborated exclusively on lyrics, rather than music, so my close readings of these Dylan-Levy efforts acknowledge the partnership, even though I occasionally use shorthand such as "Dylan's speaker," merely for the sake of concision.

out *Planet Waves*'s forecast in 'Dirge' and 'Wedding Song.' The artist was in torment. [...] *Blood* is about impermanence and fragmentation of remembrance and relationships" (440).[5] It is important to note that, while all three albums emphasize the impermanent and fractured, key *Desire* songs at least imagine harmony in the domestic sphere.

"Isis" concerns just such a severed relationship and opens with the line, "I married Isis on the fifth day of May / But I could not hold on to her very long." Since Dylan married Sara in November of 1965, the song is not straight autobiography, but the *Cinco de Mayo* setting suggests a tension between independence and strength via unity that links it to Dylan's disintegrating marriage. *Cinco de Mayo* is frequently mistaken by Americans, especially non-Latina/o Americans, as a celebration of Mexican independence; in fact, beginning in the immediate pre-Civil War years, this is precisely how Latinos in the U.S. conceived of the holiday, as "an expression of [...] support for freedom and democracy throughout the Americas" (Hayes-Bautista 2012, 190).[6] For contemporary Mexicans, however, the holiday actually celebrates the unification of Mexican armies against French invaders at the first battle of Puebla, and the juxtaposition of autonomy and strength in community is central to the "Isis" narrative. As such, "Isis" is a composition that allows for several threads of this essay to be pulled together via another Dylan western and its exploration of the fraught collision between the outlaw and domesticity.

Reportedly the first Levy/Dylan song collaboration (Barker 2004a, 175), "Isis" was introduced by Dylan during the 1975 Rolling Thunder tour in this way: "This is a song about marriage."[7] Even though the song references the title character, who is both the speaker's marriage partner and named after an Egyptian goddess, Isis fails to play a prominent role in the main narrative, aside from thoughts of her prediction in verse six that "things would be different the next time we wed." So what does the narrative recount? Dylan's speaker rides "straight away" from Isis, arriving at a "high place of darkness and light," where he is approached by another outlaw-type who promises "somethin' easy to catch." The business proposition, such as it is, involves the raiding of a tomb for the treasures buried

---

[5] Shelton considers the three albums in question—*Planet Waves, Blood on the Tracks* and *Desire*—to be so closely linked thematically that he speaks of them as a "trilogy" (2003, 462).

[6] For more on the history of Cinco de Mayo, see Hayes-Bautista (2012).

[7] One live version of "Isis" with this intro was recorded on 4 December 1975 in Montreal, Quebec, and later released on the 1985 compilation *Biograph*.

within. Given the song's title, as well as the location of this "body" in the pyramids, one might surmise that we are far removed from the American west. However, according to Levy, the Egyptian iconography was mere cover: "[the pyramids] were a substitute for the hills of Wyoming" (qtd. in Barker 2004a, 179). Predictably, the robbery is a failure ("There was no jewels, no nothin'") and the speaker's outlaw friend dies mysteriously during the raid. Anxious to escape the failure and the "outrageous" snow (yet another clue that the setting is not North Africa), Dylan's speaker rides "back to find Isis to tell her [he] love[s] her."

When Jane Tompkins (1992) writes that the western "is about men's fear of losing their mastery, and hence their identity" (45) by distancing themselves from the feminization of church and home—the two places Tompkins writes that women are welcome—such a description largely fits the Dylan western in the pre-*Desire* era.[8] However, many of Dylan's outlaw protagonists in 1975 ("Isis" was recorded in July of that year) have far more ambivalence about home. In fact, the narrative of "Isis" concludes with a reunion of the speaker and title character—or at least the promise of one: "She said, 'You gonna stay?' I said, 'Yeah, I jes might.'" In the final verse that follows, Dylan returns to thoughts of *Cinco de Mayo*, and as clear a statement as possible about the push and pull of the outlaw's love for his partner: "What drives me to you is what drives me insane." Dylan's speaker experiences insanity at Isis's side, but recall, too, that the earlier tomb-raiding scheme was also described in similar terms: "When I took up his offer I must-a been mad." The larger context for the dual forms of madness explored in "Isis"—both at the side of a romantic partner and in the world of masculinized outlaw adventures—is, of course, mirrored in Dylan's attempts to balance life as a touring musician and family man, especially after his return to touring in 1974 and 1975. Such an ambivalence has been explored in countless westerns, among them Nicholas Ray's *The Lusty Men* (1952), in which the protagonist, Wes Merritt (Arthur Kennedy), navigates the friction when his attachment to the rodeo leads him to break a promise to his wife Louise (Susan Hayward) to remain on the physically punishing rodeo circuit only as long as it takes for him to earn the money needed to purchase a home. In this way, Wes resembles the Dylan who had forsaken the road in 1966 in order to raise a family in upstate New York, and then later in Manhattan. By 1975, however, in the

---

[8] Tompkins, Jane. *West of Everything: The Inner Life of Westerns.* Oxford: Oxford UP, 1992.

words of Dylan's "Rolling Thunder" tour bandmate Rob Stoner, Dylan was driven mad by career and home life: "The marriage was falling apart, and this thing which had seemed so exciting and promising—Rolling Thunder—that wasn't [working], and he couldn't figure out why" (qtd. in Heylin 2001, 437).

Back in 1973, when Dylan had returned from scoring and shooting *Pat Garrett* and considering a move to the west coast—Malibu, specifically—the songs that Dylan wrote after a nearly three-year creative drought reflect the domestic ambivalence that characterizes all of the Dylan westerns. On the one hand, there are songs from the album *Planet Waves*—such as "Forever Young," inspired by his son Jesse (Heylin 2009, 427), or "Wedding Song," inspired by an even more obvious source ("You gave me babies one, two, three, what is more, you saved my life"). Less rooted in domesticity, however, are other songs from this same album—such as "Tough Mama" that speak of escape and aggressive masculinity in not so subtle tones, including brandishing the "badge of the lonesome road" and a speaker who plans to "go down to the river and get some stones."[9] Another example of the desire to assert masculine independence appears in "Going, Going, Gone," in which the speaker releases no small measure of frustration: "I been playin' it straight / Now, I've just got to cut loose / Before it gets late." What is clearly at work in all of the pre-*Desire* westerns, whether framed as western narratives or not, is a distinction delineated by Martin Pumphrey (1988): the western "makes an absolute and value-laden division between the masculine and feminine spheres. While it links masculinity with activity, mobility, adventure, emotional restraint and public power, it associates femininity with passivity, softness, romance and domestic containment" (181). In this way, the feminine becomes not only honored but also a kind of honorable threat. And thus, the tension for the western hero: both drawn toward, and yet resistant to, the domestic.

CONCLUSION

A month before I completed the initial draft of the present chapter, I stumbled upon a familiar type of article; the title alone suggests a dilemma shared by many Dylanologists: "Just Like a Woman: I'm a Feminist and I Love Bob Dylan—Even Though I Know I Shouldn't" (March 2016).

---

[9] According to the *Oxford English Dictionary*, "stones" have been synonymous with testicles since the twelfth century.

Along similar lines, the aforementioned Barbara O'Dair (2009) concludes in "Bob Dylan and Gender Politics" that Dylan is a member of a distinct generational sub-group: "pre-feminist men who are just as confused by their own roles in the free world as they are by the women who surround them" (84), while also suggesting that much of the purported misogyny in his work is merely a pose or "acting" (84). For the past decade or so, any number of scholars have wrestled with the gender ideology in Dylan's work, and many have concluded that, in addition to occasional misogyny ("Just Like a Woman" [1966] is frequently cast in this way), many songs by Dylan are more nuanced in their exploration of gender and power than some would expect from this "pre-feminist" artist. With this Dylan/gender discourse in mind, I want to conclude with some reflections on the evolution of the Dylan western and the ways in which the outlaw figure at least considers closer ties to the domestic.

I will begin with the enhanced alignment with domesticity on display in *Desire*; songs such as "Isis" and "Romance in Durango," which may reflect the (slightly) more progressive gender views that Pamela Thurschwell (2003) notes when comparing two mid-1970s songs from the same sessions as "Lily, Rosemary and the Jack of Hearts." On the one hand, the woman referred to in "Shelter from the Storm" (1975) offers the remedy for "a man's longing for completion in the feminine ideal even if that ideal is always retrospective, always already lost" (Thurschwell 2003, 270). Anyone familiar with "Wedding Song" (cited earlier) will recognize the ways in which the feminine offers refuge to the speaker in "Shelter" who is "blown out on the trail" (a phrase that might call the cattle trail to mind, incidentally). To Thurschwell's point, "what's already lost" is the inseparable divide between the protagonist/wanderer who is *offered* shelter—emphasis on the past tense—marked by a wall in the present: "there's a wall between us, somethin' there's been lost." The feminine presence is certainly idealized, a goddess figure who "took [his] crown of thorns"; and, perhaps because of her divinity, the wall between them appears to be unassailable. All of this makes the imagined reconciliation in "Isis" all the more noteworthy: in another song addressed to a goddess figure—this time to a woman explicitly linked, by name, to a goddess associated with marriage, magic, and rebirth—the song concludes with a possible reconciliation and a gender division that may be crumbling.

Thurschwell (2003) contrasts the untouchable, feminine ideal in "Shelter" with "Up to Me," a song presumably written to close *Blood on the Tracks*, although not issued until the release of *Biograph* in 1985.

Thematically, however, the songs could not be more different. Whereas "Shelter" calls for the woman to nurture and protect the protagonist, self-reliance is the prescription for romantic disappointment in "Up to Me": "I guess it must be up to me." In fact, while the male was "blown out" in "Shelter," the woman in the later song is "burned out," and the speaker suspects he is the cause. To signal a much different gender dynamic, an image of the outlaw is invoked, but it is not the male speaker with whom the outlaw is identified: "Oh, the only decent thing I did when I worked as a postal clerk / Was to haul your picture down off the wall near the cage where I used to work." Here, the speaker is "caged" like so many other of Dylan's frustrated male speakers, but it is uncertain if he was in this state because of his connection to his love interest, or by virtue of separation from her. In addition, listeners witness Dylan being playful with a familiar trope of the "Wanted!" poster and creating a fluidity with the borders dividing the masculine and feminine. And yet "Up to Me" never concluded *Blood on the Tracks*; instead, Dylan dropped the song as album closer in favor of "Buckets of Rain," possibly to shift from a tone of self-reproach to one of "hope and endurance" (Gill & Odegard 2004, 90). Instead of the bold inversion of the outlaw trope in "Up to Me," "Buckets" offers a run-of-the-mill, cool male speaker: "If you want me, honey baby / I'll be here."

By the time *Desire* was released, roughly a year after *Blood on the Tracks*, Dylan was clearly inhabiting a creative space in which proximity to the domestic possessed a greater resonance for him. Make no mistake: the Dylan westerns of *Desire* are not the revisionist, gender-bending westerns of the Bill Clinton era—films such as *The Ballad of Little Jo* (1993), *Bad Girls* (1994), and *The Quick and the Dead* (1995)—but these often-elusive narratives do point the way to some of the more surprising and playful ruminations on gender to come in the latter decades of Dylan's career. Such works include "Highlands" (1997), in which a waitress assumes that the speaker never reads women authors, putting him on the defensive after he had been admiring her legs. In the Dylan western, one would never argue for the forms of "uncertain masculinity" (to borrow Jim Kitses's term) on display in many post-classical westerns—films covering the spectrum from *Johnny Guitar* (1954) to *Pale Rider* (1985), the latter being one of the films in which Kitses applies the "uncertain" tag. Nevertheless, the ways in which Dylan's use of western tropes is developed and extended between 1967 and 1976, with an accelerated intensity in the post-*Pat Garrett* era, suggest much about Dylan's domestic uncertainty. But those increasingly complex song westerns also suggest that a "Polyvocal Dylan" is a product of the manner in which cinematic discourses collide with gender discourses at a particular moment of ideological crisis for the western and western hero. In the end, Dylan's western heroes never resolve their own state of crisis, as they seem perpetually ambivalent, even in their very occasional appearances post-1976. In "Senor (Tales of Yankee Power)" (1978), Dylan seemingly expresses the desire for autonomy and rootedness that will be familiar to anyone who has read this far: "Señor, señor, do you know where she is hidin'? / How long are we gonna be ridin'?" Of course, the ride of the Dylan outlaw (or ideal and autonomous male) rarely ends before his inevitable, violent death.

References

Barabas, SuzAnne, and Gabor Barabas. 1990. *Gunsmoke: A Complete History and Analysis of the Legendary Broadcast Series*. Jefferson, NC: McFarland.

Barker, Derek. 2004a. Apathy for the Devil, Jacques Levy, Desire, Joseph Conrad, and 'Black Diamond Bay'. In *Isis: A Bob Dylan Anthology*, ed. Derek Barker, 174–186. London: Helter Skelter.

———. 2004b. My Name it is Nothing. In *Isis: A Bob Dylan Anthology*, ed. Derek Barker, 45–52. London: Helter Skelter.

Dylan, Bob. 2004a. *Chronicles Volume One*. New York: Simon & Schuster.

———. 2004b. Interview by Ed Bradley. *60 Minutes*, CBS, December 5, 2004.

———. 2004c (1962). My Life in a Stolen Moment. In *Studio A: The Bob Dylan Reader*, ed. Benjamin Hedin, 3–7. New York: Norton.

Ford, John, dir. 1946. *My Darling Clementine*. 20th Century Fox.

Gill, Andy, and Kevin Odegard. 2004. *A Simple Twist of Fate: Bob Dylan and the Making of 'Blood on the Tracks*. Cambridge, MA: Da Capo.

Gray, Michael. 2008. *The Bob Dylan Encyclopedia*. New York: Continuum.

Guthrie, Woody. 1999 (1940). *Asch Recordings Volume 4*. Smithsonian Folkways.

Hayes-Bautista, David. 2012. *El Cinco de Mayo: An American Tradition*. Berkeley: University of California Press.

Heylin, Clinton. 2001. *Behind the Shades Revisited*. New York: HarperCollins.

———. 2009. *Revolution in the Air: The Songs of Bob Dylan, 1957–1973*. Chicago: Chicago Review Press.

———. 2010. *Still on the Road: The Songs of Bob Dylan 1974–2006*. Chicago: Chicago Review Press.

hooks, bell. 1994. *Outlaw Culture: Resisting Representations*. New York: Routledge.

Kitses, Jim. 2004. *Horizons West: Directing the Western from John Ford to Clint Eastwood*. New ed. London: British Film Institute.

Lee, C.P. 2004. *Like the Night (Revisited)*. London: Helter Skelter.

March, Anna. 2016. Just Like a Woman: I'm a Feminist and I Love Bob Dylan— Even Though I Know I Shouldn't. *Salon*, May 16, 2016.

Marqusee, Mike. 2003. *Chimes of Freedom: The Politics of Bob Dylan's Art*. New York: The New Press.

McGregor, Craig, ed. 1990. *Bob Dylan, The Early Years: A Retrospective*. New York: Da Capo.

O'Dair, Barbara. 2009. Bob Dylan and Gender Politics. In *The Cambridge Companion to Bob Dylan*, ed. Kevin J.H. Dettmar, 80–86. New York: Cambridge University Press.

Peckinpah, Sam, dir. 1973. *Pat Garrett and Billy the Kid*. MGM.

Peek, Wendy Chapman. 2003. Rethinking Masculinity in the Western. *Journal of Popular Film and Television* 30: 206–219.

Pumphrey, Martin. 1988. Masculinity. In *BFI Companion to the Western*, ed. Edward Buscombe, 181–183. London: British Film Institute.

Saunders, John. 2001. *The Western Genre: From Lordsburg to Big Whiskey*. London: Wallflower.

Scaduto, Anthony. 1973. *Dylan: An Intimate Biography*. New York: Signet.

Scobie, Stephen. 2003. *Alias Bob Dylan Revisited*. Calgary: Red Deer Press.

Shelton, Robert. 2003. *No Direction Home: The Life and Music of Bob Dylan*. 2nd ed. New York: Da Capo.

Springer, John Parris. 2005. Beyond the River: Women and the Role of the Feminine in Howard Hawks' *Red River*. In *Hollywood's West: The American Frontier in Film, Television, and History*, ed. Peter C. Rollins and John E. O'Connor, 115–125. Lexington: University Press of Kentucky.

Thurschwell, Pamela. 2003. A Different Baby Blue.'. In *"Do You, Mr. Jones?": Bob Dylan With the Poets and Professors*, ed. Neil Corcoran, 253–273. London: Pimlico.

Tompkins, Jane. 1992. *West of Everything: The Inner Life of Westerns*. Oxford: Oxford University Press.

Wilentz, Sean. 2010. *Bob Dylan in America*. New York: Doubleday.

CHAPTER 8

"I Don't Do Sketches from Memory": Bob Dylan and Autobiography

Emily O. Wittman and Paul R. Wright

Dylan's circuitous path to writing his Nobel Lecture is certainly worthy of some sort of explanation. Nine days into Dylan's two-week failure to acknowledge his Nobel win, prominent committee member Per Wastberg stated that "One can say that it is impolite and arrogant," although he also admitted "he is who he is" (qtd. in *Esquire.com* 2016). Dylan blithely continued on the Never Ending Tour that he began in 1988, even passing through Stockholm for a couple of gigs. And yet the speech—long time in coming and delivered only a couple of days before the deadline—reveals a memorable, if arguably, derivative, engagement with literature, a youthful engagement which, he argues, forcefully impacted him and influenced the course of his songwriting career and his life writ large. This was a rare moment for Dylan; the recorded speech—widely distributed across social media—is unabashedly frank, emotive, and grateful. And yet at the very moment at which he introduces us to his vivid recollections of *Moby Dick*, *All Quiet on the Western Front*, and *The Odyssey*, he foils our expectations.

E. O. Wittman (✉)
The University of Alabama, Tuscaloosa, AL, USA

P. R. Wright
Cabrini University, Radnor, PA, USA

© The Author(s) 2019
N. Otiono, J. Toth (eds.), *Polyvocal Bob Dylan*,
Palgrave Studies in Music and Literature,
https://doi.org/10.1007/978-3-030-17042-4_8

When did he read these books? Under what circumstances? Dylan opens up only to withdraw at the very moment when we dare to let ourselves hope, after all of this time, for a window into the personal, the autobiographical, and the chronological. Must we now give up? Or should we rather rethink our need for a linear narrative about Dylan's past and revelations of soul-searching and private moments and, in turn, learn to reconcile ourselves to what we *do* have: an approach to writing about the self that is explosive rather than revealing, fragmented rather than cohesive? One thing is clear; when we theorize Dylan's relationship to autobiography—whether in his songs, in his interviews, or in his ludically indirect memoir, *Chronicles*—we must turn away from traditional categories such as the autobiographical category of confession adumbrated by Augustine. By exploring Dylan's affinities with alternative forms of life-writing, we can—perhaps counterintuitively—discover highly autobiographical work in both his songs and his memoir. To do so, we must change our focus. Before turning explicitly to *Chronicles* and Dylan's place within the history of Western autobiography, a few symptomatic readings of his oeuvre will be useful to set the stage.

"I don't do sketches from memory," Dylan sings in "Highlands" (1997), opening the way for a reading of a defiant interiority unmoored from temporality. This emblematizes Dylan's seemingly perverse refusal to play it straight when it comes to narratives about himself that could be considered autobiographical work in any manner. And yet he so clearly references writing and the attempt to get a story down on the page. "Highlands" embodies the increasingly elusive later Dylan, situated between the mysterious songs of his youth and his 2004 memoir *Chronicles* (subtitled *Volume One* although no further volumes have appeared or are projected to appear), which again may be Dylan at his most coy, telling an elliptical story about himself with the promise of future elaboration, an elaboration that has yet to come, here or anywhere else.

In "Highlands," Dylan makes specific reference to the impossibility and absurdity of writing, channeling lyrics that could just as easily apply to literary narrative as to songwriting *per se*. Sharing that he "woke up this mornin' and … looked at the same old page / Same old rat race, life in the same old cage," Dylan evokes primarily frustrating questions about authenticity in asserting his incapacity to "know the difference between a real blonde and a fake." This alludes both to the relative authenticity of subjectivity and to ever-compromised possibilities of being genuinely creative. In the narrative centerpiece of this willfully workaday epic—a song which clocks in at 16 minutes and 31 seconds (Dylan's single longest studio piece)—Dylan envisions an encounter between himself and a waitress in a Boston diner. The exchange over the food order establishes a paradigm of confrontation that will define much of the song:

> I said "Tell me what I want"
> She say "You probably want hard boiled eggs"
> I said "That's right, bring me some"
> She says "We ain't got any, you picked the wrong time to come"

Bantering with Dylan in a scene vaguely reminiscent of the diner confrontation in Bob Rafelson's *Five Easy Pieces* (1970),[1] the waitress then recognizes him as a visual "artist" and proceeds to challenge him to "draw a picture" of her. In songwriting terms, this would be the equivalent of asking the musician to compose a song about her on the spot—a more predictable narrative maneuver for Dylan. The positioning of Dylan as a visual artist is significant for its autobiographical dimensions that we will explore further below.

Just as the waitress revels in disappointing the narrator's food order, he in turn demurs at her request to be drawn, offering a series of excuses that include his insistence that "I don't do sketches from memory." Challenging him to see her as anything but a distant memory given she is standing right before him, the waitress has an answer for each increasingly absurd excuse (e.g., "I know but I don't have my drawin' book"; "Yes I could but I don't know where my pencil is at"). At last, she provides the narrator with both a napkin and a pencil "out from behind her ear." Upon the narrator producing the demanded sketch, the waitress (now figured as critic and not merely subject) contentiously insists, "That don't look a thing like me." Escalating the confused argument over verisimilitude, the waitress then shifts the aesthetic ground to literature, suggesting to Dylan, who is not quite sure he is hearing correctly, "You don't read women authors, do ya? ... Ya just don't seem like you do." Offended and indignant, he insists that she is "way wrong." The episode ends as she challenges him to name even one female author. His only answer is "Erica Jong."

---

[1] This iconic scene is now the most memorable moment from Rafelson's portrait of Bobby Dupea (Jack Nicholson), a disaffected piano prodigy who has rejected his life of privilege for the rootless life of an oil-rig worker, only to be called home to see his dying father. Confronting a rules-driven diner waitress insistent on "no substitutions" in customer orders, Dupea engages in an escalating confrontation over the bureaucratized menu of the establishment, leading to his violent sweeping of glasses and silverware from the table.

With the refrain ("My heart's in the highlands") and song title echoing Robert Burns's 1789 poem, "Highlands" uses this extended narrative interlude as an opportunity to interpolate a host of issues that have both haunted and animated Dylan's career. The tension between the visual and the verbal arts, the relationship between literature and songwriting, and even longstanding critiques of Dylan as misogynist circulate here in the dizzying repartee between him and the waitress, who may or may not recognize Dylan. Cycling between artful play and genuine contentiousness, Dylan ultimately refuses to "settle" or even solidify the grounds of the debate between himself and the potentially fictional waitress, instead offering only the punchline that his engagement with women is limited to Jong's pop-chronicles of the sexual revolution and second-wave feminism. Forced to do "sketches from memory," an exasperated Dylan expresses his resentment at being forced to make any declarations of skill, intent, or ideology. Being asked to "compose" on the spot evokes Dylan himself being invariably asked to raid his own songbook for reliable "classics," as opposed to his continual penchant for solitary self-reinvention at his own pace and in his own evolving idiom.

In the exchange on Jong and "women authors," Dylan also attempts both to acknowledge and to downplay his construction of a decidedly masculine folk persona that is paradoxically both authoritative and self-deprecating. Adding a special frisson to this moment may well be the echoes here of one of the sources of trouble in Dylan's failed marriage to Sara Dylan (born Shirley Noznisky): Dylan's insistence in 1974 on commuting from Malibu to New York City to train as a visual artist with guru-painter Norman Raeben. Aside from Sara's concerns about the distance and possible infidelities, there was also, according to Dylan at least, a fundamental disconnect between them on the meaning and significance of his aesthetic paradigm shift.

As recounted in Howard Sounes's (2001) controversial biography, *Down the Highway: The Life of Bob Dylan*, connecting with Raeben jump-started Dylan's "ways of seeing," to borrow from John Berger's ([1972] 2008) classic formulation. In an almost Buddhist tableau of masterly object lessons, Dylan recounts being shown a vase by Raeben which was then abruptly snatched out of sight by the painter, who exhorted him to immediately paint it from memory. Realizing that "he had looked at the vase but not really seen it" afforded Dylan "an important lesson in art and also a perspective that he might apply to life in general" (Sounes 2001,

328). Dylan—mesmerized by the challenge of shifting aesthetic gears and media—began sleeping in Raeben's studio like a dutiful apprentice or acolyte, describing the artist as "more powerful than any magician." Part of Dylan's fixation on the "magician" Raeben included the fact that, initially, Raeben had no clue who Dylan was. As friend Jacques Levy offered, "Bob really likes the idea that people don't really know who he is, or don't respond to him in that starry-eyed, awestruck way" (qtd. Sounes 2001, 328). In addition to suggesting Dylan appreciated Raeben's refusal to be star-struck, this may well also allude to Dylan's fundamental instinct to be and to remain unknown in an existential sense.

To the consternation of Sara, Dylan had seemingly been seduced by a new art as much as by any earthly lover. Dylan offers that "my wife never did understand me ever since that day" and "that's when our marriage started breaking up. She never knew what I was talking about, what I was thinking about. And I couldn't possibly explain it" (qtd. in Sounes 2001, 328). The aesthetic dilemma and siren call of meeting Raeben's challenge with the vase—what Dylan would in "Highlands" later call "sketches from memory"—was seemingly one of many marriage deal-breakers with Sara, thereby forming a direct through-line from this 1974 period of experimentation in painting to Dylan's late 1990s meditations on the relations between art and authenticity, male-female dynamics, and the mutually implicating roles of the visual and verbal arts. Perhaps the greatest difference between the period of "infatuated" (Sounes 2001, 328) apprenticeship to Raeben and the spirit of "Highlands" two decades later is just how resolutely resistant to performing on command Dylan has become. "Highlands" presents a narrator—who is in this instance songwriter, singer, storyteller, and visual artist all at once—playfully exasperated at being asked to craft and share his art outside the confines of a sanctioned artistic venue (or rather, *inside* what he deems the safe zone of daily life and the laidback "diner culture" evoked in the song). It is almost as if Dylan is here repudiating the cult of automatism that had helped to shape modernist approaches to both painting and literature, and in turn repudiating a younger incarnation of himself that had been so taken with all of that. What remains consistent, it would seem, is the calculated evasion of anything like self-revelation except through an indirection that is both its own medium and message.

POLITICS AND THE POETIC SELF

In considering the expansive sweep of Dylan's songwriting in the years leading up to "Highlands" and the *Chronicles* autobiography we discuss at length below, we turn now to trace some key early efforts that demonstrate Dylan's preoccupation with self-revelation as a pitfall of vulnerability—a trap both sought after and shunned. Perhaps the least apparent choice of an early Dylan work that touches on self-revelation would be the iconic protest song, "The Lonesome Death of Hattie Carroll" (1964). No Dylan protest song in the 1960s folk vein would seem further removed from engagement with the self than this one, rooted as it so hauntingly is in the February 1963 murder/manslaughter of African-American mother and "maid of the kitchen" Hattie Carroll at the hands of the drunken William Zantzinger, scion of a wealthy Maryland family. Along with "The Death of Emmett Till" (1962), "Only a Pawn in Their Game" (1963), and "Hurricane" (1975), "Hattie Carroll" ranks among Dylan's signal achievements in responding to the civil rights movement and racist abuses of African-Americans. Covering both the act of violence that cost Hattie her life and the trial that ended in a shocking six-month sentence for William (in part, it was said, to keep him out of a largely black prison population at institutions established for longer sentences), the song has remained a touchstone into the present day. It has of course garnered as much attention for the minor errors in Dylan's account (e.g., the seemingly intentional misspelling of Zantzinger's name as "Zanzinger"; the assertion that he was charged with first-degree murder when in fact it was second-degree and later reduced to manslaughter)—none of which in any way diminish the power and essential truth of Dylan's song, or of the horrors visited on Hattie.

Literature scholar Christopher Ricks (2003), for decades a well-regarded explicator of everything from John Milton to the Romantic and Victorian poets, famously took on the task of making the case for Dylan as a major literary artist in his book *Dylan's Visions of Sin*. A master-study in prosody and versification, Ricks's book may well have gone a long way toward influencing the eventual selection of Dylan for the Nobel Prize in 2016. In a study that frames its poetic analysis with a consideration of classical virtues and vices as organizing principles to understand Dylan's verse, Ricks highlights "The Lonesome Death of Hattie Carroll" in an extended case-study of Dylan's conception of justice. Ricks points out that the song "is a supreme understanding of the difference between writing a political song and writing a song politically" (233). Favoring the latter approach as Dylan's essential achievement (and likening it to T. S. Eliot's distinction between religious poems and "writing poems religiously"), Ricks finds in Dylan's effort a fundamental and calculated restraint that is at turns unexpected, unsettling, and an incitement to a moral embrace of grieving as a political act. Finding the animating genius of the song in Dylan's control of tone and cadence, Ricks finds that "the double challenge to the song lay in its duty not to yield to the anger that had seized Zanzinger, and in its duty to resist melodrama and sentimentality" (222). For Ricks, a genuine hallmark of the song in terms of meeting the degree of difficulty set for it—in addition to exposing and condemning the criminal mistreatment of Hattie Carroll herself—is Dylan's "exquisite self-control" and "refusal to commit the sin that is Zanzinger's anger—however much such righteous anger might have claimed to be all in the good cause of giving a bad man some of his own medicine" (227).

While Ricks (2003) does not put it in quite these terms, it would seem that he views Dylan as orchestrating an almost classically Greek management of the passions in the narrative economy of catharsis—except that this catharsis is framed as refuting a merely purgative function in favor of stimulating both grief and outrage that are hoped to inspire change. Where we would like to press and challenge Ricks's analysis is the extent to which it succumbs to this carefully crafted image of Dylan the poet who is the measured exemplar of bardic self-restraint. In fact, there are important ways in which the refrain of "Hattie Carroll" operates to foreground and then deconstruct precisely that posture of controlled response to the unspeakable and unbearable waste of Hattie's life. Consider here the refrain of "Hattie Carroll." In the first three stanzas, we get the following: "But you who philosophize disgrace and criticize all fears / Take the rag away from your face / Now ain't the time for your tears." In the last stanza, however, the final two lines are recalibrated: "Oh, but you who philosophize disgrace and criticize all fears / Bury the rag deep in your face / For now's the time for your tears." The question of Dylan's own interiority and stance as commentating bard hinges on the shifting referents implied by "you who philosophize disgrace and criticize all fears." The Ricksian reading of "Hattie Carroll" presumes that Dylan the supremely controlled poet is addressing us and calling on us to restrain our grief until we have taken the time to hear the entire sordid and heartbreaking tale. The songwriter is similarly restraining his own grief in order to get through composing and performing the song, thereby modeling a

modus vivendi for horrific times. In the opposition between the early stanzas' insistence that we "take the rag away from [our] face" and the last's
that we "bury the rag deep" and allow the tears their due, it would seem
that both the listener and poet are exhorted to internalize their pain until
such time as it can be overwhelmed by an informed and righteous grief
(and perhaps a righteous anger to follow).

This reading works well as far as it goes, but what it presumes is that
Dylan is engaged in a rather uncomplicated self-presentation as the bardic
grief-counselor we did not know we needed. If that were merely the case,
the song would lose so much of its lasting power and relevance. What is
lost in this univocal reading is the possibility that "you who philosophize
disgrace and criticize all fears" refers to the hypocrites in the making that
we *all* threaten to become in the face of miseries like Hattie Carroll's. The
"philosophers of disgrace" certainly include all those who rationalize and
try ludicrously to adjudicate the horrors of what happened to Hattie—
attempting to put a number to the loss endured by her ten children. Here
are included quite obviously the judges "in the courtroom of honor," who
pound "their gavel / To show that all's equal and that the courts are on
the level," perpetuating the lie that enabled Hattie's mistreatment in the
first place. The "critics of fears" suggest not only those who are heartbro-
ken by Hattie's fate and dissuaded from action against it by fear of the
consequences, but also those very racists who would suppress civil rights
activism and outrage in the name of white supremacy masquerading as
social order.

And yet Dylan's refrain—to the extent that it preaches to a choir of the
fellow outraged—never once lets off the hook those listeners of goodwill
to whom the poet sells his song. If the audience for "Hattie Carroll"
includes a self-selecting, liberal-minded white elite—Dylan's equivalent of
the Miltonic "fit audience … tho'few" (Milton [1667] 2003, VII. 31)—
we are reminded that they too are capable of sophistry as a way of evading
the fully social dimensions of their own grief and the call to transformative
action such grief entails. And if the philosophers of disgrace and critics of
fear are meant to include all social agents posing as helpless, crying witnesses to injustice (or in the case of judges, measured mediators), it is
impossible not to think that Dylan potentially numbers himself among
them, or at least recognizes in the first instance the inherent moral dangers
of a poetic intervention in a pernicious evil. In the cause of forcibly bringing evil to our attention, the song runs the risk of exploiting and trivial-
izing—particularly when it deals with a specific and fully humanized being

enduring that evil. It is the primal tension between Hattie Carroll and "Hattie Carroll" of which Dylan is all too aware. If that challenge is met honorably in "Hattie Carroll," it is not because Dylan is the restrained poet in control of his own grief and anger, as Ricks (2003) argues; instead, it is because Dylan understands his own compromised position in the rhetoric of outrage and self-presentation. In this way, "Hattie Carroll" is a deeply self-revelatory song, but only insofar as it posits position-taking as a quagmire of intellect, emotion, vulnerability, and the politicization of real suffering.

Following on the heels of the album that included "Hattie Carroll," came *Another Side of Bob Dylan* (1964), a collection often seen as Dylan's riposte to both the folk protest movement at large and to his own participation in shaping its musical genre. While this discontinuity is often overstated by divided critics and assorted other partisans of Dylan's ever-multiplying "eras," a song like the oft-covered "My Back Pages" certainly affords ample evidence of disenchantment and a new direction. The frustration Dylan conveys in this album is not merely about political certainties and the kind of songwriting they engender—perhaps more importantly, this turn reflects Dylan's disillusionment with being viewed as the "poster boy" for any kind of ideological art. If any Dylan song can be deemed overtly "autobiographical," then "My Back Pages" certainly seems to fit the bill. And yet as we saw with "Hattie Carroll" (a song that has been remembered for us as purely political and yet has very important dimensions of self-exploration hinted at in our discussion above), "My Back Pages" proves to be a similar kind of poetic paradox. In this instance, we have a song remembered for us as defiantly personal and resolutely apolitical, something in the vein of Whitman's famed parenthetical line in "Song of Myself": "(I am large. I contain multitudes.)" ([1855] 1961, sec. 51).

And yet, this snarling manifesto of a song includes among its tropes some clear instances of a self-continuing to be shaped by contemporary politics, but through an entirely new prism of morally opportunistic cooptation. What supports the usual contention that "My Back Pages" is a repudiation of politics is how it directly echoes and even parodizes the melodies and harmonies of "Hattie Carroll" in what seems a very self-conscious effort to footnote and undermine Dylan's own genre allegiances. In the conventional narrative of Dylan rejecting his recent past as the voice of a movement, these lines of the refrain are most often singled out: "Ah, but I was so much older then / I'm younger than that now." The jab here at the pretensions (and pretended political maturity) of the folk movement lands hard, and it turns on Dylan embracing a reverse aging into the naivete of youth in an era of increasingly polarizing political commitments. In a sense both anticipating and warping free speech activist Jack Weinberg's 1965 dictum that "we have a saying in the movement that we don't trust anybody over 30" (qtd. in Benet 1964, 6), Dylan's refrain distrusts the usurped authority of elders too—but in this instance, being "older" is a state of mind and an endemic intolerance for ambiguity. By reveling in the possibilities of aging backward out of intransigence, Dylan certainly seems in the refrain to be planting a solitary flag far removed from the cultural battlefields of his moment.

Still, just as it is a mistake to view "Hattie Carroll" as a purely political song, it is equally misguided to see no political sensibility or commitment at all in the individualist dissatisfaction of "My Back Pages." Above all, we find that the real targets of Dylan's ire in this song are the seductions of the songwriting, poetic self as a social construct, and we must be careful to see that this too is a political claim of which Dylan is fully aware. "My Back Pages" is less a rejection of the political than a recontextualization of it. To be sure, the song critiques facile movements and ideological gestures for which Dylan had been made a symbol, but he is crystal clear about his own complicity in that process. The sarcasm of the tune is equal opportunity and self-directed, and it is very squarely trained on the lure of easy answers that emerge *from the self* and are not simply imposed or peddled by others. There is no better example here than Dylan acknowledging how he "Pounced with fire on flaming roads / Using ideas as my maps." When ideas are road mapped, they are not merely concretized; they are instrumentalized and fetishized—denuded of vitality in the name of purity. The song reminds us that the blame for this falls fundamentally on the subject that submits to this factionalized mental re-engineering. In allowing that "Lies that life is black and white / Spoke from my skull," Dylan is not indicting a movement as much as the troubadour who looks for a movement out of which to craft (and market) a poetic persona.

The self-gratifying motivations of easy sex for a movement-troubadour are also exposed here as carnal frauds as the singer admits that "Girls' faces formed the forward path / From phony jealousy / To memorizing politics / Of ancient history." The song in turn evokes Dylan the movement-troubadour as the wannabe intellectual who pontificates ("A self-ordained professor's tongue / Too serious to fool"); the cantankerous warrior spoiling for any fight ("In a soldier's stance, I aimed my hand / At the mongrel dogs who teach"); and the ever-paranoid revolutionary ("Yes, my guard stood hard when abstract threats / Too noble to neglect / Deceived me into thinking / I had something to protect"). Among the lines most often adduced as Dylan's rejection of political songwriting and the folk movement are his admissions that he was caught in a cycle of "Fearing not that I'd become my enemy / In the instant that I preach." What seems to be lost in the collective remembrance of "My Back Pages" is the scathing self-indictment of the piece here—which itself constitutes a new kind of political act at a moment when white liberal collectivist activism had so disenchanted Dylan.

Indeed, in his (in)famous 1964 interview with Nat Hentoff for *The New Yorker*, Dylan averred that he was done with "finger-pointing songs" and that he did not "want to write *for* people anymore" as some kind of "spokesman" (Dylan 2017, 17). To read this as an apolitical championing of self-indulgence or apathy (as so many in the folk movement did even prior to Dylan "going electric" in 1965) is to miss the fundamentally *political* nature of the sea-change Dylan was signaling both in the interview and his music. The key distinction here is illuminated when we consider what appear to be the most controversial lines of "My Back Pages"—Dylan's suggestion in the fourth stanza that among his troubadour sins are how he

> Spouted out that liberty
> Is just equality in school
> "Equality," I spoke the word
> As if a wedding vow

Some might be tempted to read these lines not merely as a move away from political songwriting like "Hattie Carroll" toward a personal aesthetic, but as a willful disconnection from the very civil rights movement whose "soundtrack" Dylan had been purportedly helping to write. To assume this, however, is to miss a vitally important element of Dylan's recalibration of himself as political poet. The word "just" in the second line quoted above is essential here, reminding us that Dylan is not abandoning the cause of liberty, but is moving away from those who would view it "just" as a matter of desegregation or any other discrete social reform, however sorely needed. The reduction of liberty to a platform or a slogan is the surest way to delay or sabotage it. Again, the emphasis is on self-indictment—Dylan is the one posited as speaking "equality" as a "wedding vow" that he hardly intends to honor, or at least hardly feels capable of honoring, much as he might want. Liberty and equality are not abandoned as social goods or objectives here, but they are richly complicated beyond the truisms of easy reform programs and their troubadour-spokesmen.

The Hentoff interview again brings home the deeply *political* sensibility behind Dylan's decision here. While the bits about transcending "finger-pointing" get the most attention in the interview, just as important is the very next statement by Dylan:

> Like I once wrote about Emmett Till in the first person, pretending I was him. From now on, I want to write from inside me, and to do that I'm going to have to get back to writing like I used to when I was ten—having everything come out naturally. The way I like to write is for it to come out the way I walk or talk. (Dylan 2017, 17)

Dylan fully acknowledges here the compromised and politically problematic gesture of speaking not only *for* another but also *as* another. This is especially vexed when considering the tortured dynamics of racial subjectivity and racist objectification, and the issues Dylan raises here remain contemporary problems today in the contested notion that movements such as "Black Lives Matter" can have genuine allies among the white community—and if they can, what the contribution and positionality of white allies ought to be. It is almost as if in talking about his Emmett Till song, Dylan is newly internalizing and repurposing the sentiments of his previous album's Medgar Evers song, "Only a Pawn in Their Game." In that tune, the "pawn in their game" was Evers's assassin as a hateful pawn of white supremacy writ large. In the Hentoff interview comments on Till, Dylan is in essence admitting that speaking for (or worse, as) Till (and thereby the African-American experience) not only risks poetic inauthenticity, but also courts a kind of arrogant assumption of voice that is itself a clearly political sin. It is in this light that we need to understand Dylan's positionality in "My Back Pages"—disillusioned with the movement-troubadour's assumption of others' voices like some false "wedding vow," Dylan as songwriter wishes to age backward and into his own authentic language at last.

"Idiot Wind" and Self-Obfuscation

If "Hattie Carroll" is a political song with a deeply autobiographical dilemma, and "My Back Pages" a personal and individualistic manifesto with a far more nuanced political purpose than is often assumed, perhaps a few lines from a later Dylan touchstone can encapsulate the paradoxes at work and play here. As we begin to shift our discussion to Dylan's *Chronicles* as his only prose experiment in explicit (yet highly evasive) autobiography, we are reminded of "Idiot Wind," a memorable entry from Dylan's next period, 1975s *Blood on the Tracks*. As the album most often described (even by some in his family circle) as Dylan's most personal effort in the wake of his crumbling marriage to Sara, *Blood on the Tracks* encapsulates all the tropes of self-presentation and self-obfuscation that we identified above in his classic period. To grasp the challenge posed by any exegesis of *Chronicles* as an autobiographical exercise, we do well to recall Dylan's tempestuous rage in "Idiot Wind" at all efforts to reduce him (or his interlocutor in the song) to biographical narrative and gossip. (For Dylan, these are quite often essentially one and the same.) Raging with the power of King Lear on the heath in Shakespeare's stormy tragedy, Dylan seemingly indicts Sara, the media, and himself for all the emptiness of their revelations, promises, and threats made as the marriage devolves: "Someone's got it in for me, they're planting stories in the press / Whoever it is I wish they'd cut it out but when they will I can only guess." He goes on to lament that "People... just can't remember how to act" when they "see" him: "Their minds are filled with big ideas, images and distorted facts." By the second stanza, the listener is implicated as well: "Even you, yesterday you had to ask me where it was at / I couldn't believe after all these years, you didn't know me better than that." Dylan seemingly chastises us for not knowing him well enough, despite decades of calculated evasion. Yet there is also the desire to be transmuted from one self to another altogether: "I can't feel you anymore, I can't even touch the books you've read / Every time I crawl past your door, I been wishin' I was somebody else instead." The narrator here is torn between, on the one hand, being recognized and appreciated for who he fundamentally remains and, on the other hand, fleeing all prior selves for some happier realm of continual reinvention. If as the singer concludes, "We're idiots, babe / It's a wonder we can even feed ourselves," the question remains: what good can self-examination bring?

We find Dylan owning a similar kind of calculated reticence even in his earliest literary efforts to "present" his life. Dylan's reluctance to be pinned down or categorized began as early as his name change from Zimmerman to Dylan and includes a clear rejection of confessional modes. "My Life in a Stolen Moment" (1962), a ludic poem included in the program for a 1963 concert at New York's Town Hall, clearly demonstrates that his desire to obscure his origins was an early one. From a rather frank depiction of his home town Hibbing, he turns to spurious claims about running away from home multiple times while growing up. From there, he paints a farcical story of himself as a proto-hobo "jailed for suspicion of armed robbery" and "held for four hours on a murder rap." These fictitious accounts, mixed in with factual details, paint the story of a kid in trouble with his family and the law, more the character of a folk tune than the young man from a middle-class home who leaves Hibbing and then the Twin Cities for the music scene in New York. And yet, at the end of the poem, he makes some concessions: he simply does not have the time "to go back an' see why an' where." This claim doubles as an excuse for the exaggerations in his poem but also—poignantly—for why he has not gone back to Hibbing to visit his family. Swept up in the heady blur of early fame, he takes extreme liberties with his pre-New York life, while being direct about his life in the big city and his encounter with the folk scene that brought him recognition:

> I got recorded at Columbia after being wrote up in the Times
> An' I still can't find the time to go back an' see why an' where
> I started doing what I'm doing
> I can't tell you the influences 'cause there's too many
> To mention and I might leave one out
> An' that wouldn't be fair
> Woody Guthrie, sure
> Big Joe Williams, yeah
> It's easy to remember those names
> But what about the faces you can't find again

Even when he is forthcoming, Dylan adopts a self-conscious demotic idiom, more Dust Bowl than Midwest. Already he is foiling readerly expectations. He would be well aware that the audience at the Town Hall would be eager to know his story but, a few weeks shy of his 22nd birthday, he already knew how he would respond. Or rather, he knew how he would not respond. The poem ends with a reiteration of his claim that he ran away from home multiple times from age ten to eighteen and was "brought back all but once." This strategy of deflection and disruption also clearly serves a self-marketing purpose for Dylan, as cultivating an air of incongruous mystery through self-mythologizing lore no doubt drew him even more attention in the New York music scene of 1963.

By the time we reach Dylan's 2004 *Chronicles*, then, we have an explicit point of departure for a discussion of Dylan's engagement with autobiography as a form. We argue that Dylan explicitly moves away from the Augustinian mode of autobiography, which is characterized by the dual moves of confession and conversion, as well as a chronological coherence that permits the autobiographer the distance to speak about the past as a finished event with a telos. The past is revisited and reconstructed in Dylan's corpus more along the lines of Rousseau's ([1782] 2011) achronological *Reveries of a Solitary Walker*, in which the past is brought up, without apology or confession, or even a linear narrative, as a means to think through the present. By situating Dylan in that autobiographical vein, we can do justice to his own efforts in *Chronicles* to position himself in an intellectual tradition, not merely a musical genealogy. This effort is of course underscored by his letter to the Nobel Prize committee in which he acknowledges his debt to the world of letters. In what follows, we define the distinctive character, construction, and preoccupations of Dylan's explicitly autobiographical work, including questions of ancestry and tradition. Just as we situate Dylan within a historical tradition of self-reflection inflected by aesthetic experimentation, we can also identify the ways in which he parted from that tradition and contributed greatly to rethinking and reworking the very genre of autobiography itself.

Also, of critical interest when making this comparison, both Rousseau's *Reveries* and Dylan's *Chronicles* assume a knowledge of the subject at hand. *Chronicles* is a book for a person who has an understanding, however modest, of Dylan, and knowledge about his career. Both books thus, de facto, assume a strong interest on the part of the readership. Dylan follows his eighteenth-century precursor in writing for what is in essence a fan base. *L'ami* Jean-Jacques, as Rousseau was known in his day, can arguably be recast as Dylan, the mysterious and intriguing songwriter who had been foiling his audience's curiosity for—at the time of *Chronicles'* publication—nearly 50 years.

And yet Dylan goes one further, dipping also into the genres of the *Bildungsroman* and the *Künstlerroman*, books—autobiographical or fictional—which detail the growth of a young person into intellectual, emotional, and artistic maturity. *Chronicles* begins as the young folk singer arrives in New York City. But, as we shall see, Dylan will foil us here too, leaving off right at the moment when he began to reach artistic maturity and jumping forward in time to a period in the eighties when his career was flagging, and he hoped to reinvent himself. Again, like Rousseau's *Reveries,* Dylan's *Chronicles* refuses to follow the structure of artistic development or any other form of growing season. Indeed, if we were to assign a specific genre to *Chronicles* it would not, ironically, be a chronicle but rather a manner of anti-*Bildungsroman*, a book that foils our understanding of the development of an artist by moving from beginnings straight into the complexities of a seasoned artist, an artist who—like Rousseau—reflects back on a life that is unfinished and deeply colored by the present. This in turn allows the book itself to become another incarnation of Dylan's self-reinvention—a Whitmanesque "song of myself" without a linear chronology as crutch.

CHRONICLES AND SELF-REVELATION

Chronicles begins not with Dylan's birth or childhood, but rather *in medias res* at Leeds Music Publishing Company. Dylan (2004) tells what might be an apocryphal story about Lou Levy introducing him to the boxer Jack Dempsey, who teasingly treats Dylan as a new heavyweight contender. But Lou then brings him into his office where Dylan realizes, after looking in awe at all of the signed photos on the wall, that he might be in the process of making it. What follows, not in chronological order, is an account of the agent John Hammond offering him a contract. Dylan ponders the artists "who had created music that resonated through American life" (5). "I could hardly believe myself awake," he writes, "him signing me to Columbia Records was so unbelievable" (5). He recognizes that Hammond had taken a chance with him, signing a folk musician at a time when "folk music was considered junky, second rate" (5).

Dylan's gratitude is palpable as Hammond "explained that he saw me as someone in the long line of a tradition, the tradition of blues, jazz and folk and not as some newfangled wunderkind on the cutting edge" (2004, 5). *Chronicles* thus begins somewhat deceptively as the story of the rise to fame of Bob Dylan, the musician and artist that the reader knows. We are alerted to his youth and experience as he—much to his own regret later—signs his contract with Columbia without reading it. "I would have gladly signed whatever form he put in front of me" (2004, 5), he recalls. But even here,

Dylan the ingenue rejects candor when it comes to his personal history. When John calls in Billy James, the head of publicity at Columbia, Dylan is already cagey, lying to this man who annoys him because he "looked like he'd never been stoned a day in his life, never been in any kind of trouble" (5). Dylan immediately starts dissembling to this man who "tried to get me to cough up some facts, like I was supposed to give them to him straight and square" (5). He fabricates everything he tells James; he says he is from Illinois, where he "had a dozen jobs" (5) before working construction in Detroit. Right from the get go, Dylan is defensive and protective about his family: "He asked me about my family, where they were. I told him I had no idea, that they were long gone" (7). Dylan also claims to have been kicked out of his family home.

And thus, within the first pages of *Chronicles*, Dylan outlines his approach to life-writing. There are things he will not discuss, and he is unapologetic about it—this is the way it is going to be going forward. He is as indirect as he was in his early manifestos: "I hated these kind of questions. Felt I could ignore them. Billy seemed unsure of me and that was just fine. I didn't feel like answering his questions anyway, didn't feel the need to explain anything to anybody" (2004, 7). These observations pave the way for the rest of the book. It is key to note that this interlude takes place before "My Life in a Stolen Moment," the pseudo-autobiographical poem in the program at New York's Town Hall in 1963. We can thus see that Dylan's famous evasiveness dates back at least as early as his first record signing, at least insofar as he lets on. At this point the reader might rightfully ask: What is this book going to "chronicle" if he will not answer "these kind of questions"? He also gives Billy the familiar story of riding in on a freight train, "pure hokum—hophead talk," he confesses to the reader (8). And then, suddenly, he becomes candid, forthright at least to the extent that we can believe his sincerity.[2] He came from the Midwest in

---

[2] It is worth noting that the veracity of the book has been questioned by some who suggest that key incidents are invented out of whole cloth. As we saw above, the book is indeed quirkily selective in the eras and the vignettes that Dylan chooses to explore, thereby defying usual expectations of comprehensiveness in narrating an eventful life. Above all, this is a book that refuses to tie up loose ends and square accounts, and is equally recalcitrant about chronology, its title notwithstanding. Dylan's writing is stubbornly and proudly both improvisational and impressionistic. And yet this is precisely why *Chronicles* remains an autobiographical endeavor—each of these apparent departures from the expectations of the genre are in fact hallmarks of autobiographical creativity and evasion from Augustine to Rousseau and beyond.

an Impala and arrived, bewildered, in New York City in the middle of winter: "At last I was here, in New York City, a city like a web too intricate to understand and I wasn't going to try" (9). After just a few pages into *Chronicles*, the reader is justified in anticipating a truth-teller, but a reluctant and sidestepping one at that.

In this way, Dylan alerts the reader that he will be forthcoming only on his own terms, and *Chronicles* reads, for a while at least (as we saw above), like a *Bildungsroman*, the account of an artist who "was at the initiation point of square one but in no sense a neophyte" (2004, 9). Dylan recounts this "initiation" into the burgeoning folk music scene beginning with daytime gigs (9). He keeps to himself, does not talk about himself, nor discusses his life story. As he writes of Freddy Neil who books the daytime gigs at the Café Wha?: "We were very compatible, didn't talk personal" (13). So Dylan, the chronicler, will be candid, but this will be the chronicle of a man who does not like to "talk personal." Curiously, Dylan abhorred playing alone. He needed other people, needed an audience; he just did not want to tell the audience his personal story. As he describes the lean years: "I could never sit in a room and just play all by myself. I needed to play for people and my whole life was becoming what I practiced" (16). Dylan's hell seems indeed to be other people, but, at the same time, his hell is his proving ground.

Dylan's (2004) account of his early life in New York is punctuated by two realizations. First, he is aware that he is unique, that he has something the other performers do not have. He might not play as well or sing as well, but he is bringing something new to the table, even if he is not yet writing his own songs: "There were a lot of better singers and better musicians around these places but there wasn't anybody close in nature to what I was doing" (18). He describes this as "putting the song across" (18). After he meets Dave Van Ronk, he muses: "I'd come from a long ways off and had started from a long ways down. But now destiny was about to manifest itself. I felt like it was looking right at me and no one else" (22). The other realization, which is intimately connected to the first, is that there are elements of the present that simply do not interest him. He is unique, but he is unable or unwilling to affiliate himself with the "madly complicated modern world." For him, folk songs *are* the present: "What was swinging, topical and up to date for me was stuff like the Titanic sinking, the Galveston flood, John Henry driving steel, John Hardy shooting a man on the West Virginia line" (20). The subject matter of the traditional songs that he plays is more important to him than whatever else was going on in New York City or, for that matter, the world, at that time; nevertheless, he is aware of his place in time and, at least with respect to this, is willing to see himself in a group portrait with his contemporaries. He foregrounds his uniqueness and his personal destiny, but not at the expense of his generation: "I was born in the spring of 1941.[...] If you were born around this time or were living and alive, you could feel the old world go and the new one beginning. It was like putting the clock back to when B.C. became A.D." (28). Although he only chronicles his very early songwriting, we can see the skeleton of the ideas that grew into the single "Blowin' in the Wind" (1963) and the entire album *The Times They Are a-Changin'* (1964).

The first part of *Chronicles* details Dylan's early artistic development. Dylan (2004) recounts his growth as a musician, singer, and songwriter. We are treated to his first years in New York City as he clicks with the folk scene, finds friends, and scrounges places to play. He is still careful when talking to people about himself, and he still does not give us any clear reason why. As he writes of Izzy Young, the proprietor of the Café Wha?: "I was very careful when talking to outsiders, but Izzy was okay and I answered him in plain talk" (20). As interlocutor-readers of this text, our status is still arguably uncertain. Are we getting the "plain talk" or are we getting the obfuscation? The puzzle of Dylan attempting something like *Chronicles* is already in the forefront. If he was suspicious about "plain talk," then why did he write this book? Is he telegraphing that we are only getting a part of the picture, and that this is as much as we are ever going to get? Dylan signals to us from the first few pages that *Chronicles* is a book by a man who abhors sharing and answering personal questions. So, what exactly is he chronicling? In the beginning, it is his introduction to the folk scene in New York City and the work there that led him to his first record contract. But where can such a book take us from here if it is so resolutely laconic?

Although he will cut us off prematurely, Dylan's next move in *Chronicles* is to detail his early education in books. We have already learned that that there is something unique about Dylan (and his place and time), but now we discover that he needs to supplement his talent with an education that he will find haphazardly in the library of his friend Ray Gooch. Reminiscent of his account of his youthful reading in his Nobel Prize lecture, Dylan (2004) recalls formative experiences in Gooch's library. Like the folk songs, the classics of literature are more present to him than the vagaries of the modern world and "mainstream culture" that was "lame as hell and a big trick" (35). As Dylan writes,

> It was said that World War II spelled the end of the Age of Enlightenment, but I wouldn't have known it. I was still in it. Somehow I could still remember and feel the light of something about it. I'd read that stuff. Voltaire, Rousseau, John Locke, Montesquieu, Martin Luther—visionaries, revolutionaries... it was like I knew those guys, like they'd been living in my backyard. (30)

It is clear from these passages that Dylan—at this point at least—hoped to connect his songs with the world of books rather than mainstream culture. His awe of the high culture of canonical works is crucial to his development as an artist, perhaps as much so as his mastery of folk songs and their mysterious tales of days of yore. His exalted praise for books is noteworthy: "They were my preceptor and guide into some altered consciousness of reality, some different republic, some liberated republic" (34) where "you couldn't help but lose your passion for dumbness" (35). Books thus served as both escape and guide, but above all, as an antidote to a culturally prescribed idiocy. Dylan's autobiographical effort can arguably be understood to showcase similar aspiration.

"Up until this time I'd been raised in a cultural spectrum that had left my mind black with soot" (35–6), Dylan (2004) muses. At this point in his life, he is consciously looking for material to write about, admitting that he is particularly compelled by war and, surprisingly, that he had at one point hoped to attend West Point: "I'd always pictured myself dying in some heroic battle rather than in bed" (41). While aspiring to write folk songs of his own, he leaves Ray Gooch's library for the New York Public Library and starts reading articles in newspapers on microfilm from the pre-Civil War to the Civil War—ruminating on the origins and nature of the conflict. He had no particular use for the information at that point, but he knew that learning about it was formative for him as he "locked it away in my mind out of sight, left it alone. Figured I could come send a truck back for it later" (86). In this way Dylan was prescient, anticipating the album *Modern Times* (2006) which would follow *Chronicles* by two years.[3] Arguably, this reading also influenced his early masterpieces about the poison of conflict—for instance, "Masters of War" (1963), which ties together specificities of Dylan's contemporary moment while also digging deep into the psycho-pathology of military conflict throughout history. In formulating this perspective on conflict, Dylan grants the Civil War pride

---

[3] For more on how *Modern Times* builds on Civil War-era literature, see Hermes (2017).

of place in his artistic development: "The godawful truth of that would be the all-encompassing template behind everything that I would write" (86). This should remind us of how often Dylan's autobiographical mode is not merely a form of self-presentation, but also a quest to mine the world around him for templates that lend self-narration a discernible configuration.

Although Dylan often limits our access to the particulars of the evolution of his songwriting, he does account for the inception of his craft with a certain candor. He describes it as a fluid process, claiming, in fact, that he cannot even remember when it occurred to him to write his own songs (2004, 51). In order to take this leap in his process, he analyzes folk songs, starts reading long poetry, and tries to understand what makes a good folk song tick. Dylan gives a convincing account of his musical and poetic education, making clear that songwriting is a difficult and intimidating task, one that requires both vision and bravery. He stresses this at the outset:

> It's not like you see songs approaching and invite them in. It's not that easy. You want to write songs that are bigger than life. You want to say something about strange things that have happened to you, strange things you have seen. You have to know and understand something and then go past the vernacular. (51)

His realizations make him even more aware of the talent of the old folk singers to which the early part of *Chronicles* is, in so many ways, an homage. He honors the "chilling precision" with which his precursors wrote, poignantly evoking his discovery of the classic folk song, "I Dreamed I Saw Joe Hill." He likens that song to literature as he reads pamphlets about Joe Hill the man: "What I read could have come out of a mystery novel" (52). But after seeing Mike Seeger play at Alan Lomax's flat, he realizes that it is his turn to compose: "The thought occurred to me that maybe I'd have to write my own folk songs, ones that Mike didn't know" (71). So, in a sense, Dylan contradicts himself, arguing that he didn't know when he decided to write folk songs; yet, a scant 20 pages later, he offers us a clear account of exactly when he decided to do so. And, at this point in *Chronicles*, Dylan also acknowledges the difficulty that came with an awareness of his artistic vocation and the realization that music, if he wanted to "stay playing it [...] would have to claim a larger part of myself" and become center stage, forcing him to "overlook a lot of things—a lot of things that might even need attention" (72).

Another step that Dylan took, a more controversial step in terms of understanding his autobiographical efforts, was to change his name from Bobby Zimmerman to Bob Dylan. Dylan addresses this act, about which there has been so much speculation, in a manner that is as evasive as it is explanatory. If we hoped to understand the reason for the name change— wondering, for instance, if he was hiding his Jewish heritage—*Chronicles* will not help us out. Indeed, the very issue lumps us back together with Billy James, the advertising executive at Columbia who bordered on asking too much. Dylan will not be forthright and we are thus, as readers, lumped together with the people with whom he can't "talk personal." It is a moment that interpellates us as readers, challenging our preconceptions, while also frustrating what the author seems to cast as nosiness. Dylan, of course, was not alone in changing his name; countless singers and actors did so at the time. In fact, it was arguably *de rigeur*. The choice to adopt Dylan is clarified as an homage to Dylan Thomas, but as for the disappearance of the last name "Zimmerman," Dylan is evasively playful, telling us a story whose twist is almost balletic. There was another Bobby Zimmerman and he is going to tell us of his fate:

> As far as Bobby Zimmerman goes, I'm going to give this to you right straight and you can check it out. One of the early presidents of the San Bernadino Angels was Bobby Zimmerman, and he was killed in 1964 on the Bass Lake run. The muffler fell off his bike, he made a U-turn to retrieve it in front of the pack and was instantly killed. That person is gone. That was the end of him. (2004, 79)

This is classic Dylan, and this passage, in many ways, emblematizes his approach to sharing. At the very moment it seems that he will open up on a hot button issue, he frustrates our expectations. Yet Dylan does give away more than the passage might suggest at first blush. Bobby Zimmerman the biker died in 1964, long after Dylan changed his name. The Bobby Zimmerman story is an *ex post facto* story, one—it would seem—that was taken from the news to answer the question Dylan had been asked about since the initial name change.

Despite this will to anachronism, the story of Bobby Zimmerman the biker affords a narrative opportunism in connection to Dylan's own biography as he later suffered a nearly fatal motorcycle accident, which legendarily is viewed as changing Dylan's life and outlook although numerous questions remain about the accuracy of that event as he described it. That alleged motorcycle accident, regardless of its veracity, is nonetheless a centerpiece of the third chapter of *Chronicles*, a chapter that skips right over his early successes and achievements and cuts straight to a time when, married and a new father, he hoped to pull back from his career almost entirely and concentrate on his family: "I was determined to put myself beyond the reach of it all. I was a family man now" (2004, 109). And so we jump forward in time, from the Dylan of the first two chapters who was hoping to write his own songs, to the consummate artist who aggressively dodged the fans who followed him up to Woodstock, the very place where he claims that he sought refuge for himself and for his growing family from the "rat race" (114). At this juncture, the book departs from the conceit of youthful *Bildung*, in favor of achronological sections that highlight his unwitting debt to the fragmented and seemingly random structure of Rousseau's autobiographical *Reveries*. In the *Reveries*, Rousseau hides on an island to escape his enemies and naysayers. At this point in *Chronicles*, Dylan is hiding as well, hiding from the "soot" of the modern world, but also from his fans and the public at large who persist in seeing in him a protest singer and, more significantly, the voice of a generation—an issue we discussed above in relation to "The Lonesome Death of Hattie Carroll" and "My Back Pages." Here in *Chronicles*, Dylan is even more frank on this score:

> I had very little in common with and knew even less about a generation that I was supposed to be the voice of. I'd left my hometown only ten years earlier, wasn't vociferating the opinions of anybody. My destiny lay down the road with whatever life invited, had nothing to do with representing any kind of civilization. Being true to yourself, that was the thing. (115)

We have jumped here from the burgeoning artist to the provisionally retired artist who is fleeing the fame that his ensuing art has brought him. Attendant to his ducking out of the musical scene is the possibility that Dylan became successful precisely due to cultivated misperceptions of his work, and that it might be he who sent out the false cue with his account of the motorcycle accident.

Dylan in this period of reinvention in late 1960s flirts instead with high culture, considering taking up Archibald MacLeish's request that he write some songs for an upcoming play. Ultimately, Dylan decides that he has no vocation for the task. Dylan has tried to escape the Dylan that brought him his early fame, but the escape will not be in the orbit of high culture:

After listening intently, I intuitively realized that I didn't think this was for me. After hearing a few lines from the script, I didn't see how our destinies could be intermixed. This play was dark, painted a world of paranoia, guilt and fear—it was all blacked out and met the atomic age head on, reeked of foul play. (2004, 113)

In spite of this criticism, Dylan's admiration for MacLeish grows as he finds in the playwright a man who had truly found his vocation in a way in which Dylan has not yet. MacLeish, we are told, was "a man who had reached the moon when most of us scarcely make it off the ground" (131). Yet, in finding "foul play" in the high culture he was initially awed by, Dylan recognized that the entire era was steeped in bad faith on all levels. If he was going to take up music again, it would have to be in a very different vein. Dylan would need, once again, to reinvent himself, but it would not be in response to the demands of the public, in particular not those of the "rogue radicals" who came to Woodstock "looking for the Prince of Protest" (116).

Dylan begins the next phase of reinvention with an attention-grabbing trip to Israel, where he is photographed in a skullcap at the Western Wall. This leads to "all the great rags" announcing that he has become a Zionist: "This helped a little," he offers (2004, 122). Overall, this is a period of self-reflection, but also a period of recovery from his overnight success, one that brought him fame at the expense—he suggests—of his soul. He had learned to write the songs that he dreamed of in his first years in New York City, but they had fished up the wrong audience and the wrong reception. He found himself where he never wanted to be: pinned down, defined, and misunderstood.

It is no accident then that *Chronicles* moves jarringly yet directly into the recording of his mid-career album *Oh Mercy* (1989), with a brief detour into *New Morning* (1970)—skipping the years when his albums would bring a new and more personal Dylan back into the public eye and heading straight to Dylan's forties when the task at hand would be, once again, reinvention, finding new ways to write songs, and perhaps even finding a wholly new audience. The chapter of *Chronicles* titled "Oh Mercy" details the travails of an artist who many—perhaps even himself—believe is well past his best years:

I hadn't actually disappeared from the scene, but the road had narrowed, almost was shut down and was supposed to be wide open. I hadn't gone away yet. I was lingering out on the pavement. There was a missing person inside of myself and I needed to find him. Now and again, I did try a few times, tried hard to force it. (2004, 147)

In this, Dylan's *Chronicles* has moved decisively away from the *Bildungsroman* or *Künstlerroman*. For it is precisely at the moment of success where most autobiographies of artists trail off or switch course to cover the surprises and antics of fame and success. *Chronicles* details what seems, for a moment here at least, to be a downhill slide. We have yet to learn how Dylan wrote his first songs. Now we learn, in detail, the difficult process by which he wrote songs during his overlooked middle period. Instead of an in-depth description of how Dylan composed one or another of his earlier and more commercially successful albums, we are treated to the recording of his comeback, *Oh Mercy*, his 26th studio album, to which he devotes an 80-page chapter of the autobiography (141).

The "Oh Mercy" chapter is filled with setbacks. Dylan has suffered a grave hand injury. He is alienated from his early work, whose "raw nerves" he can no longer touch. "It wasn't my moment of history anymore" (2004, 148), he notes ironically. Following the previous chapter, we can wonder if this is not in fact what Dylan was looking for all along, the possibility to create without being labeled a prophet or seer or voice of a generation. Yet he searches for a new kind of music, a new audience, a new vocal technique, new visions, and new ways of composing and playing. In this chapter, we are finally treated to the discussion of craft, composition, and technique that was so conspicuously absent in the earlier chapters. And through it all, Dylan suggests that this turn was, in fundamental ways, an accident. Had he not been in bed with a hand injury, he might not have started writing songs: "Maybe I wouldn't have written them if I wasn't laid up like I was" (165).

The Dylan of *Oh Mercy* is a consummate songwriter. From the folk singer of the first chapter who plays covers and traditional songs, Dylan is transmuted into an artist who, much like his younger self, writes upward of 20 songs in a month. How he got here, he will not tell us, but he will let us in on the nitty-gritty details of recording his comeback album. If there is *Bildung* here, it is middle age *Bildung*, the search for new beginnings in the Dantesque midpoint of life's journey. In fact, the *Oh Mercy* chapter is perhaps the most traditionally autobiographical chapter in *Chronicles* in its details, including an extended recollection of a visit with his then-wife to a country store in rural Louisiana from which he departs with a WORLD'S GREATEST GRANDPA bumper sticker. The chapter offers genuine insight into the process of conceiving and recording an album, including working with other people, the nature of studio recording, and knowing when a song is as good as it is ever going to be. *Oh Mercy* offers a thorough description of the joys and tedium of recording an album—not to mention the joys and tedium of autobiographical practice.

Indeed, the topic of autobiography is broached head on in the chapter when Dylan recalls recording the song "Everything is Broken." "Everything is Broken" would become the hit of the album, but at the time of its recording, it did not seem headed in that direction. Legendary producer Daniel Lanois thinks it might be a "throwaway" (2004, 198). The session band is in disarray. As Dylan notes, turning again to the politics of recording, "When you cut a song like this with a group of musicians, it's rare to get a day when all five or six feel good in the same kind of way at the same time" (198–9). Dylan's concern is revealing: "Critics usually didn't like a song like this coming out of me because it didn't seem to be autobiographical. Maybe not, but the stuff I write does come from an autobiographical place" (199).[4] Although Dylan does not specify why and how "Everything is Broken" is autobiographical, this statement alone gives us a warrant to treat his lyrics, older and more recent, as at least a guarded gesture toward self-revelation.

Ultimately, Dylan is forced to return to the concerns that characterized his early career. Although the recording with Lanois was ultimately successful, it was also bumpy. Dylan explains his relationship with Lanois in a familiar refrain: "I know that he wanted to understand me more as we went along, but you can't do that, not unless you like to do puzzles" (2004, 218). Here Dylan obfuscates his agency and his coherence as a self, as he has done so many times before. His songs are autobiographical, but you will be thwarted if you try to figure him out. Are they puzzles of Dylan's own creation or are they an inalienable part of his being? Is Dylan intimating and subscribing to an ethics of interpersonal communication? Lanois functions here as the reader of *Chronicles* might, patiently taking the Dylan he can get, but wanting more—more answers, more details, more insight.

Lanois as producer also suffers from wanting the younger Dylan back, but the artist who composed this new record bears little relation to that

---

[4] This seems to directly contradict Dylan's claim on 122 that *Blood on the Tracks* was not autobiographical at all, but rather based on a cycle of Chekhov stories.

icon: "The voice on the record was never going to be the voice of the martyred man of constant sorrow, and I think in the beginning, Danny had to come to terms with that, and when he gave that notion up, that's when things started to work" (2004, 200–21). In the middle of an extended rumination on whether he still has it, Dylan makes it clear that he does not want to go back in time. If he still has it, he wants to move forward, keep innovating. At the same time, he realizes that times have, quite literally, changed and that "The kind of music that Danny and I were making was archaic." His contemporaries are now Public Enemy, N.W.A., Run-D.M.C.: "They were beating drums, tearing it up, hurling horses over cliffs" (219). The group portrait of the 1960s has changed, and Dylan does not know where he fits into the new one, if at all.

Life as Lyric

The jarring jump backward in time that characterizes the final chapter of *Chronicles*, "River of Ice," returns Dylan to his attempts to join in the New York folk scene and also brings us back to the beginning of the book. It takes off where the first two chapters end. We are once again at the beginning of Dylan's career. Here Dylan has turned the logic of the *Bildungsroman* on its head, ending with the beginning although—once more—ending before his story starts. He has finally begun writing his own songs, but is still unsure of where they will take him:

> I didn't have many songs, but I was making up some compositions on the spot, rearranging verses to old blues ballads, adding an original line here or there, anything that came into my mind—slapping a title on it. I was doing my best, had to thoroughly feel I was earning my fee. Nothing would have convinced me that I was actually a songwriter and I wasn't, not in the conventional songwriter sense of the word. (2004, 227)

Now Dylan lets on that the reason John Hammond had brought him to Leeds Music—where *Chronicles* begins—is because of a song he wrote about Woody Guthrie, which amounts to Dylan's admission of both cultural debt and genealogy.

From this moment, we go backward in time still further—more remotely than the book has yet gone—back to Dylan's childhood in Minnesota. The story of young Dylan comes at the end of *Chronicles*, reversing the order of the *Bildungsroman*, and recalling the extremely non-linear "promenades" of Rousseau's solitary walker. We find Dylan biding his time through the activities of a small Midwestern town, playing ice hockey and shooting rubber-guns. We get glimpses of his childhood, his parents' youth, his childhood activities, his family, his move to the Twin Cities at 18. We follow him through his discovery of folk music and the folk music scene, which he finds far more interesting than anything he had encountered in Hibbing, deciding he has "little in common with anyone not like-minded" (2004, 236). We are told about his discovery of Woody Guthrie, which is nothing short of an epiphany: "It was like I had been in the dark and someone had turned on the main switch of a lightning conductor" (245). In the last few pages of *Chronicles*, we see Dylan moving to New York City, succeeding and recording in the music world.

"River of Ice" thus has a two-fold approach. It takes us back to the first chapter and gives us both a before and after, but in samples and impressions. The foiled *Bildung* of the last four chapters has been resolved at the end. Dylan had recorded his first songs. Except for one about Woody Guthrie, they are not necessarily completely original songs: "Sitting in Lou's office I rattled off lines and verses based on the stuff I knew" (2004, 228). But Dylan is making it in the folk scene and he is on his way, with destiny on his side: "The road out would be treacherous, and I didn't know where it would lead but I followed it anyway" (292). Significantly, Dylan already knows that the future will take him away from folk music into an entirely different musical world: "The folk music scene had been like a paradise that I had to leave, like Adam had to leave the garden. It was just too perfect" (292).

Chronicles ultimately works against the Augustinian tradition in which the past is unyielding and final, in which the break between what was and what will be is absolute and coherent. As we have suggested earlier, the more fitting precursor is Rousseau, whose work oscillates in a speculative, unpredictable, and dynamic fashion between past, present, and future. Like Rousseau's *Reveries of a Solitary Walker*, *Chronicles* is joyously picaresque. In the final pages of *Chronicles*, Dylan nods toward the future and all of the sweeping changes ahead. Juggling and jumbled between the past and the present, Dylan finds the point of departure for his later accomplishments, challenges, and accolades. Yet this closing account is no Archimedean point of leverage through which traditional conversion narratives and autobiographies master the telling and the meaning of a life; instead, this is an envisioning rather than a pure evasion, a point of no return and no regrets—the autobiography as song fragment and the life as lyric.

References

Benet, James. 1964. Growing Pains at UC. *San Francisco Chronicle*, November 15, 1964.

Berger, John. (1972) 2008. *Ways of Seeing*. New York: Penguin Books.

Dylan, Bob. 2004. *Chronicles. Volume One*. New York: Simon & Schuster.

———. 2017. *Bob Dylan: The Essential Interviews*. Edited by Jonathan Cott. New York: Simon & Schuster.

Hermes, Will. 2017. Modern Times. In *Bob Dylan: The Complete Album Guide*, 82–83. New York: Rolling Stone.

Milton, John. 2003 (1667). *Paradise Lost*. New York: Penguin.

Rafelson, Bob, dir. 1970. *Five Easy Pieces*. Columbia Pictures.

Ricks, Christopher. 2003. *Dylan's Visions of Sin*. New York: Ecco.

Rousseau, Jean Jacques. 2011 (1782). *Reveries of a Solitary Walker*. Translated by Russell Goulbourne. Oxford: Oxford University Press.

Sounes, Howard. 2001. *Down the Highway: The Life of Bob Dylan*. New York: Grove Press.

Whitman, Walt. 1961 (1855). Song of Myself. In *Leaves of Grass: The First (1855) Edition*, ed. Malcolm Cowley, 25–86. New York: Penguin.

CHAPTER 9

Beyond Genre: Lyrics, Literature, and the Influence of Bob Dylan's Transgressive Creative Imagination

Nduka Otiono

Growing up in Nigeria, America invaded our world largely through fragments of culture: books and music.
(Pius Adesanmi, "Don Williams: Fragments of Memory")

For over half a century, the jury has been very busy deliberating on Bob Dylan's transgressive creative imagination to determine whether indeed his works qualify as poetry. Reviewing Bob Dylan's 1966 concert in Dublin, an *Irish Times* contributor argued that "Mr. Dylan is a poet, and though he might be a minor one, were he to publish in slim volumes without the assistance of guitar, harmonica and publicity machine, it is something to sell poetry to a mass audience at all" (Smyth 2011). The debate over Dylan's credentials as a poet understandably turned into a din following his receipt of the Nobel Prize in Literature in 2016. Yet, having already won a string of honors going back as early as the 1963 Tom Paine Award—including induction into the Rock & Roll Hall of Fame in 1988, a Grammy

N. Otiono (✉)
Institute of African Studies, Carleton University, Ottawa, ON, Canada

© The Author(s) 2019
N. Otiono, J. Toth (eds.), *Polyvocal Bob Dylan*,
Palgrave Studies in Music and Literature,
https://doi.org/10.1007/978-3-030-17042-4_9

Lifetime Achievement Award in 1991, and a Pulitzer Prize in 2008 in Special Awards and Citations "for his profound impact on popular music and American culture, marked by lyrical compositions of extraordinary poetic power"—it should be of little surprise that the unpredictable artist would continue to receive prestigious honors for his artistic expression. Still, the announcement of Bob Dylan as the first-ever musician/song writer to win the 2016 Nobel Prize in Literature for "having created new poetic expressions within the great American song tradition" evoked controversy and harsh criticism as to whether his works should be considered literature. Although not Dylan's first encounter with the Nobel Committee—visiting professor of English at Washington and Lee University, Gordon Ball, nominated Dylan on multiple occasions starting in 1996 (Ball 2016)—the idea of Dylan being celebrated alongside American literary greats such as Ernest Hemingway, William Faulkner, John Steinbeck, and Toni Morrison seemed too much for some literary genre purists to swallow.

Despite Ball's (2007) argument that "Poetry and music have shared common ground, from the Greeks to Pound and Ginsberg" (25), the dismissal of Bob Dylan as a poet is not new. The popular American novelist and journalist Norman Mailer once scoffed at the idea of Dylan as a poet: "If Dylan's a poet, I'm a basketball player" (Leland 2002, 142). On October 13, 2016 (when the Swedish Academy announced Dylan's Nobel win), a slew of novelists and writers quickly took to Twitter to share their feelings on Dylan receiving the prestigious Prize.[1] According to reporters at Reuters, the announcement of Dylan's win at the Royal Academy Hall in October 2016 was met with gasps and even bits of laughter (Sennaro and Scrutton 2016).

As an American artist, Dylan's work has been criticized from a Western lens, categorized into American traditions of folk, rock, and, to an extent, gospel music. The Nobel Prize committee used similar categories when critically reviewing his work as pieces of literary cannon.

But what about Bob Dylan's influence outside of these "traditional" or American/Western spheres of popular culture? This is the central question that this chapter seeks to answer from an African perspective, using a focus group of Nigerian writers as case study. The criticism unleashed on Dylan's role as a literary figure following the Nobel Prize award refocuses attention on the barriers of who can be recognized, accepted, and celebrated within various spheres of creative and cultural production. It also prompts

---

[1] Some of these tweets are discussed in the introduction to this book.

reflections on how Dylan's work and persona transcends geographical space and how his music cast a spell on a group of African writers in the late twentieth century—the latter being my organizing focus here. Such reflections will enable me to bring into global critical conversations on Bob Dylan that yet uncharted influence of Dylan in Africa—specifically on the small group of Nigerian poets who found in him a patron saint.

Dylan, though not a writer or poet in the "traditional" sense, produces works that transcend genre and align with an unusual theoretical approach which Khatija BiBi Khan (2017) identifies as "soetry." According to Khan, soetry's "clear features... are manifest in the poetry in the song and the song in the poetry" (71) or, put differently, in "the fusion of poetry and song" (72). In a similar vein, Lebold (2007) conceptualizes Dylan's transgressive lyrics as the "*performed song*" (59),[2] while Betsy Bowden (1982) identifies Dylan's eclectic genre as "performed literature" (4).

The poetic craft and personal accounts of the Nigerian poets given below justify this idea of "soetry" and help us to see Dylan's work beyond a traditionalist/academic view of poetry as *just* words/lyrics. This, in fact, is the import of Khan's (2017) analysis of Niyi Osundare's poetry. Although the works of the Nigerian poets discussed here do not share the same degree of traditional oral poetry resources as Khan demonstrates in his analysis of Osundare's poetry, the poets in the circle composed and performed their poetry fully informed by the same tradition.

A defining feature of the poets in the group on focus is the landmark publication of six volumes of poetry by members of the group known as the "Update poets" which preceded the release of Dylan's mid-career album

---

[2] In a related vein, Christopher Ricks (2016a) warns against "reducing" Dylan's work to literature: "The art of song is a triple art, a true compound. And it doesn't make sense to ask which element of a compound is more 'important': the voice, or the music, or the words? (Which is more important in water, the oxygen or the hydrogen?) And that therefore there is a danger, even while we are very grateful this time to the Nobel Committee, if we simply allocate Dylan's art of song to literature or Literature, of our privileging the words, as though song were not a triangle and often an equilateral triangle." Ricks (2016b) further discusses Bob Dylan as a poet in an hour-long podcast produced by Eleanor Wachtel for the Canadian Broadcasting Corporation (CBC). Indeed, the relationship between Dylan's lyricism, poetry, and musical production has been analyzed by many in academic circles. These include: Canadian poet and Emeritus Professor of English at the University of Victoria, Stephen Scobie (1999, 2003); former Oxford Professor of Poetry, Sir Christopher Ricks (2003); an edited collection by Neil Corcoran (2003), the former King Alfred Professor of English Literature at the University of Liverpool; and Aiden Day (1988), former Professor of Nineteenth Century and Contemporary Literature at the University of Edinburgh.

Oh Mercy (1989). Named after the publisher, Update Communications, Lagos, the group comprised the following poets who were specially published by the writers' guild of Nigeria, the Association of Nigerian Authors (ANA): Uche Nduka (*Flower Child* [1988]); Afam Akeh (*Stolen Moments* [1988]); Idzia Ahmad (*A Shout Across the Wall* [1988]); Esiaba Irobi (*Cotyledons* [1988]); Emman Shehu Usman (*Questions for Big Brother* [1988]); and Kemi Atanda Ilori (*Amnesty* [1988]). Of the six Update poets, only three fit squarely into the circle that I focus on in this chapter—Akeh, Ahmad, and Nduka. Among the six, Ilori happens to be the only poet that is not part of the group discussed here. While I shall provide more insight into the profile of the group below, as well as on members of the extended circle (including me), and how Bob Dylan wielded historic influence on the group, it is important to note at the outset that, oddly enough, Africa is one of the continents in which Bob Dylan has never played a concert—although Africa features in my favorite Dylan song, "Man in the Long Black Coat" (1989), discussed in detail below. Yet, Dylan's persona and work have enthralled unlikely disciples in some corners of the continent. As Ryan Book (2015) adroitly observes about places Dylan has played,

> The folk icon has been enrolled on his "Never Ending Tour" since 1988, and the statistics demonstrate just how far he's gone. As of a report from 2013, Dylan had played 2,500 shows in more than 800 cities and travelled more than 1,000,000 miles... enough to have travelled to the moon and back by bus... twice. With a travel log like that, it's even more interesting to check out where the performer hasn't been, versus where he actually played.

Among the prominent places Dylan has not played are Alaska, the Middle East, India, the Caribbean, and Africa. Appraising possible reasons why Africa has not featured in Dylan's three-decade "Never Ending Tour" diary, Book (2015) ruminates:

> Although it's not at all surprising that he's skipped playing in Antarctica as part of some promo, it's rather shocking that he hasn't once played a gig in Africa during the last 27 years. We're not going to make light of the many reasons why no Western performer sets long African runs: Poverty makes attending concerts an absurd notion for much of the population and regional conflicts make it plain dangerous. Putting on a show in Nigeria or Kenya is not outside of the realm of possibility for someone of Dylan's stature however, even if it was a free show. Perhaps he protested playing South Africa during the early '90s due to Apartheid, but those days have passed. Egypt

has a reasonable GDP, and other of Africa's 10 richest nations—such as Morocco and Algeria—are literally less than 100 miles from where Dylan has performed in Spain.

The omission of Africa from Dylan's thousands of concerts in over fifty-four countries[3] is more telling considering the continent's near omnipresent status in the charity or benefit concert genre curated by Western music icons such as Bob Geldof, Paul McCartney, and Bono, via Band Aid, Live Aid, and other such projects. Yet, Dylan was part of the United Support of Artists (USA) for Africa organization that emerged from the hit single "We are the World" charity concert of 1985 championed by Harry Belafonte, activist and King of Calypso, to alleviate poverty in Africa and the United States. Dylan also featured in the first-ever benefit concert, The Concert for Bangladeshi in 1971 (organized by the Beatles' George Harrison and Ravi Shankar). But Dylan has never played in Africa. So how did Dylan become the centripetal artistic force that inspired the group of African poets upon whom I focus in this chapter? To answer the question, I shall take a personal angle.

A CIRCLE OF POETS UNITED BY DYLAN

Although I do not recollect the exact date I encountered Bob Dylan's work in Lagos, Nigeria's densely populated commercial and cultural capital city, I remember the circumstances that brought the inimitable artist into my consciousness. I had graduated from the University of Ibadan, Nigeria's premier university, and had moved to Lagos to pursue a career in journalism and creative writing. It was in the early 1990s and Lagos—like other cities that serve as cultural hubs (such as New York, San Francisco, Paris, Dublin, and London)—was the dream site for young people determined to "make it big" in life. My extensive knowledge of the city had been defined by hanging out with friends in various parts of the city while working as a journalist in various media houses. While enjoying a peripatetic existence, I encountered some cultural denizens who inhabited the literary spaces in the Surulere and Ikeja sections of the city. Besides the Update poets, the other denizens of Lagos's creative space born around the independence

---

[3] See Eric Jaffe's statistical and interactive guide to all the cities and set lists Dylan performed over the past 25 years as of June 7, 2013: "808 Cities, 2,503 Shows, and 1,007,416 Miles: The Staggering Geography of Bob Dylan's 'Never Ending Tour.'"

and postindependence turbulent period of 1960s in Nigeria who consti-
tuted the circle included: Eyakatang Carlos Udofia, poet and estate sur-
veyor; Demola Babajide, civil servant and vagrant poet with a trademark
baritone voice; Ike Okonta, fiery journalist and writer of whom Oguibe
wittily noted in a poem that the God that robbed him of speech gave him
a fiery pen in return; Sanya Osha, philosopher and prolific writer whose
essay on Prince is one of the most unflattering critiques of the Purple Rain
King[4]; E.C. Osondu, winner of a Caine Prize for African Writing; and
Anthony Akika, attorney, human rights activist, and literary enthusiast in
whose Surulere, Lagos, home we congregated and held many impromptu
literary salons in the early 1990s.

A close-knit group of emerging writers and intellectuals, the love of
literature and ideas defined the many literary fêtes and salons we held in
dingy *bukatarias* and beer and peppersoup lounges (e.g., Busy Bees and
Shindig) in Surulere, Lagos. There were others also who, although they
were not resident in the Lagos-Ibadan axis, were strongly linked to the
group through a shared interest in Dylan—especially from the "Nsukka
school" (a reference to University of Nigeria Nsukka). The latter included,
chiefly, Olu Oguibe, a scholar and artist, and Esiaba Irobi, poet, playwright, critic, and author of about a dozen books.

It was within this group that I encountered Bob Dylan, already vener-
ated and worshipped by Idzia [also Izzia] Ahmad and Uche Nduka as poet-
prophet and patron saint. Not only were the duo writing poetry inspired by
Dylan and keeping literary diaries, they were imitating Dylan's bohemian
lifestyle and singing Dylan's "Mr. Tambourine Man" like an anthem.[5] As
Sanya Osha recalls, "Idzia... in fact wrote an entire collection... modelled
on Dylan's songs beginning with 'A Simple Twist of Fate.'"[6] For his part,
Uche Nduka wrote poems inspired by Dylan's taut elliptical style, while
producing prose pieces with Dylanesque confessional tones and epistolary
bent; such inspiration is on full display in *Belltime Letters* (2000), in which

---

[4] See Sanya Osha, "Why Prince is Over-rated." *Pambazuka*, June 9, 2016.

[5] So enchanted by "Tambourine Man" was Uche Nduka that he alluded to Dylan as "king
of the tambourine" in his second collection of poems, *Second Act* (1994, 12).

[6] Email message to author, March 19, 2018. For more on Idzia Ahmad see the special issue
of *Sentinel Literary Quarterly* (March 2003) dedicated to the poet. The online publication
contains tributes by seven contemporaries—Olu Oguibe, Nnorom Azuonye, Uche Nduka,
Obiwu, Amatoritsero Ede, Sanya Osha, and Emman Shehu Usman—celebrating Ahmad who
died in 2003 at the age of forty-three (see www.sentinelpoetry.org.uk). Also see the tribute by
Omale Allen Abdul-Jabbar (2007) entitled "Carlos Izzia Ahmad: The Man and His Poetry."

Nduka evokes his multiple selves like Dylan: "My life revolves around trying to make peace among my squabbling selves; to unceasingly assure the different pieces of me that they need not fear or detest or patronize each other in their quest for space and expression" (8). It seemed inevitable to have been bitten by the Dylan bug while associating with Nduka and Ahmad. And bitten I was, and memorably baptized into the Dylan cult through a ninety-minute audio cassette gifted to me by Ahmad, "worker in the ministry of poetry" (Nduka 2003). It was a compilation of Dylan's songs that included the album, *Oh Mercy* (1989), the ten-tracker with disquieting songs such as "Political World," "Everything is Broken," and "Disease of Conceit." Like a besotted lover, I would repeatedly play the songs, especially my all-time favorite, "Man in the Long Black Coat" (1989), with its enchanting opening lines and allusion to Africa (i.e., "African trees / Bent over backwards from a hurricane breeze"), until the sound quality began to fade and I had to duplicate the cassette.

For me, there couldn't be a better introduction to Dylan than "Man in the Long Black Coat," a conviction that was years later reinforced while reading Dylan's glowing reflections on the song in *Chronicles* (2004a, 215–16). The song's hypnotic narrative bent, the lyricism, the imagery, and the direct invocation of Africa worked like some hard drug that got me hooked on Dylan. Not surprising, the song—better still, the poem—was one of my earliest textual choices to teach in a first-year course (i.e., Literature in Global Perspectives) during my doctoral program at the University of Alberta. The positive response I received from my students reinforced my immersion in Dylan, so much so that I did not realize how and when one of Dylan's songs, "Love Sick" (1997), reincarnated in *Love in the Time of Nightmares* (2008)—the collection of poems I wrote during my Alberta years.[7] The song's tormenting lines had evidently stuck in my consciousness: "I'm sick of love, I wish I'd never met you / I'm sick of love, I'm trying to forget you." In stanzas four and seven of my own "Lovesick," the poet-persona laments in tercets:

> it's mysterious how love's melodies change,
> how its temper fluctuates like tidal waves—
> flourishing at one moment then retreating.

[7] In my earlier poetry collection, *Voices in the Rainbow* (1997), I identified with Dylan's controversial allusive and intertextual modernist style through my experimentation with heteroglossia, best theorized by the great Russian philosopher and literary critic, Mikhail Bakhtin, in his ground-breaking essay, "Discourse in the Novel" ([1934] 1981).

> i'm lovesick, tired of the politics of our lives;
> my love can be as stubborn as the moon, now
> u see her now u don't & the cycle continues. (34)

Back to my pre-Alberta days in Lagos—and still very much till this day: Lagos is a city of contradictions: of sadness and joy; of inspiration and asphyxiation for the young artist; of opportunities and lynched illusions. So challenging is living in Lagos that in a documentary on Nigeria, the novelist Chinua Achebe described living in Lagos as "living in a war front." But it is a war front that paradoxically nurtured and tormented the artist, especially the unemployed one scavenging hostile streets for the bare bones of survival and the scaffolds upon which to build a career and a future. Obi Nwakanma (2006) captures "Lagos of the poets" in a graphic newspaper article:

> POETRY walks on the streets in Lagos. It is in the incredible dynamic of life which enacts, like some incandescent power, the moment of each living hour: it is in the sense by which, living in this city, a poet glimpses a whole new form of life, and an alternative way in which to experience it fully. This vast, tense and bristling city, its social tendon tautly held by imprecise impulses, reverberates in the poetic propensities which she inspires.

The importance of the city to the creative imagination of the writers is further reflected in the works of poets such as Afam Akeh. In a melancholic poem, "Mid Year Blues" (n.d.), the poet laments the infrastructural decay that contributes to making living in Lagos a daily struggle:

> Every rain, every rain,
> the water flushes the guts of Lagos
> and writes a poem of pain
> …
> Each great wind echoes the dream
> until in the drenched moments
> there is a thirst for sunlight,
> and in the air a lament is born
> for the prosperous paths not taken.

For members of the writers circle then, Lagos was like the New York that Bob Dylan evoked in his unusual letter of apology to the Emergency Civil Liberties Committee following the controversial acceptance speech he gave for the Tom Paine Award in which he compared himself to Lee Harvey Oswald:

contrary t rumors, I am very proud of where I'm from an also of the many blood streams that run in my roots. But I would not be doing what I'm doing today if I hadn't comet New York. I was given my direction from new york. I was fed in new york. I was beaten down by new york an I was picked up by new york. I was made t keep going on by new York. I'm speakin now of the people I've met who were strugglin for their lives an other peoples'. ([1963] 2012)[8]

Like Dylan's New York, Lagos was the metropolitan beast where artists armed only with their talents and dreams struggled to find the muse and direction in life. It was not difficult, therefore, to see why Dylan cast a spell on our small Lagos group. Besides Dylan's artistic ingenuity and counter-cultural disposition, our group was drawn to artists whose rebellious and anti-establishment personae advertised the kind of fierce creative tempera-ment that we aspired to possess. Nigeria in the late 1980s and 1990s writhed in the death pangs of military dictatorship and a torturous process of transi-tion to democratic governance. Writers, journalists, activists were jailed for their work. The writer and environmental rights activist, Ken Saro-Wiwa, was gruesomely executed by hanging within this period. So, more than ever before, writers found therapy in their art, while some sought escape through liquor or fled into exile. The period was marked by student protests against military dictatorship, the SAP (Structural Adjustment Program) riots, and massive brain drain involving Nigerian intellectuals and other professionals. Hence, apart from Dylan, the group was fascinated by Dambudzo Marachera, the unorthodox Zimbabwean writer and author of the award-winning collection of short stories *The House of Hunger* ([1993] 2009); the tortured soul poet Sylvia Plath; Christopher Okigbo, the poet-soldier who fought and died for his beliefs in the Nigerian/Biafra war; members of the Beat Generation; John Coltrane; John Lee Hooker; Jimi Hendrix; Bob Marley; and quite remarkably, Fela Anikulapo Kuti, the Afrobeat King. The group found inspiration in Kuti's artistic ingenuity and iconoclastic defiance of convention which blended with the experimental and freewheeling artis-tic temperament that Dylan later captured in *Chronicles* (2004a), and in his Tom Paine Award "apology" letter (cited above) in which he refuses to apologize: "no I do not apologize for being me nor any part of me." In his personal reflections—reproduced in full below—Uche Nduka recalls that

---

[8] I am quoting the speech as it is transcribed in a *Letters of Note* article (2012): "I do not apologize for being me nor any part of me." *Letters of Note* is edited online by Shaun Usher.

"Some of us even took to playing the harmonica and dressing like our American artist-hero. His songs such as 'Blowin' In The Wind,' 'Like A Rolling Stone,' 'Visions of Johanna' and 'Jokerman' emboldened us in our fight against political tyranny and boredom." Among those who took to playing the harmonica was Olu Oguibe; and Idzia Ahmad and Emman Shehu Usman were noted for their love of the acoustic guitar, with which both accompanied their poetry performances.

Although *Chronicles* and Dylan's many interviews (along with innumerable biographies and articles) highlight the traits that made him such a favorite of our group, that experimental epistolary apologia to the Emergency Civil Liberties Committee, complete with its idiosyncratic spelling style, stands as one of the best examples of what (about Dylan's work) most delighted us. In lines that capture the philosophy of writing for survival which underpinned the creative spirit of writers in my circle then, Dylan ([1963] 2012) helped define the inexplicable and tempestuous creative impulse of writing "in order to keep from going insane":

> I'll return once again t the road
> I cant tell You why other people write, but I write in order to keep from going insane.
> my head, I expect'd turn inside out if my hands were t leave me.
> but I hardly ever talk about why I write. an I scarcely ever think about it. the thought of it
> is too alarmin
> an I never ever talk about why I speak
> but that's because I never do it. this is the first time I am talkin about it…an I pray the last the thought of doing it again is too scary
> ha! it's a scary world
> but only once in a while huh?

As if inspired by Dylan's lines above, in his book-length poem "Chiaroscuro" (also the title of the collection, *Chiaroscuro* [1997])— which narrates the story of his generation through a quasi-autobiographical protagonist named Abali—Uche Nduka unapologetically bursts forth:

> I won't have you outdrink the fish
> and outsmoke the chimney.
> I will pull you to where poems
> quell the rage of booze and smoke. (2)

And in *Stolen Moments* (1988), which Akeh thinks may have borrowed airs from Dylan's autobiographical "My Life in Stolen Moments" (1962), but is not directly connected to it, the Nigerian poet deploys the same tone of disappointment that characterizes Dylan's long poem:

> The world is
> a stolen moment of rustling leaves.
> Still I am arid,
> cannot write the poem of my dreams (8).

Although Dylan's sexual innuendo tends more implicit than overt—as in his sensual ballads "Lay, Lady, Lay" (1969) and "You're Gonna Make Me Lonesome When You Go" (1974)—Uche Nduka and some members of the Nigerian circle of writers deployed what Nduka calls "the audacity of assertion"[9] to produce shocking (yet still Dylanesque) erotic lines such as "The penis has no bone / It's the will that makes it stand" (Oguibe 1992, 85).[10] As noted already, besides Dylan, the circle was concurrently under the influence of the Afrobeat King and radical critic of the Nigerian military, Kuti. His sexually charged, explicit lines in songs such as "Na Poi"[11] and his revolutionary lifestyle inspired the poets (I even wrote a sequence inspired by Kuti's songs in, and dedicated to him, my first collection of poems, *Voices in the Rainbow* [1997].) Contacted to offer their reflections on the spell of Dylan while working on this chapter, three of my contemporaries from the group submitted the following *testimonies* which I am inclined to reproduce in full as these offer remarkable insights regarding the group's poetics and artistic romance with Dylan.

[9] Uche Nduka, email to the author, March 19, 2018.

[10] Both Esiaba Irobi and Uche Nduka composed similar lines around which we joked and which I still remember but cannot easily trace their specific citations: "O Cynthia, Cynthia, thy thighs are tight" (Irobi), and "Half in, half out, / the penis questions the thigh" (Nduka). Nduka has more of such lines in "Four Poems" (n.d.).

[11] A brief description of the song in felakuti.bandcamp.com states: "The 'Na Poi' album contains a later version of Fela's scandalous hit 'Na Poi' in which Fela details what happens between a man and a woman behind closed doors. Originally banned by the Nigerian Broadcasting Company for its taboo sexual lyrics, the version on this eponymous album interchanges spoken word and sung lyrics over the Africa 70 horn play, spanning not only the complete a-side of the record, but the first part of the b-side as well—clocking 25 minutes."

REFLECTIONS BY UCHE NDUKA

Author of nearly a dozen books of poetry and prose, the latest of which is a collection of poems Living in Public (2018), *Nduka is perhaps the most prolific poet of his generation from Nigeria. He obtained his BA from the University of Nigeria and his MFA from Long Island University, Brooklyn. A poet, essayist, song writer, and adjunct professor, he currently lives in Brooklyn, New York, having spent over a decade in Germany and Holland. His award-winning poetry has been translated into German, Romanian, Italian, Finnish, Serbo-Croatian, and Dutch.*

I first heard the music of Bob Dylan in Kano, Nigeria, in 1981. A first-year undergraduate, I was initially both fascinated and repelled by his voice in the album titled "Nashville Skyline." However, repeated listening to those love and marital songs won me over. Since then, I have been an ardent fan of the acoustic and electric troubadour. I sensed nurturance, risk, adventure in his words and musicality. His melodic and narrative generosity overthrew my timidity and caution.

Many years later, after graduating from the university, I discovered that I was not the only member of my generation of writers in Nigeria in thrall of Dylan's artistic magic. Esiaba Irobi, Idzia Ahmed, Sanya Osha, Nduka Otiono, Ogaga Ifowodo, Olu Oguibe, Obi Nwakanma, Ike Okonta were all under the spell of his songs and mystique.

One of the most interesting things about Bob Dylan is his ability to see himself and his country without recourse to falsehoods or flattery. "Trying to Get to Heaven," "The Times They Are a-Changing," "Positively 4th Street," "Just Like a Woman," "Mr Tambourine Man," "Temporary Like Achilles" are songs that called for intuitive responses and assertions in our writings/poems.

Bob Dylan's poetic gifts were particularly important to me while I was writing my first (*Flower Child* 1988) and second (*Second Act* 1994) volumes of poems. Needless to say, his work has been in conversation with mine for many years now. His musical assemblages have been sources of inspiration and renewal for me. I feel energized by his seemingly outsider's perspective on politics, love, spirituality, war, art, freedom.

I cherish the electricity of attention in his lyrics that opens the door to memory, desire, history, vision, prophecy, and passionate moments. For him, home is wherever he finds himself. He is a nomad who prefers not to rob the sea of its handwriting. Inside his voice, the ends of roads are the beginnings of roads. This is about knowing that there is a love that moves sideways. It is also about how to survive correspondences and severances.

Love your craft and let your craft love you, he seems to say. The subject throughout Bob Dylan's songs is metamorphosis. Constant change is integral to his lyrical and narrative formations. His is a quest for what is perceptible to the insatiable shadow; an art linked to growth, exploration, and self-transformation. I like his inclination not to rest on past creative achievements, his desire to always be on the roll/road.

Each period in his work leans on the unforeseen. He milks the possibilities of the unrefined and the unpolished. He is driven to variety and innovation. In this way, he goes beyond witnessing to expand the territory of his writing and singing.

Bob Dylan is not weighed down by praise and hero-worship. He signals a freshness that connects to restless evolving necessity. Sometimes he asks: How far must you go to smear grief? Listen to "Sad Eyed Lady of the Lowlands," "One of Us Must Know (Sooner or Later)," "Ballad of a Thin Man," and "Desolation Row."

In my work some poems and periods call for the audacity of assertion. Dylan helped me discover the importance of a kind of assertion that does not condemn one to a circle of explanation.

For me and my generation in Nigeria, the music of this inscrutable bard was the soundtrack to our travels throughout the country, our courtships, our flirtations, our political protests. He helped me discover myself as an artistic wayfarer. His example made us refuse to write a poetry of restraint.

He is still urging us to zestfully stoke our artistic fires.[12]

REFLECTIONS BY AFAM AKEH

Akeh has held positions in literary journalism, church leadership and university administration. He published his first volume of poetry, Stolen Moments *in 1988, and his second,* Letter Home and Biafran Nights *in 2013. A Political Science graduate of the University of Ibadan, Nigeria, he also holds an MA in Creative Writing and a Graduate Diploma in Publishing from Oxford Brookes University. Akeh has lived in Oxford, England, since 1992, from where he continues to indulge his passions for poetry and critical commentary on the arts.*

Bob Dylan's work is still inspiring ardent followers and mimic practices across aesthetic, ideological and other representational divides. A great survivor of the culture wars, he can apparently be anything ideologues imagine him as—iconic 1960s radical, folk hero, feminist, born-again Christian, rock star, or country blues and gospel music artist.

[12] Uche Nduka, email to the author, March 19, 2018.

At given periods of his career, he has possibly identified as all of these, but Dylan was always uniquely Dylan, not another radical Joan Baez or Peter Seeger or Bob Marley. His music was sometimes in tune with radical causes, especially in early career, but he was primarily about making and selling music. Some who want more from him, who want him as their hero, become disillusioned when they can't definitively tick their preferred boxes for him. Many continue to love his music and retain precious memories of their fan years, but brand him an enigma.

I was reminded of all these, and of my own journey as his fan, by some unhappy responses to Dylan's 2016 Nobel Prize in Literature, and, more recently, his promotional visit to England, to sell his line of Whiskey products. In my earliest encounter with Dylan as a cultural icon, I remember hearing "Blowin' in the Wind" and "Knockin' on Heaven's Door" in Church gatherings. I thought they were gospel music songs before I knew they were part of the Dylan oeuvre.[13] In my heady earlier days of student activism, before the fall of communism, I also imagined Dylan as a committed culture warrior and political activist—just like Fela Kuti and Bob Marley—because of songs like "The Times They Are a-Changin'" and "Like a Rolling Stone."

Poetry would come calling in an urgent tone, and with it, a greater interest in the lyrics and writing life of Dylan. Did work by or on Bob Dylan influence my writing, especially my 1988 volume of poems, *Stolen Moments?* It would be easy to say no, because there was no conscious effort to imitate or even engage Dylan, but he was one of our significant presiding spirits, the poetry of his life, all that outsider aesthetics and free-spirited life which found expression in him, the Beat Generation and Andy Warhol's Factory.

It was the 1980s, and a new generation of writers was being nurtured at the University of Ibadan and elsewhere in Nigeria, the poets among them soon to be published for the first time. Some of us—and that would include Uche Nduka, Esiaba Irobi, Amatoritsero Ede, and Idzia Ahmad—were determined not to write like the literary generations before us. We felt that African Poetry had become mired in tradition and ideological strictures, so we were especially open to other airs and idioms, and for what would from our liminal time seek to deregulate African creative practices in accordance with our cosmopolitan experience. This shift in perspective and practice was influenced by many factors, including the transnational presence of significant cultural icons like Bob Dylan.[14]

[13] Akeh's association of "Blowin' in the Wind" with gospel music is understandable as indeed the song was "built on the melody of the old spiritual 'No More Auction Block'" (Alan Light 2017, 13).

[14] Afam Akeh, email to the author, June 18, 2018.

REFLECTIONS BY OLU OGUIBE

Educated at the University of Nigeria, Nsukka and the School of Oriental and African Studies of the University of London, Oguibe is the author of four volumes of poetry including A Gathering Fear *(1992), which won the Christopher Okigbo All-Africa Prize for Literature, and* I am Bound to this Land by Blood *(2013), as well as several volumes of critical writing including* The Culture Game *(2004) and* Uzo Egonu: An African Artist in the West *(1995). Also a celebrated visual artist, art historian, and curator, Oguibe's honors include the State of Connecticut Governor's Arts Award for Excellence and Lifetime Achievement (2013) and the Arnold Bode Prize of the City of Kassel (2017).*

I think it was Esiaba Irobi that began the 1960s children's interest in Bob Dylan and his work, and passed it on to myself and several others. This was mid- rather than late 1980s. Before that, I think people were mostly into the Country and Western singers, and of course, funk and soul, without connecting any of it to literature. I remember someone like James Taylor was also very popular, but none of us connected his lyrics to poetry. Even a real-life poet-singer-songwriter like Kris Kristofferson wasn't so popular and it wasn't until I left Nigeria before I got into Kristofferson's work and eventually made the literary connection. But Irobi had not just tons of Dylan's music, if I recall correctly, he also had his first book of lyrics and drawings, a copy of which I would buy later. So, from the word go, he associated the music to writing and poetry, and the music was his life. He talked nonstop about Dylan, he cited Dylan in his notes and letters to friends, and his writing was deeply impacted by Dylan's symbolist inclinations as well as his politics. When I first met the writer and journalist Ike Okonta, for instance, he was more a Madonna guy. *Material Girl* and the like. I believe it was our association with Esiaba Irobi that put Dylan on his radar.

Most of the guys who made up the Anthill literary circle in Nsukka in the mid- and late 1980s were into Dylan and occasionally performed his songs at the famed cabaret. Almost all of them were performers or amateur singer-songwriters, people like the journalist Dulue Mbachu, Usman Shehu, and Jachimike Adiele. The proprietor of the cabaret, Gbubemi Amanoritsewor or Amas as he was called, was a recorded musician and part of the 1970s/1980s campus rock explosion in Nigeria. So, they were all familiar with Dylan, years before "The Man in the Long Black Coat." We were more about *Highway 61 Revisited* and *Blood on the Tracks.*

My own deep interest in Allen Ginsberg—I wouldn't say the Beat poets generally because I was ever only interested in Ginsberg and LeRoi Jones/Amiri Baraka—was, in fact, in a rather circuitous way, kindled through Bob

Dylan. And yes, my return to the harp, also, which is an instrument that I learnt as a kid but grew out like most kids do. All this, as you know, was happening in a huge miasma of youthful search and curiosity, and unlike young people out here in the West, we took in influences from far and wide. My own path led more directly to the modernists, to Eliot and Ezra Pound, but also to the African cultural nationalists and revivalists; Okot P'Bitek, Kofi Awoonor, Christopher Okigbo, Chinweizu, and I was always careful not to get carried away too far by the outside influences. However, turning to Igbo forms in my search back then, to Abigbo Mbaise and Ekpe and Ekereavu from Ngwa, to popular musicians and performers like Sir Warrior and the Oriental Brothers, to Ezigbo Obiligbo, Mike Ejeagha, Area Scatter, I saw instant parallels between those and not just Bob Dylan's work but Bob Marley's also, at the center of which in every instance was the trope of the casual aphorism.

Writers and critics have written quite a bit about Dylan's biblical references, especially the ubiquity of New Testament sources in his writing, but to my knowledge none has remarked on the uniqueness of his employment of the aphorism as a trope, something that no other American singer or writer of his or any other generation has employed quite as profusely and something that is, of course, akin to the Igbo penchant for aphorisms or the so-called proverb as an essential part of everyday speech. You cited earlier my line "the penis has no bone; it is the will that makes it stand" in *A Song from Exile*, for instance, which is an aphorism that I'd never considered erotic until now. Such wit is quite replete in my poetry as, indeed, it is in Igbo speech. It was this particular feature, this proclivity for uncommon wit, for proverbs and adages and biblical parables that made his work even more admirable to me, and more relevant to my own writing and work, and has sustained my interest in his music to the present day.[15]

The Ecstasy of Influence[16]

Clearly, these testimonies demonstrate how Dylan became a creative spark that ignited the poetry and lifestyle of some of the postindependence Nigerian writers born in the roaring 1960s as African countries gained independence from colonial rule. The testimonies throw more light on Dylan's direct and indirect influence on these writers and how his eccentric lifestyle and cerebral sounds turned him into a subject of hero-worship.

[15] Olu Oguibe, email to the author, March 23, 2018.

[16] Borrowed from the title of Jonathan Lethem's 2012 book, *The Ecstasy of Influence: Nonfictions, Etc.* Part III of the book on Plagiarism offers particularly poignant insights into the fundamental complexity of influence and creativity.

From the group, Uche Nduka and Esiaba Irobi seem to have been most influenced by "The Dylan Mystique" (Hampton 1986, 149), and the way he wrote songs with "astonishing rapidity" (Marshall 2007, 49), as well as "astounded his followers with a swift succession of stylistic, political, and personal transmutations—from folk neophyte to protest singer to rock 'n' roll poet to wise old country sage" (4–5). For while the promising career of Irobi—who Oguibe writes so glowingly about in his testimony above—was, like Ahmad's, prematurely abridged by death, Nduka's and Irobi's prolificity and eclectic oeuvre have established them as the most productive writers of the group, both operating like troubadours across the world and respectively publishing about a dozen books that span various genres, themes, and styles.

A major force of Dylan's appeal to not just the Nigerian circle of poets, but generally, is captured in Robert Shelton's ([1986] 2010) profiling of Dylan as "a myth-maker, a myth-taker and a myth-breaker" whose story shows "how a song-poet became a public dreamer who mythologized the dreams and nightmares of a generation" (13). In Dylan, then, the Nigerian poets found a muse, secret sharer of the hidden transcripts of our struggles, and a quintessential example of the composite artist who straddles our polyvocal creative aspirations. Akeh powerfully sums it up in his reflections above: "[Dylan] was one of our significant presiding spirits, the poetry of his life, all that outsider aesthetics and free-spirited life which found expression in him, the Beat Generation and Andy Warhol's Factory."

Cognizant of Oguibe's assertion above and echoed by Akeh that Nigeria's youths tend to absorb influences from far and wide, a loudly missing point from the three recollections is the influence of country music which Dylan flirted with especially in "Nashville Skyline" (1969). Pius Adesanmi, author of the Penguin Prize for Africa-winning book, *You Are Not a Country, Africa* (2011), eloquently fills this lacuna in an interesting essay, "Don Williams: Fragments of Memory" (n.d.). The opening lines of the essay foreground the complicated relationship between the imperial powers, postcolonial cultural experience, and subjectivity in these words on the epigraph above: "Growing up in Nigeria, America invaded our world largely through fragments of culture: books and music."[17] The epigraph also calls attention to America's soft popular cultural imperialism in an age of globalization evident not only through literature and books but also through cinema as represented by Nigeria's popular Nollywood film industry.

[17] For more details, see Pius Adesanmi (2009), "Don Williams: Fragments of Memory."

Notwithstanding the influence of Bob Dylan on the Nigerian poets highlighted in this chapter, it is important to relativize the nature of such influence in line with the instructive cynicism about "influence" which Dylan himself promoted, say, in the closing lines of "My Life in a Stolen Moment" ([1962] 2004b),[18] and which scholars of comparative literature maintain. Rikka Rossi (2010), for example, observes, "If the concept of influence is susceptible to overemphasizing originality, colonialist conquest, and nationalist interests, then intertextuality raises problems concerning the limits of the resemblances between texts and thus risks losing a historical perspective" (375). Oguibe recognizes such limitations: "One might say that these things [influences] happen without intention. I obviously make numerous biblical references in my work, just like Dylan or James Baldwin, but that's also because of my own background as a child preacher, and not just because of the influence of Bob Dylan and his social engagement. But it's definitely in there."[19] Further plumbing Dylan's influence with regard to producing socially conscious art, Oguibe alludes to his own predicament following his award-winning but controversial artistic installation in Kassel, Germany (in 2017), entitled "Das Fremdlinge und Fluchtlinge Monument" ("Monument to Strangers and Refugees"). The installation became a lightning rod for confrontations between German far-right nationalists on one hand, and immigrant and refugee advocates and proponents of multiculturalism and freedom of expression on the other (Batycka 2018). And like Dylan, Oguibe resists labels—of heroism or messianism:

> I've found [Dylan's] example very useful as I try to continue to deal with social issues in my work without becoming part of any movements or groups, or becoming a "spokesperson." Since the work in Germany, you have no idea what pressure I've been under to become more or less the face of the immigrant rights movement, which I don't necessarily wish to be. I've turned down an offer to make a television documentary about my work, I've

---

[18] Dylan confesses: "I started doing what I'm doin / I can't tell you the influences 'cause there's too many to mention an' I might leave one out / An' that wouldn't be fair." Elsewhere, in "11 Outlined Epitaphs," Dylan (1964) proclaims: "Yes, I am a thief of thoughts." This latter declaration would seem to be a perfect response to accusations of plagiarism against Dylan, especially in *Chronicles* and his albums *Love and Theft* (2001) and *Modern Times* (2006). In this regard, see Scott Warmuth's (2008) "Bob Charlatan: Deconstructing Dylan *Chronicles: Volume One*."

[19] Olu Oguibe, email to the author, March 24, 2018.

disappointed lots of eager PhD students writing dissertations on the refugee problem, etc, etc, because all I really want is to do my work and have my say and do so quietly. I don't wish to be anyone's hero. In the thick of it all, I've often thought of Dylan's similar predicament in the '60s as he navigated the temptations of the civil rights era. Lots of people were disappointed that he didn't want to be another Joan Baez or Pete Seeger. That came out in songs like "It Ain't Me, Babe," etc. So, looking at an artist's struggle with the lure of messianism even before I was born, imagining what it was like for him, and seeing how he struggled to deal with it; I find all that both instructive and inspiring.[20]

Indubitably, the same response to influence cannot be said of the other writers in the group. Indeed, as we see in the extended passage reproduced above, Oguibe, who was very close to Irobi, notes that "Irobi had not just tons of Dylan's music... he also had his first book of lyrics and drawings... So, from the word go he associated the music to writing and poetry, and the music was his life." Oguibe further recalls that Irobi "talked nonstop about Dylan, he cited Dylan in his notes and letters to friends, and his writing was deeply impacted by Dylan's symbolist inclinations as well as his politics." And as far as I can recall, Ahmad was truly enraptured by Dylan. More than any other poet in the group, Ahmad saw himself more in the mold of Dylan's minstrelsy, and spent a lot of time writing songs, rehearsing them, and playing his acoustic guitar at various fora. Particularly noteworthy in Ahmad's *A Shout Across the Wall* is the final section, Part Three: An Iron Voice—which the poet dedicates to Anthony Akika, our mutual friend introduced earlier. Memorable poems such as "Between Index, Fore and Thumb" (82–5) and "I Stopped Her Dead Against the Railings" (97–8) resonate with the narrative temperament, tortured sensibility, wry humor, philosophical reflections, and dense allusions typical of Dylan's stylistic devices which critics have contested.

The relationship between lyrics, music, and literature that is embodied in Dylan's repertoire, and that influenced the work of members of the Lagos circle in the late twentieth and early twenty-first centuries, has continued to be the subject of controversy among the literati and consumers of popular culture. The controversy, as validated by the individual accounts of my contemporaries in this chapter, stems from stunted academic thinking that narrowly focuses on analyzing lyrics from a purely Western perspective. But we know that "Dylan's words are performed: music, voice,

[20] Olu Oguibe, email to the author, March 24, 2018.

and words come together to create a distinctive cultural artefact and not a verbalized poem" (Marshall 2009, 101). The obsession with separating Dylan's lyrics from his music also reflects the inability of those well-versed in written literature to view poetry-in-performance as *soetry*. The idea of *soetry* as indicated above, I should re-emphasize, is not only justified by the traditional African conception of spoken word, but also underscored by the textual analysis of exemplary works of Dylan and the poets of the Nigerian circle sampled in this chapter. Critics of Dylan such as Stephen Metcalf (2016) disclaim Dylan as a literary figure, stating that "the distinctive thing about literature is that it involves reading silently to oneself. Silence and solitude are inextricably a part of reading, and reading is the exclusive vehicle for literature."[21]

However, ultimately, poetry has often been associated with oral tradition, and such traditions are meant to be shared or performed among peoples and communities, allowing for collective participation. It is not just a creative act executed in tranquility. The group of African poets discussed in this chapter is familiar with the oral nature of poetry, and spoken word performance is a staple of the literary soirees staged by the Nigerian poets. Such soirees and a shared love of performance poetry further align the Nigerian poets discussed in this chapter to Dylan as part of a community of transnational verbal artists operating beyond geographical boundaries.

As noted already, Dylan's lyrics attest to his ability to mesh "folk idiom" with poetic ballad traditions. Lethem (2016) shows that Dylan's poetic signature "is in the slippages, which his critics ironically fault him for—the crush of extra syllables in an overloaded line, the distortions, like that of the word 'mirror' into 'meer' to force a rhyme, the repeated collapse of a pretty lyric into abject plea or insult." Much of the lyrical poetry influences that shaped Dylan's folk music in the 1960s were complemented by Dylan's immersion in Christian and Jewish texts, and which in turn partly influenced the reception of Dylan by some of the Nigerian poets. As Akeh testifies above, "I heard 'Blowin' in the Wind' and 'Knockin' on Heaven's Door' in Church gatherings. I thought they were gospel music songs before I knew they were part of the Dylan oeuvre."

---

[21] Metcalf also calls Dylan's lyrics "colloquial, spare, painterly, and without the accompanying music, inert" in comparison to other American musicians such as Richard Wilbur, who he considers a poet.

Beyond Akeh's recollection of the religious influence of Dylan above, Gilmour (2004) demonstrates how "Bible-soaked" Dylan's songs are, a fact that implicates how such religious influences appealed to Akeh and other members of the circle. Dylan's well-known involvement with Christianity began in the late 1970s. He was baptized in a Pentecostal church in 1979 and went on to attend Bible school (Häger 2008, 47). His music during this period as reflected in *Trouble No More* (2017), which is part of the Bootleg series, confers the status of gospel singer on him, and his references to the Bible are ample. Gilmour (2004) notes the obvious references to the Bible in specific Dylan songs such as "God on Our Side" (1964), "Shot of Love" (1981), and "Caribbean Wind" (1985).

Akeh's assumption that Dylan's lyrics were gospel music songs is not surprising—because we both witnessed the rise of Pentecostalism in Nigeria in the late twentieth and early twenty-first centuries and Akeh, like some other youngsters, had been smitten by the Holy Spirit. In fact, the period marked the rise of Rev. Chris Okotie's ministry, Household of God. Okotie, a celebrated pop artist who became "born again" and launched a gospel ministry that appealed strongly to some members of our literary circle—especially Ahmad, Akeh, Nduka, and I believe, Toyin Adewale (the only prominent female affiliate of the group, and author of *Naked Testimonies* [2006] and co-editor of *Breaking the Silence: An Anthology of Women Writers* [1996]).[22] A further proof of the immersion of members of the group in Christianity was Ahmad's dedication, in *A Shout Across the Wall*, of a poem entitled "Panam Percy Paul"[23] to a local Nigerian gospel artist who appealed to various members of the Lagos group.

---

[22] The absence of female writers in the group points to the relative minority status of women in such intellectual and cultural affairs in the country at the time. Not surprising, Toyin Adewale played a pivotal role in addressing this marginalization of women through the establishment of the Women Writers Association of Nigeria (WRITA), and the ground-breaking publication of an all-female anthology of short stories symbolically entitled *Breaking the Silence* edited by Toyin Adewale and Omowunmi Segun (1999). The situation has since improved, with some of the more visible contemporary writers being women—such as Chimamanda Adichie, Chika Unigwe, Sefi Attah, and so on.

[23] Panam Percy Paul is one of the outstanding gospel artistes from the Middle Belt of Nigeria known for his pithy lyrics, vocal powers, and memorable live concerts, some of which are recorded on commercial DVDs. His kind of music has been described as "gos-pop"—that is, combining gospel and popular genres.

Conclusion

In appreciating Dylan's religious alignment, powerful lyrics, and musician-ship, we should not gloss over his role as an activist in the era of civil rights and leftist traditions[24]—or that his work as a folk artist is very much grounded in borrowing from oral cultures of folk music, and from rural white Americans as well as African American rhythms and blues (Mellers 1981, 143). His respect for African American sounds is further high-lighted by his revelation that in his later years he was drawn to the African American rap genre, particularly the works of Ice-T, Kurtis Blow, Public Enemy, N.W.A., and Run-D.M.C. (Dylan 2004a, 219).

Apparently, Bob Dylan's commanding position within popular culture and in the Nigerian context explored in this chapter is hard to miss when the multidimensional influences on his work and the ways in which he has shaped folk, rock, and gospel music, as well as the literary arts, are considered. The root of confusion about classifying Dylan for most academics and critics is a reluctance to accept his role within multiple and multifaceted forms of popu-lar culture that includes his lyricism and poetic expression, music, and perfor-mance. What is so interesting about the Nobel win is that the academy and various academics, the "high" culture or more bourgeoisie institutions that Dylan's folk persona has so vehemently worked to be distanced from, are the ones acclaiming and defending his work, while the criticism he encountered came mostly from "popular" figures producing for the masses. Divided as the responses of Dylan's listeners and critics are, especially after the Nobel, Boucher and Browning (2009) offer compelling reasons for Dylan's contin-ued appeal in their introduction to *The Political Art of Bob Dylan*:

> The endurance of the appeal of Bob Dylan over decades to an audience that spans the generations is testimony to his undeniable talent, but also to the ingenuity of his management and of Dylan himself. The five decades of Dylan's ever changing persona are projected in multiple media in a never ending present in which the many faces of Bob Dylan are simultaneously juxtaposed. (4)

---

[24] Dylan's role as an activist is also seen within his relationship to folk traditions, which is widely accepted as the music of the middle-class and 'leftist tradition' in America (see Butler [2003] 2010, 59). Thus, folk singers are supposed to act as community leaders who echo the lived experience of those listening to their music (Dunlap 2006, 564). Dylan himself has been a prominent figure in speaking out against injustice in America, and indeed, "had to warm up for Dr. King before he made his great 'I Have a Dream' speech—the preacher preceded by the pilgrim" (Bono [2008] 2017, 46).

That Dylan's Nigerian influence is partly subsumed in his general appeal highlighted in the above excerpt is commonsensical; he would *not* have affected artists in Nigeria had he been just another traditional literary artist. It is his willingness to confuse musical and literary genres—and to explore a variety of voices which Bono ([2008] 2017) identifies as "howling, seducing, raging, indignant, jeering, imploring, begging, hectoring, confessing, keening, wailing, soothing, conversational, crooning"—that made him so influential. Besides, it is no secret that literature is widely regarded as a form of written work, and thus lyrics occupy a gray area in the genre of poetry, their literary weight always in doubt. Hence as Shelton ([1986] 2010) poignantly observes, "Definitions of 'literature' had to be expanded in new and exciting ways to encompass Dylan's art. It included his stage and page writing, his novel, *Tarantula* [1971] 2004c, his early 'journalism,' and his development of all forms of media as valid writers' vehicles, his duels with the press, his famed anti-interviews, were, in themselves, a form of literary performance" (15). An even foggier area is that of oral literature. If we focus on the importance of oral literature, we open up the possibility of looking past American/Western critics of Dylan, and even past the Nobel Prize Committee, as a means to validate Dylan as a poet.

The significance of Bob Dylan's influence in Africa as evident in this chapter, therefore, stems from his maverick artistic persona, from his transgressive art, and, perhaps most importantly, from the power of his *songs* as underscored in his Nobel Prize acceptance speech (2016): "I've made dozens of records and played thousands of concerts all around the world. *But it's my songs that are at the vital center of almost everything I do.*[25] *They seemed to have found a place in the lives of many people throughout many different cultures and I'm grateful for that*" (my emphasis). From the shores of his homeland in America, through the metropolitan centers of the world, Dylan's works have strongly reverberated, and will continue to play in the hearts and art of my contemporaries in Africa and beyond. The centrality of the songs/lyrics to the *essence* of Bob Dylan cannot be overemphasized. Bowden (1982) notes in her pioneering book-length study of Dylan that "the sociological approaches of popular culture studies barely skim the surface of the best Dylan songs. Nor do musicologists have much to say, for without words most Dylan melodies

---

[25] Howard Sounes (2000) reinforces the point being made here in his biography of Dylan, *Down the Highway: The Life of Bob Dylan*, when he affirms that "Dylan would occasionally open up to girlfriends. But it was in his songs that he really revealed himself" (100).

and chord changes would be boring" (1). The debate around Dylan's literary credentials may not have been settled even as the artist remains productive in his late seventies,[26] but his life and art will continue to provoke further interest afield, and to surprise in their "soetry" and allusive turns. Understood this way, Dylan's parody of one of Shakespeare's most memorable quotes in his letter to the Emergency Civil Liberties Committee cited earlier points to the "open window" that his works continue to invoke and to invite haters and lovers alike to enter: "out! out! brief candle / life's but an open window / an I must jump back thru it now."[27] Indeed, Hampton (1986), echoing the Boucher and Browning (2009) quote above, asserts that Dylan's greatest asset has been his "longevity as a popular singer"—and of the four guerrilla minstrels studied by Hampton, he is the only one still living (199). The consequence of this longevity and his influence on a recent generation of Nigerian poets is implicated in Uche Nduka's testimony above: "For me and my generation in Nigeria, the music of this inscrutable bard was the soundtrack to our travels throughout the country, our courtships, our flirtations, our political protests. He helped me discover myself as an artistic wayfarer. His example made us refuse to write a poetry of restraint. *He is still urging us to zestfully stoke our artistic fires*" (my emphasis).

Being alive and continuing to be productive well into his twilight years mean that the last is yet to be heard about Bob Dylan's African influence. More so, when viewed through the prism of the African philosophical concept of *Ubuntu:* "I am because we are." Although the new generation of writers and artists may not be wired into Dylanesque lyrics, performance, and aesthetics—a number of them are already pursuing a renewed form of spoken word genre[28]—the attention refocused on Dylan's life and work by the Nobel Prize may yet inspire Africa's creative youth to find new ways of re-engaging with the non-conformist artist about whom David Yaffe (2011) has written: "Indeed, it's hard to know where, precisely, to place him" (2). Or, perhaps, to re-engage with an artist whose songs, Robert Santelli (2005) declares, "were strikingly original statements of a world mired in absurdity" (6).

---

[26] Even as we were concluding work on this book project Dylan was playing his 2018 concert tour. I witnessed my first-ever Dylan concert in Rochester, New York, on November 14, 2018.

[27] See Shakespeare's *Macbeth*, Act 5, Scene 5.

[28] Various spoken word slams and poetry festivals are burgeoning across Nigeria. Notable artists who have, in fact, released some poetry/music CDs and DVDs, as well as established YouTube channels, include the Nigerian-Canadian Beautiful Nubia and the Lagos-based poet and journalist Akeem Lasisi.

References

Abdul-Jabbar, Omale Allen. 2007. Carlos Izzia Ahmad: The Man and His Poetry. https://www.africanwriter.com.

Adesanmi, Pius. 2009. Don Williams: Fragments of Memory. *Maple Tree Literary Supplement*, no. 3. www.mtls.ca.

———. 2011. *You are Not a Country, Africa: A Personal History of the African Present*. South Africa: Penguin Books.

Adewale, Toyin. 2006. *Naked Testimonies*. N.p.: Mallory International.

Adewale, Toyin, and Omowunmi Segun. 1999. *Breaking the Silence: An Anthology of Women Writers*. N.p.: WRITA, Women Writers of Nigeria.

Ahmad, Idzia. 1988. *A Shout Across the Wall*. Lagos: Update Communications Ltd.

Akeh, Afam. 1988. *Stolen Moments*. Lagos: Update Communications Ltd.

———. n.d. Mid Year Blues. nwokolo.com.

Bakhtin, Mikhail. 1981 (1934). *The Dialogic Imagination: Four Essays*. Edited by Michael Holquist and translated by Caryl Emerson and Michael Holquist. Austin: University of Texas Press.

Ball, Gordon. 2007. Dylan and the Nobel. *Oral Tradition* 22 (1): 14–29.

———. 2016. I Nominated Bob Dylan for the Nobel Prize More Than a Dozen Times. *Washington Post*, October 14, 2016. https://www.washingtonpost.com.

Batycka, Dorian. 2018. Dispute Erupts over Artist's 'Monument for Strangers and Refugees' in Germany. https://hyperallergic.com.

Bono. 2017 (2008). Voice of Ages. In *Rolling Stone Bob Dylan: The Complete Album Guide*, 46. New York: Rolling Stone.

Book, Ryan. 2015. Where Has Bob Dylan Not Played in 'Never Ending Tour'? Alaska and Africa Craving Some Attention. *The Music Times*, April 15, 2015. https://www.musictimes.com.

Boucher, David, and Gary Browning. 2009. *The Political Art of Bob Dylan*. 2nd ed. Exeter: Imprint Academic.

Bowden, Betsy. 1982. *Performed Literature: Words and Music by Bob Dylan*. Bloomington: Indiana University Press.

Butler, Christopher. 2010 (2003). Dylan and the Academics. In *Do You, Mr. Jones? Bob Dylan with the Poets and Professors*, edited by Neil Corcoran, 51-70. New York: Penguin Random House.

Corcoran, Neil, ed. 2010 (2003). *Do You, Mr. Jones? Bob Dylan with the Poets and Professors*. New York: Penguin Random House.

Dunlap, James. 2006. Through the Eyes of Tom Joad: Patterns of American Idealism, Bob Dylan, and the Folk Protest Movement. *Popular Music and Society* 29 (5): 549–573.

Dylan, Bob. 1964. 11 Outlined Epitaphs (liner notes). *The Times They Are a-Changin'*. Columbia Vinyl Record.

———. 2004a. *Chronicles Volume One*. New York: Simon & Schuster.

———. 2004b (1962). My Life in a Stolen Moment. In *Studio A: The Bob Dylan Reader*, edited by Benjamin Hedin, 3-7. New York: Norton.

———. 2004c (1971). *Tarantula*. New York: Scribner

———. 2016. Banquet Speech. *The Nobel Prize*, December 10, 2016. https://www.nobelprize.org.

———. 2017. Nobel Lecture. *The Nobel Prize*, June 5, 2017. https://www.nobelprize.org.

Gilmour, Michael J. 2004. *Tangled up in the Bible: Bob Dylan and Scripture*. New York, NY: Continuum International Publishing Group.

Häger, Andreas. 2008. Bob Dylan and Religion. In *Postmodern Spirituality*, ed. Tore Ahlbäck, 44–60. Finland: The Donner Institute for Research.

Hampton, Wayne. 1986. *Guerrilla Minstrels*. Knoxville: The University of Tennessee Press.

Ilori, Kemi Atanda. 1988. *Amnesty*. Lagos: Update Communications Ltd.

Irobi, Esiaba. 1988. *Cotyledons*. Lagos: Update Communications Ltd.

Jaffe, Eric. 2013. 808 Cities, 2,503 Shows, and 1,007,416 Miles: The Staggering Geography of Bob Dylan's 'Never Ending Tour'. *Citylab*, June 7, 2013. https://www.citylab.com.

Lebold, Christopher. 2007. A Face Like a Mask and a Voice that Croaks: An Integrated Poetics of Bob Dylan's Voice, Personae, and Lyrics. *Oral Tradition* 22 (1): 57–70.

Leland, John. 2002. It's Only Rhyming Quatrains, but I Like It. In *Da Capo Best Music Writing 2002: The Years Finest Writing on Rock, Pop, Jazz, Country and More*, ed. P. Bresnick and J. Lethem, 141–150. Cambridge, MA: Da Capo Books.

Lethem, Jonathan. 2016. Novelist Jonathan Lethem on Bob Dylan's 'Mad-Scientist Audacity'. *Rolling Stone*, December 9, 2016. https://www.rollingstone.com.

Light, Alan. 2017. The Freewheelin Bob Dylan. In *Rolling Stone Bob Dylan: The Complete Album Guide*, 10–13. New York: Rolling Stone.

Marachera, Dambudzo. 2009 (1993). *The House of Hunger*. N.p.: Knopf Canada.

Marshall, Lee. 2007. *Bob Dylan: The Never Ending Star*. Cambridge: Polity Press.

———. 2009. Bob Dylan and the Academy. In *The Cambridge Companion to Bob Dylan*, ed. Kevin J.H. Dettmar, 100–109. Cambridge, UK: Cambridge University Press.

Mellers, Wilfred. 1981. God, Modality and Meaning in Some Recent Songs of Bob Dylan. *Popular Music* 1: 143–157.

Metcalf, Stephen. 2016. Bob Dylan Is a Genius of Almost Unparalleled Influence, but He Shouldn't Have Gotten the Nobel. *Slate*, October 10, 2016. https://slate.com.

Nduka, Uche. 1988. *Flower Child*. Lagos: Update Communications Ltd.

———. 1994. *Second Act*. Lagos: Journoblues Communications Ltd.

———. 1997. *Chiaroscuro*. Bremen: Yeti Press.

———. 2000. *Belltime Letters*. Bremen: Newleaf Press.

———. 2003. Izzia Ahmad: Worker in the Ministry of Poetry. *Sentinel Poetry Movement*, March 2003. http://www.sentinelpoetry.org.uk.

———. 2018. *Living in Public*. N.p.: Writers' Collective of Kristiania, Inc.

———. n.d. Four Poems. Accessed June 2, 2018. expoundmagazine.com/four-poems-uche-nduka/.

Nwakanma, Obi. 2006. Nigeria: Lagos and a Life of The Poets. *Vanguard*, January 15, 2006. https://allafrica.com.

Oguibe, Olu. 1992. For You, Homeland. In *A Gathering Fear*, 84–85. Bayreuth: Verlag Norbert Aas.

———. 2010. Esiaba Irobi: The Tragedy of Exile. *Maple Tree Literary Supplement*, no. 7. www.mtls.ca.

Osha, Sanya. 2016. Why Prince is Over-rated. *Pambazuka*, June 9, 2016. https://www.pambazuka.org/arts/why-prince-over-rated.

Otiono, Nduka. 1997. *Voices in the Rainbow*. Lagos: Oracle Books Ltd.

———. 2008. *Love in a Time of Nightmares*. Baltimore, MD: PublishAmerica.

Pulitzer Prizes, The. 2008. The 2008 Pulitzer Prize Winner in Special Awards and Citations. www.pulitzer.org/prize-winners-by-year/2008.

Ricks, Christopher. 2003. *Dylan's Visions of Sin*. Edinburgh, UK: Canongate Books.

———. 2016a. Bob Dylan is a Genius—But Reducing His Songs to 'Literature' is Dangerous. *Telegraph*, October 14, 2016. https://www.telegraph.co.uk.

———. 2016b. Christopher Ricks on Bob Dylan. *CBC*. Podcast, Writers and Company, Produced by Eleanor Wachtel. October 13, 2016. https://www.cbc.ca/player/play/2696240152.

Rossi, Riika. 2010. Influences, Intertextualities, Genres: History of Naturalism and Concepts of Comparative Literature. *Canadian Review of Comparative Literature* 37 (4): 370–381.

Santelli, Robert. 2005. *The Bob Dylan Scrapbook, 1956–1966*. New York: Simon & Schuster.

Scobie, Stephen. 1999. *And Forget My Name: A Speculative Biography of Bob Dylan*. Victoria, BC: Ekstasis Editions.

———. 2003. *Alias Bob Dylan Revisited*. Markham, ON: Red Deer Press.

Sennaro, Johan, and Alistair Scrutton. 2016. 'Greatest Living Poet' Bob Dylan Wins Nobel Literature Prize. *Reuters*, October 13, 2016. https://www.reuters.com.

Shehu, Usman. 1988. *Questions for Big Brother*. Lagos: Update Communications Ltd.

Shelton, Robert. 2010 (1986). *No Direction Home: The Life and Music of Bob Dylan*. Milwaukee, WI: Backbeat Books.

Smyth, Gerry. 2011. Is Bob Dylan Really a Poet? *Irish Times*, April 16, 2011. https://www.irishtimes.com/culture/music/2.681/is-bob-dylan-really-a-poet-1.574161.

Sounes, Howard. 2000. *Dylan Down the Highway: The Life of Bob Dylan*. London: Black Swan.

Usher, Shaun, ed. 2012 (1963). I Do Not Apologize for Myself Nor My Fears. May 24, 2012. www.lettersofnote.com.

Warmuth, Scott. 2008. Bob Charlatan: Deconstructing Dylan *Chronicles: Volume One*. *New Haven Review* 6: 70–83.

NOTES ON CONTRIBUTORS

Damian A. Carpenter recently completed a postdoctoral fellowship at East Tennessee State University. He is the author of *Lead Belly, Woody Guthrie, Bob Dylan and American Folk Outlaw Performance* (2018). Some of his other Dylan-related publications appear in *The Life, Music, and Thought of Woody Guthrie: A Critical Appraisal* (2011) and the forthcoming *World of Bob Dylan* (2019).

Astrid Franke is Professor of American Studies in Tuebingen. She is the author of *Keys to Controversies: Stereotypes in Modern American Novels* (1999) and *Pursue the Illusion: Problems of Public Poetry in America* (2010), and co-editor of *Civilizing and Decivilizing Processes: Figurational Approaches to American Studies* (2011) and *Transatlantic Negotiations* (2007). She is a member of the Collaborative Research Center "Threatened Orders" with a project on the resilience of the racial order in the US. Other research interests include popular culture, cultural history and theory, and, as an underlying thread, intersections of literature and sociology.

Charles O. Hartman is Lucy Marsh Haskell '19 Endowed Professor of English and Poet in Residence at Connecticut College. He has published seven books of poetry, including *New & Selected Poems* (2008), as well as books on jazz and song and on computer poetry. He is the author of *Free Verse* (Northwest University Press, 1981—still in print) and *Verse: An Introduction to Prosody* (2015). He plays jazz guitar.

© The Author(s) 2019
N. Otiono, J. Toth (eds.), *Polyvocal Bob Dylan*,
Palgrave Studies in Music and Literature,
https://doi.org/10.1007/978-3-030-17042-4

John McCombe is Professor of English and Director of the University Honors Program at the University of Dayton. His teaching and research interests include twentieth-century British literature, film, and popular music studies. His work has appeared in journals such as *Modern Fiction Studies*, *Cinema Journal*, and the *Journal of Popular Music Studies*. His most recent publication is a chapter entitled "'Getting Better All the Time': A Multidisciplinary Exploration of Beatles Mythology" in *Teaching the Beatles* (2018).

Keith Nainby is Professor of Communication Studies at California State University, Stanislaus. He studies listening as a communicative act, exploring recorded musical performances by artists such as Bob Dylan and Miles Davis. His previous scholarship on Dylan has appeared in the journal *Contemporary Theatre Review* and in the book *Political Rock* (2013).

Nduka Otiono is an Assistant Professor at the Institute of African Studies, Carleton University. He is a writer; along with two volumes of poetry and a collection of short stories, he is co-editor of *We-Men: An Anthology of Men Writing on Women* (1998) and *Camouflage: Best of Contemporary Writing from Nigeria* (2006). Prior to turning to academia, he was for many years a journalist in Nigeria. His works have appeared in *Journal of Folklore Research*, *African Literature Today*, *Journal of African Cinema*, *Transfers: Interdisciplinary Journal of Mobility Studies*, *Wasafiri*, among others. He is winner of a Capital Educator's Award for Excellence in Teaching.

Josh Toth is Associate Professor of English at MacEwan University. Along with articles on critical theory and American literature in journals such as *Cultural Critique*, *Critique*, *Lit*, *Mosaic*, and *MELUS*, he is author of *The Passing of Postmodernism: A Spectroanalysis of the Contemporary* (2010) and *Stranger America: A Narrative Ethics of Exclusion* (2018). He is also co-editor (with Neil Brooks) of *The Mourning After: Attending the Wake of Postmodernism* (2007).

Katherine Weiss is Professor of English at East Tennessee State University whose research interests are in modern and contemporary drama and theatre. Her accomplishments include a collection of essays titled *Samuel Beckett: History, Memory, Archive* (co-edited with Seán Kennedy, Palgrave Macmillan, 2009), an edited student edition of Tennessee Williams's *Sweet Bird of Youth* (2010), a book, *The Plays of Samuel Beckett* (2013), and an edited volume, *A Student Handbook to the Plays of Tennessee Williams* (2014). Most recently, she co-edited *Samuel Beckett and Contemporary Art* (2018) with Robert Reginio and David Houston Jones.

Emily O. Wittman is an Associate Professor at the University of Alabama where she is Director of the Program in Comparative and World Literature. She has published extensively on autobiography and in the field of translation studies. She is co-editor, with Maria DiBattista, of *Modernism and Autobiography* (2014) and the *Cambridge Companion to Autobiography* (2014). She has previously published, with co-author Paul R. Wright, two essays on Bob Dylan and pedagogy.

Paul R. Wright is Assistant Provost for International Affairs at Cabrini University. He has presented and published on diverse subjects across media boundaries, including ground-breaking American television series such as *The Wire* and *The Sopranos*, the music and life of Bob Dylan, and the films of Akira Kurosawa and Martin Scorsese. He has also been an invited speaker internationally on the subject of "cultural copyright" in world cinema, as well as the work on income inequality done by Thomas Piketty and its connections to representations of social class in American media. In addition to his administrative work at Cabrini University, Wright also teaches regularly at the Bryn Mawr Film Institute.

Index[1]

---

[1] Note: Page numbers followed by 'n' refer to notes.

© The Author(s) 2019
N. Otiono, J. Toth (eds.), *Polyvocal Bob Dylan*,
Palgrave Studies in Music and Literature,
https://doi.org/10.1007/978-3-030-17042-4

9 783030 170417